PRESENCE AND PLEASURE

Presence and Pleasure

The Funk Grooves of James Brown and Parliament

ANNE DANIELSEN

Wesleyan University Press
Middletown, Connecticut

Published by Wesleyan University Press, Middletown, CT 06549

www.wesleyan.edu/wespress

Printed in the United States of America

5 4 3 2

Library of Congress Cataloging-in-Publication Data

Danielsen, Anne.

Presence and pleasure : the funk grooves of James Brown and Parliament /
Anne Danielsen.

    p. cm. — (Music/culture)

Includes bibliographical references and index.

ISBN-13: 978-0-8195-6822-9 (cloth : alk. paper)

ISBN-10: 0-8195-6822-8 (cloth : alk. paper)

ISBN-13: 978-0-8195-6823-6 (pbk. : alk. paper)

ISBN-10: 0-8195-6823-6 (pbk. : alk. paper)

1. Funk (Music)—History and criticism. 2. Brown, James, 1928–

3. Parliament (Musical group) I. Title. II. Series.

ML3527.8. D36 2006

781.644—dc22   2006010987

Contents

Preface

This book grew out of my doctoral study at the University of Oslo from 1995 to 2001, but in more than one way, it started long before that. Almost twenty years ago, in the mid-1980s, I was part of a band that played soul, r&b, rock, and funk. While I was always deeply engaged in the funk tunes we made and played—for me they were among the most meaningful things we did—I eventually realized that we were not managing them very well after all. I realized that funk was a difficult thing to play properly, because it should in fact be played everything *but* properly. Indeed, it should be "dirty," and in exactly the right way. Put simply, I realized that funk is a very complex groove, and that it should not be taken for granted that a funk groove really is funky.

The reason for my almost lifelong fascination with funk, however, lies even further back in time. It stems from the dance-floor experiences of a young woman conquered by the wave of black dance music that swept over the international music scene in the late 1970s. I did not reflect upon the difference in style and character between funk and other dance music at that time—I probably did not even label funk as funk—but I certainly knew the difference when engaging with the rhythms on the dance floor. Some grooves simply moved the body, not the other way around. Some grooves were "edgy" in a certain way, offering a simultaneously dense and openly spaced fabric of rhythms that brought me into a highly pleasurable state of being, a presence in both the music and the body at once.

This state of being and the musical magic of the funk groove are themes that run throughout this book. Both are unwriteable as such. Knowing this, however, does not prevent me or any other interpreter from understanding or writing, but it may encourage us to write with the awareness that there is no way around this basic condition. Though there is resistance implied in this knowledge, we can hope that we are still able to make resonant the hidden experience of being in the funkiness of a funky groove.

Acknowledgments

This book is based on a doctoral study that was made possible by financial support from the Norwegian Research Council. Additional support from the council enabled a stay at the University of California, Los Angeles, in the first half of 1997. The council has also supported this publication.

The completion of the book would never have been possible without the help and support of numerous people. I want to express my gratitude to Ståle Wikshåland, my supervisor during my doctoral studies at the University of Oslo, for his thorough, critical reading and strong support throughout the whole process, and to Robert Walser for his generous support and valuable feedback in the process of transforming the text from dissertation to book.

For their helpful comments on drafts and parts of this text, I thank Alf Bjørnberg, Arne Melberg, Arnfinn Bø-Rygg, Anne Britt Gran, Stan Hawkins, Tellef Kvifte, Anders Danielsen Lie, Preben von der Lippe, Erling Guldbrandsen, Jørgen Langdalen, and Gisela Attinger. Gisela Attinger also made my handwritten notation readable, and Ellen Glimstad and Peter Knudsen assisted with the illustrations. Moreover, I thank Gaute Drevdal for generously sharing his views and literature on funk, Odd Skårberg for informative discussions on popular music, and Alf Bjørnberg, Christian Refsum, and Hallgjerd Aksnes for their valuable references. Thanks also go to the Department of Musicology, University of Oslo, which has been my place of work during this process, and to Suzanna Tamminen and Eric Levy at Wesleyan University Press, as well as to copyeditor Nils Nadeau, whose careful readings improved the text as regards both content and structure. Thanks also to the press's anonymous readers for their constructive and critical readings.

My family and friends have generously supported me along the way. Very special thanks go to Tellef, Tobias, Signe, and Hans.

A. D.

I

Black and/or White

Introductory Perspectives

1

Whose Funk?

Funk is a "bad" word. But as with so many of the bad words of black American English, bad may be both good and bad. Funk is one of these bad words whose meaning has been inverted. And both as good and as bad, it seems to be at the extreme. In the *Black Talk* dictionary of Geneva Smitherman, it is defined as (1) the musical sound of jazz, blues, work songs, rhythm and blues, and African American music generally; (2) the quality of being soulful, funky; (3) a bad smell; an unpleasant odor, or (4) a euphemism for *fuck,* in its sexual meaning.[1] On the one hand, it connotes the dirtiest of the dirty; on the other, it seems to be in touch with the fundamental essence of life.

The word "funk" seems to have been related to musical qualities from the outset. Funk as a distinct musical style, however, did not emerge until the late 1960s. Stylistically, it may be placed in the lineage of rhythm and blues, jazz (more precisely, the so-called "hard bop" of Art Blakey and Horace Silver), and the rough southern soul that developed on the Stax label in Memphis. Both James Brown and Sly and the Family Stone have been named founders of the style, the former more prominent in African American accounts and the latter in Anglo-American rock discourse.[2] Sly and the Family Stone's songs "Dance to the Music" (1968) and "Thank you (Falettinme Be Mice Elf Again)" (1970) were among the first songs that introduced funk to a white audience.[3]

In the first half of the 1970s, funk became increasingly popular among African Americans. At the same time, as a musical style, it evolved in several different directions. George Clinton and his groups Parliament and Funkadelics took funk in the direction of heavy grooves and cosmic stage shows, while Earth, Wind, and Fire, Ohio Players, Kool and the Gang, and others developed a more disco-influenced style. Earth, Wind, and Fire, at least, may be seen as a precursor to the wave of disco that was to come, resulting in a formidable crossover for black dance music, which suddenly became hot with the white dancing audience—artists like Michael Jackson, Diana Ross, Donna Summer, and Chic, to mention only a few, had big international hits in the late 1970s. At the same time, old-school funk artists almost vanished from the charts.

The 1980s were almost free of funk, at least as far as the international pop scene was concerned. Prince was certainly funky, but he did not promote himself as a funk artist. In the 1990s, however, funk was redis- covered, due to rap and hip-hop and a general revival of groove-based dance music. The grooves of the golden age of funk in the 1970s became the prime source of samples for hip-hop, while some new dance music, such as acid jazz and trip-hop, recirculated the old grooves in new wrappings. In line with this, the old grooves themselves were also re- vived for older and newer fans.[4]

This book concentrates on what might be described as the golden age of funk, namely the late 1960s through the 1970s. I approach the subject from a double perspective. On the one hand, I focus on musical production—more precisely, on two of the artists/bands that were sem- inal in the process of inventing the new style, and that hold a special position with regard to both musical and cultural impact in what might be called the African American story of funk: James Brown and his bands, and George Clinton and his group Parliament, reformed in the 1980s under the name P-Funk All-Stars. On the other hand, I explore the reception of funk with regard to a certain historical situation, namely how funk was experienced and understood by the generation of mostly white, pop- and rock-confident Western fans whose relationship with it started with the crossover of black dance music during the 1970s. As a white, middle-class Scandinavian woman born in the early 1960s, I was part of this audience, and my teens were accompanied by disco, funk, and discofunk. Today it is easy to see why those years were formative with regard to my musical preferences.

James Brown's activities in the ten years following "Papa's Got a Brand New Bag" (1965) are and always will be prominent in the history of funk as well as the general history of African American music. During this period Brown and his musicians delivered a series of grooves that was outstanding with regard to both innovation and quality. From the mid-1970s, George Clinton and Parliament holds an equally crucial position in the history of funk, developing the funk groove to the extreme, at least with regard to its funkiness, and providing fans and followers with the "philosophy of P-Funk."

The musical products of both the James Brown organization and the P-Funk camp continue to fascinate today. (They are also the most sampled grooves of the funk era.) Before diving further into the issues, I will thus briefly introduce the artists behind the musical forces that are at the core of this book.

James Brown and Parliament—A Short History

In his article on James Brown in *The Rolling Stone Illustrated History of Rock 'n' Roll,* Robert Palmer writes: "What drives a man like James Brown, a man who could have retired in 1965 or 1975, but who has kept on trying to outdo himself instead? Perhaps the goal has been forgotten and the struggle itself is the reward; perhaps it always was."[5]

Born in 1933 in a one-room country shack in the woods outside Barnwell, South Carolina, James Brown grew up poorer than the poor, lacking almost everything that a child needs: love and care, and sometimes even food and clothes. Soon his parents split up and his mother went away; he would not see her again for twenty years. At the age of four he was left alone in the woods while his father was out working: "I don't think you can spend much time by yourself as a child and not have it affect you in a big way. Being alone in the woods like that, spending nights in a cabin with nobody else there, not having anybody to talk to, worked a change in me that stayed with me from then on: It gave me my own mind. No matter what came in my way after that—

prison, personal problems, government harassment—I had the ability to fall back on myself."[6]

A few years later, his father handed his upbringing over to James's great-aunt and they moved to a new home in Atlanta, a whorehouse that also accommodated gambling and an illegal liquor trade. At the age of sixteen he was imprisoned for petty theft. In 1952 he was turned loose on parole after three years in prison. He got in touch with the Byrd family and soon began to sing in church with Sarah Byrd, then joining the group of her brother Bobby.

Named James Brown and the Flames, the group had its first hit with "Please, Please, Please" in 1956. It was the pop-gospel ballad "Try Me" (1958), however, that really opened doors. After a few years Brown took control of the band and his own career with regard to both music and business. In 1963 he released the first live recording from the Apollo Theater, a project he funded himself, due to a lack of support from King, his record company. It became the second-bestselling album in the United States. In 1965 "Papa's Got a Brand New Bag" became a big hit, and in the following years James Brown and his orchestra, later renamed the JBs, started working on a new style that surfaced for the public with "Cold Sweat" in 1967. Brown and his musicians then followed with a series of remarkable tunes, including several number-one r&b hits.

For many years the band of James Brown was considered the best within the r&b/soul/funk branch of black American music. Its different line-ups included many of the legendary musicians of the time, such as drummers Melvin Parker, Clyde Stubblefield, and John "Jabo" Starks, saxophonist Maceo Parker, trombonist Fred Wesley, and bassist Bootsy Collins, to mention only a few. Playing with the James Brown band was the dream of many musicians. In the words of Bootsy Collins: "James Brown had heard about us over at King, so we were his new choice when he had problems with his original band. We were considered hot. Actually we had developed a cockiness like we were God's gift to the world. So when I met Mr. Brown, I was cool, probably the coolest—on the outside. But inside I was like, 'Dang, I'm dreamin.'"[7]

Bootsy Collins and his brother Phelps "Catfish" Collins played with James Brown for one year before leaving for the P-Funk party. The rigorous orderliness of Brown's band was probably not their style, but before leaving they made their stamp on songs such as "Sex Machine," "Super Bad," "Talkin' Loud and Saying Nothing," and "Get Up, Get Into It, Get Involved," which were all recorded in 1970, as well as "Soul Power" from 1971.

On the side, James Brown sponsored programs for ghetto youth, spoke at high schools, and invested in black businesses. He played live on television to calm the black population after the murder of Martin Luther King Jr. He played for the troops in Vietnam, and he and his wife had dinner with Vice-President Hubert Humphrey. He had, in other words, come a long way from his aunt's home in Atlanta; he had become an American, almost as American as apple pie.

The P-Funk story seems to be different. Parliament started as a doo-wop band in 1956, and, according to George Clinton, the whole band was motivated by the fact that the doo-woppers had girls running across the stage. From the 1960s onward, they met in the Silk Palace, George Clinton's barbershop in Plainfield, New Jersey. Clinton recalled, "I was making a thousand dollars a week and spending it all making records. That was the only way I could get to do my own thing, was to pay for it."[8]

The hippie influence of the late 1960s inspired the group to change its style both musically and visually, Clinton noted: "First we were straight. Straight suits and clean. Then, when the hippies came, we took it to exaggeration. We wore sheets, we wore the suit bags that our suits came in. And it was funny to us, 'cause we come from a barbershop, we knew how to make you look cool, so we never felt uncool. We had fun doing it. Plus, I knew Jimi Hendrix did it. To me, that's the ultimate, Jimmy James. If he done changed to get that deep, 'Oh, okay. Here's another style.'"[9] The psychedelic, acid-influenced rock version of the group was called Funkadelic, while Parliament was still recording as Parliament.

At this time funk was still a bad word. Shows could not be promoted on the radio, and according to P-Funk's cover artist, Ronald "Stozo" Edwards, the mainstream black audience did not like the distorted guitar sound and nasty attitude. But in the coming years funk would be accepted as a musical alternative.

In 1971 the Collins brothers joined the P-Funk organization, encouraging its shift toward funk. They had been at the James Brown school of funk, and as Bootsy remarked, "James made us more aware of the One and dynamics, which Funkadelic had never experienced before."[10] For a while, Bootsy Collins left the group for a solo career, but he returned when Parliament was revived in 1975 and was probably the main person responsible for the funk development in the P-Funk camp in the mid-1970s:

Sly was my hero. Jimi had died and I had been with James Brown, so Sly was a good individual to try to live up to. And his music was working on blacks and whites. That's what I wanted. So I began messin' with that vibe because he was all over the radio. I had no idea what hit records was, but I could relate to Sly.

Eighty percent of the P-Funk songs I worked on was tracks I put together. That's what I was used to doing, and that's what George wanted at the time. George knew how to use what he had. He was music chef.[11]

The relaunching of Parliament was also the start of the "P-Funk cosmology." Their heavy funk grooves were combined with a spectacular live show, the result, according to Clinton, of yet another attempt to keep up with the times: "Since we'd had to come out of the hippie vibe of the sixties and do something new, it was time to be glitter again."[12] Clinton created the otherworldly Dr. Funkenstein character, who landed on stage in "The Mothership Connection" spaceship. All of the income from hits like "Chocolate City" (1975), "P. Funk (Wants to Get Funked Up)" (1975), "Give Up the Funk (Tear the Roof Off the Sucker)" (1975), and "Do That Stuff" (1976) was spent on these spectacles, which moreover turned Parliament/Funkadelic into one of the first black arena acts in pop history: "We took all of the money from the hit record, [and] half of the band left 'cause they thought we had been workin' all that hard to get a house and a car. I said, 'You get the house or the car. Can't get 'em both 'cause we gotta get a spaceship.'"[13]

The incredible stage shows of Parliament/Funkadelic were, however, more than a way of getting attention within the music business. These shows, together with the whole philosophy of funk developed by George Clinton at the time, were in fact highly political, or perhaps spiritual, projects.[14] They constituted a response to setbacks within the African American community, which found itself at the time in a rather precarious situation. The vital civil rights movement had faded, conditions in the black ghettos were getting even worse, and its leading star, the symbol of hope, freedom, and a different, better future, was gone.

Whose Funk?

For me and for many other white funk fans in the 1970s, funk was thrilling. It sounded different, and it offered a different experience. In hindsight it is plausible to connect the thrills of this difference to a notion of blackness, a notion that came into being as part of an interracial relation of black and white (I will return to this in chapter 2). At the time, however, the fact that funk was deeply embedded in the culture and history of black America seemed ultimately unimportant. We did not fully recognize the music as specifically linked to a black identity, and we were not particularly familiar with the musical practice that preceded funk. Racial matters were still distant at that time, at least in Scandinavia. And even though we were quite well informed about the history, as well as the musical traditions, of the African American population in the United States—our school lessons in history included the history of black America from its very dark beginnings in European colonialism to the civil rights movement and Martin Luther King in the 1960s—we did not link the new funk sounds to this history. Funk was exciting and different, but we did not see it as a genuine expression of a black experience or a black aesthetic. First and foremost it was part of the latest fad of dance music in the Anglo-American world of popular music, and when it was talked about, it was largely in terms of the body and sex.

By "the Anglo-American world of popular music" I mean the sphere historically and geographically limited by its link to the global construction of rock music in the 1960s and 1970s. As Simon Frith has pointed out, rock was essentially British as well as American, and during this time "the flow of sounds (and dollars) back and forth across the sea was equally strong in each direction."[15] The audiences for the music, culture, and ideology produced by this Anglo-American axis of rock and pop were, however, not limited to the geographical territories suggested by this labeling. In Scandinavia in this period, this tradition was extremely powerful: "pop and rock" meant pretty much British and American pop and rock. Thus, when I use expressions such as "the Anglo-American world of pop and rock" or "the Anglo-American-influenced audiences for funk" in this book, I use them in their cultural, rather than geographical, meanings, and they are meant to include Scandinavia and most of Northern Europe as well.

The cultural and historical context for this study of funk encompasses how funk was experienced by the generation of white Western fans who came to know it when black dance music crossed over to this world of pop and rock in the late 1970s. In such a context, funk is situated between African American musical traditions and the international, Anglo-American–dominated range of popular music, or, to put forward a far too black-and-white account of the picture: between black and white. Despite its worldwide exposure, funk had close historical and cultural connections to black America, yet it was refracted through the values and cultural horizon of a white, Western, middle-class audience. However, upon closer inspection either side of such a cultural polarization is itself rife with conflicting values and different cultural orientations. To start with the black side: African American culture is clearly situated within the West, in that African America is a part of North America, both geographically and culturally, and shares its values, history, and cultural horizon with the Western world to a considerable extent. At the same time, in some accounts of African American music and culture, such as, for example, the 1960s black nationalist texts on African American music and culture discussed in chapter 2, American and African American are held to be opposites.[16] Such a perspective stresses the differences between African American and white Western cultural traditions. African American culture is thus characterized by its dual relation to the West, being both inside and outside Western culture at the same time.

Conversely, the white side in the present opposition, white Western pop and rock audiences, is not purely white in its cultural orientation, here understood to arise from the dominant and to some extent official and institutionalized values, history, and cultural horizon of the West (that is, the Western Hemisphere and Europe). If we take account of their habits of consumption, these audiences are deeply involved in both African American culture and its "opposite." Situating funk between black and white is thus a far too reductive picture of the situation, because neither side is particularly "pure."

Put differently, one might say that the cultural processes linked with African American popular music are characterized by a manifold of different, and often local, appropriations on the sides of both production and reception. Music in general often has an openness and appeal that allow new audiences to comprehend it in their own ways—it is uniquely available for local use and interpretation. This situation makes it necessary, even when one is dealing with music that seems safely situated within the African American tradition, to specify both poles of the production-reception axis—that is, to ask not only what music or what record but also for whom. This is particularly true when African American popular music enters the global marketplace. As R. Radano and P. V. Bohlman point out, "On the global musical marketplace race is a slippery signifier, for its musical capital is considerable. Musics whose origins would seem irrefutably racial are no longer bounded by a locally relevant racial framework."[17]

In this book, I explore one instance of this process, namely the cultural meeting of a listener and dancer who was deeply influenced by the dominant values, musical preferences, and listening habits of the Anglo-American world of pop and rock—the target of black crossover in the 1970s—and the musical traditions and performance practice of African American *musicking* that are at the heart of funk. Such a task ultimately implies a non-essentialist understanding of black music. The very subject matter itself is in fact a challenge to, in Radano's words, "the view, still common to our time and culture, of an immutable black musical essence that survives apart from the contingencies of social and cultural change."[18] As is made clear by this study of funk, the meaning and function of a specific musical practice may vary considerably according to the cultural and social context: its identity is not inherent in music itself, nor is it equivalent to the culture that may be said to have produced it in the first place.

Understanding Funk—Hermeneutic Challenges

Even though musical features can never be separated from cultural constraints, it is not accidental that funk fulfilled the musical role of the musical-cultural meeting at the center of this study. A main question in this book concerns the relationship between the experience of being in a funk groove and the rhythmic qualities of funk: what is it in the sounds or their organization that brings the participant into a state of "being in the groove"?

My response to this question required both an exploration of funk grooves in musical terms and a consideration of how the groove actually is experienced when it takes place in time. The latter inquiry reveals my ambition to study funk not only as objectified cultural or musical meaning but also as lived experience. Rather than elaborating on the common understandings of funk in my culture, I wanted to play up the state of "being in funk" as such—that is, the experience prior to (as well as following, of course) our speech about this music—because this was in my view necessary for grasping the uplifting qualities of funk.

There were, however, major challenges linked with such an ambition, including how to account for that very experience. Instead of overlooking or ignoring this difficulty, I wanted to deal with it, while acknowledging that the experience I wanted to investigate escapes what might be called the "domain of thought and meaning" in its traditional sense.

A concern with these questions led me to an engagement with academic texts and philosophical traditions not commonly linked with funk or African American music more generally: phenomenology and contemporary hermeneutics.[19] A main issue within these traditions is the temporal character of human life, and especially the temporal space between immediate "being in time" and an understanding of this same being. One result of this fundamentally temporal character is that the exchange between these two basic modes of experience is itself bound to unfold over time. Since these modes cannot take place simultaneously—there is no way of attending to one's own ongoing experience at a distance—there is no possible way of arriving at a systematic understanding of being as such.

The epistemological consequence of this inability is that the process of understanding how being or subjective experience is unavoidably objectified in a process of distanciation—inherent, for example, in social discourse—requires the transformation of what is to be understood into something other than what it was. The funk experience as a state of being seems to be especially difficult to grasp, primarily because the very process of grasping it tends to conceal the distinctive qualities of its initial events. Also, because of the highly processual character of its meaning, funk is about how things are in "real time"—how the groove unfolds in performance, right then and there.

Cultural-critical discussions, as well as musical-analytical investigations, are no doubt important to the understanding of funk. However, such academic discourses often fail to address the phenomenological qualities linked with the experience of music—that is, how things are when they happen. Moreover, these discourses often convey the impression that understanding, in the sense that they represent it, is all there is. In a way they are right, because from an intersubjective perspective, there is nothing but understanding: we are simply left to understand, and then to communicate our experiences after the fact. The difference between how things are when they happen, in time, and how they are immediately afterward, in the process of understanding, is impossible to transcend: it cannot be leveled out. Still, we can try to make this impasse a part of the process of understanding and communicating. There are, thus, differences among various discourses regarding the extent to which they downplay, or attempt to highlight, their underlying bases in subjective being.

My engagement with phenomenology and hermeneutics encouraged me not to forget my initial interest in the funk experience as such.

In other words, I found a theoretical and methodological reason for my interest in approaching what I call the "funk experience" from a position within subjective experience. As I argued above, such a starting point does not imply any form of subjectivism or solipsism. Rather it concerns the problem of funk, or any other event, for that matter, *coming to one's senses*. Individual, subjective experience is in fact the only access we have, not only to the subjective aspects of musical experience but—and this is what social theory sometimes seems to forget—to its intersubjective aspects as well.

The fact that the processes of understanding, reflection, and analysis take place with subjective experience as a nontranscendable starting point means, firstly, that culture, social structures, and patterns of taste and the like do not exist apart from individual experiences and, secondly, that one cannot do away with one's own preunderstanding. In hermeneutic terms, one could say that there is no world, no others, no culture, and no history without subjective experience—without "being." The flip side of this is, as scholars of cultural studies and social theory often stress, the fundamentally social character of this being. Social and cultural patterns are part of any experience—put differently, the situatedness of being cannot be removed from an experience. As there is no position outside subjective experience, there is simply no place for an experience free of cultural, historical, and social inclinations. In terms of hermeneutics, we could say that relating (to others and to the world) is a fundamental aspect of being: being simply *is* being with others as well as being in a world.[20]

In academic texts dealing with black music, it does not always seem that this is taken fully into account. The problem is not that social and cultural patterns are overlooked. Rather there is a tendency to privilege, perhaps even ontologize, what is constructed as the original context of the music, and further to act as if one's own preunderstanding is transparent. Put differently, sometimes it might seem as if research on black music does not deal with how a particular music actually works in its own historical and social contexts but rather with how music works, or *should* work, in general, regardless of or even despite these contexts.[21] For example, the meaning of black music in Africa as determined by white ethnomusicologists is claimed to be true not only for "them" (whoever they may be) but for "us" as well. In fact, such a gesture ends up as a paradox: first, context (the African one) is claimed to be essential for the understanding of (black) music; next, context (the European one) seems to be absent (when understanding black music in Europe).[22]

In this study, my aim is not to try to merge with the African American discourse on funk in order to reinstall the "original" or most correct or true interpretational context for this music. This would actually conceal the history of the role of funk and black music for white Western audiences. My aim is rather, as pointed out earlier, to give an interpretation of funk with my own culture and experience as points of departure. However, in order to grasp this meeting of the musical and cultural horizons of these audiences and black funk as it took place in the late 1970s, it is necessary to approach the grooves from two sides: production and reception. This implies a dual ambition regarding knowledge, because it seems necessary to achieve both *self-knowledge*—knowledge of the Western pop and rock audiences—and *other-knowledge*—knowledge of African American culture and musical traditions—at the same time.[23] One has, in other words, to deal with what might be called a double hermeneutic distance. Both the cultural space between "us" and "them" and the historical distance from the moment of crossover for funk in the late 1970s must be taken into account.

In order to grasp the qualities of the funk grooves, we must seek a merging of horizons. In principal, however, this is impossible. We cannot fully do away with our own preunderstanding. Also, my account of funk as seen from *inside* the cultural situation that produced these grooves is flavored by my cultural and historical distance from those events. Bearing this in mind, however, we can still learn from the study of African American cultural and musical traditions. Moreover, in addition to an ethically based motivation for describing the circumstances under which the grooves were made and their place within the context of black struggle and black self-consciousness, an understanding of the musical traditions and culture of black America is probably the best starting point for developing the analytical tools needed to grasp funk grooves as music.

Conversely, in order to understand why these grooves were experienced and understood as they were, and to some extent still are, within my own culture, I have to focus on their reception and take into consideration the common musical habitus, as well as the common social or discursive understanding of the funk experience, among the white Western fans of this period. It is, in other words, also necessary to keep the distance intact, to keep the space between us and them open. It is not sufficient to try to adopt only the other's cultural perspective.

Nor, one might add, is it possible. It goes without saying that a total merging of horizons is utopian. Black styles may be appropriated by a non-black person, but the black *experience* is not fully understandable for an outsider. In an essay written within the context of the Black Arts Movement of the 1960s (which will be further presented in chapter 2), Julian Mayfield emphasizes the significance of approaching black aesthetics at a level *beyond* the question of black style: "For those who must create, there is a Black Aesthetic which cannot be stolen from us, and it rests on something much more substantial than hip talk, African dress, natural hair, and endless fruitless discussions of 'soul.' It is in our racial memory, and the unshakable knowledge of who we are, where we have been, and, springing from this, where are we going."[24] At this level, black aesthetics is obviously more than a way of explaining the extraordinary qualities of much black music. It is a search for a new spirituality, or, as Mayfield suggests, the recapture of an old one, "lost and buried deep in our African past."[25] It is in this sense that the Black Aesthetic Movement was in the business of making revolution, and it is in this sense that much funk, for example James Brown's, was deeply spiritual for the African American audience of the 1960s. In Mayfield's words, "We have tried everything else. Now, this the Tom Joneses and Janis Joplins cannot steal, and will not imitate. For deep in their guts they cannot feel what we have felt."[26]

James Brown was an icon of this blackness for LeRoi Jones as well. He found that James Brown's music, in form and content, identifies an entire group of people in America: "Music makes an image . . . The world James Brown's images power is the lowest placement (the most alien) in the white American social order. Therefore, it is the Blackest and potentially the strongest."[27] According to Jones, the middle classes, of any color, preferred a more respectable image of the black man than the one James Brown had to offer. They did not want to relate to the world he evoked in his music: "'The whitened' Negro and white man want a different content from the people James Brown 'describes.'"[28]

In the context of this book, however, one should perhaps add that James Brown only evokes this world when communicating with a *resonant* audience—that is, an audience that was in a position to understand the world James Brown brought with him. As I argued earlier, this was not the case with the audience represented by white European fans. In one way, we did want the content—the nonconformism, the distance from the mainstream, the experience of otherness. To us, however, that content was not threatening. The problems and the misery of James Brown's world were distant from our world, perhaps to the extent that we did not perceive them at all. The music of James Brown did not point them out for us, it pointed toward another world—our world.

It is obvious that my James Brown is different from Jones's, and that, especially today, the most exclusively black music has been embraced by many worldwide audiences and has been used for their own purposes. My claim is that even though African American rhythms have been an irreducible part of the popular music mainstream for several decades, they are probably still "hot."[29] Even though the level of discourse around these questions has considerably improved, the involvement with much African American music has remained a means of catharsis, of dealing with the "prohibited" pleasures of the body. African American rhythms still constitute a field of otherness.

Writing about black music with this as a starting point is both a difficult and a sensitive task. It may in one sense also be unethical: by repeating, and dealing with, the primitivist account of black music, one may in fact also seem to reaffirm it. On the other hand, whether one likes it or not, the blackness of black music was obviously a source for developing a fantasy of otherness, a fantasy that could help to liberate its audience from the dominant values of mainstream Western society, at least for a limited time. This otherness is probably no longer felt to be as frightening as it sometimes used to be—it is more like an alter ego or an inseparable friend—but to ignore this part of funk's history would leave us with a rather poor understanding of the subject matter while continuing to avoid some of the problematic aspects of our relationship to black music. To admit to this relationship with black music is, in my view, also to defeat the historically submitted primitivist account of black culture. The process of reflecting upon oneself may actually change something. Rather than overlooking this recent history of ours, we might instead examine this fantasy of otherness and its sources, from within, and fully disclose it.

The insights of hermeneutics and phenomenology demonstrate not only that some answers are more difficult to give than others but also that these answers—which may only be hinted at and can never be validated in a strict sense—are probably the most valid. Along these lines, this study marks out a path for understanding rather than making up a full proof system, and its field of theory is interdisciplinary and includes contributions from musicology, ethnomusicology, and cultural studies as well as philosophical traditions such as phenomenology and modern hermeneutics as represented by Paul Ricœur, Jacques Derrida, Jean-Francois Lyotard, and Gilles Deleuze, among others. These different theoretical contributions are typically presented and discussed along the way, and I do not remain faithful to any particular one of them. Rather I try to explore them all in order to understand and explain the experience of the music.

Many of the texts that became central to this study, from Chernoff's *African Rhythm and African Sensibility* (1979) and Gates's *The Signifying Monkey* (1988) to Bakhtin's "The Problem of Speech Genres" (1986), Deleuze's *Difference and Repetition* (1994), Ricœur's "The Hermeneutical Function of Distanciation" (1973), Lyotard's "The Sublime and the Avantgarde" (1991), and Derrida's "Différance" and "Signature Event Context" (1982), cultivate a more processual, performative mode of thinking and writing, or address issues of performance, or both. Likewise in their musical analyses there is a special focus on performance. As already mentioned, the musical qualities in funk are deeply embedded in performance, in the fact that a certain performer plays an actual groove in a way that makes it groove. Describing funk in general categories, without highlighting the specificity of the way things are actually done in time, seems to bypass the whole point. To identify a pattern is not enough. In fact, any musical interpretation faces this challenge. However, with regard to funk, it becomes imperative, because funk is hardly funk without a certain manner: the pattern *has* to be played to be funky.

In short, music and the experience of music have been permitted to rule my process of writing, including my use of theory. As a consequence, the various central discourses do not show up in separate chapters but are combined to inform each other throughout a more general hermeneutic reflection.

In the next chapter, I present and discuss two related but very different discourses on African American music. The first is the story of black music as an other within Western culture. This primitivist understanding of black culture is a key to understanding the role of funk within the Anglo-American–dominated field of popular music. The second offers a very different story of the musical and cultural impact of funk that grew out of the African American political movement in the 1960s.

Part II is devoted to close readings of selected funk grooves by James Brown. The tunes are chosen to suit the main focus and will, first and foremost, be considered as grooves regarding their harmonic, melodic, and timbral aspects. In chapter 3, I present a framework for the understanding of grooves. In chapter 4, I identify some important rhythmic figures in the funk grooves of James Brown, and in chapter 5 I focus on how these grooves are played. Songs like "Cold Sweat," "Sex Machine," and "The Payback" receive thorough treatments, but other tunes are also discussed according to specific points of interest.[30]

Part III concentrates on funk in the post–civil rights period. In chapter 6, I describe how funk crossed over to the white pop and rock audiences, and how this affected both the music and the public's understanding of it. Following James Brown through these years of crossover, I discuss how the new cultural climate affected both his music and his career. Chapter 7 is devoted to the analysis, interpretation, and discussion of what were probably the most important responses to this new cultural situation from the point of view of black America, namely George Clinton and his P-Funk enterprise. The rhythmic and performative shapings of the P-Funk grooves receive close attention, and songs like "Up for the Downstroke," "P-Funk Wants to Get Funked Up," "Give Up the Funk (Tear the Roof off the Sucker)," and "Do That Stuff," all reissued on *Parliament's Greatest Hits* (1984), as well as aspects of the live recording *P-Funk All-Stars Live!* (1990, recorded in 1983), are all subjects of a thorough discussion.

Part IV concentrates on different experiential aspects of funk, focusing on the connection between the musical features of funk and the funk experience This shift to a focus on experience also means a shift of context, namely to the Northern European reception of funk in the late 1970s and the historical moment when black dance music monopolized the dance rhythms of the Anglo-American world of pop and rock. I address the question of how funk is organized in time on a larger scale, as well as how this musical form is experienced while it is taking place. My musical-analytical focus is extended from investigating rhythmic patterns as these unfold on a micro-level (parts II and III) to studying funk when a rhythmic pattern is played over and over again—that is, repeated in time. In chapter 8, I present the backdrop for the inclination toward what I call song-directed listening among the white Western pop and rock audiences of the1970s. I also reflect on the important issues of time and repetition in music. Last but not least I link these reflections with the findings of the analytical investigations of part II and III. Chapter 9 is devoted to investigations into the interplay between the large-scale temporal designs of some actual songs and how they are experienced at a phenomenological level. At the core of the discussion are two different but nevertheless very typical James Brown funk tunes, "Sex Machine" and "The Payback." Both are characterized by a form and temporality that seem to prepare for what is called *the state of being in funk*—more so than the album-formatted *songs* of Parliament. They also bring into focus what modes of listening and/or participating are involved, and how the different aspects of the musical form of funk songs may be thought to have, or not have, an effect when encountering these modes. Then, in chapter 10, I reflect upon the funk experience from the "inside," assuming that the audience has reached the state of being in funk. The discussions regarding such a state of being will be extended in the direction of a more general aesthetic and epistemological reflection.

In the last chapter, I relate these analytical and experiential aspects to some basic constraints in the dominant tradition of Western thought, focusing on the relationship of the funk experience to the dominant Western understanding of this experience. How, or rather why, is the meaning of funk the way it is in a white Western context? And how does this intersect with racial ideology? These questions are now reconsidered in light of the findings of the previous chapters.

2

Two Discourses on Blackness

True "objectivity" where race is concerned is as rare as a
necklace of Hope diamonds.
—Hoyt W. Fuller

How funk is experienced—and how these experiences are explained
and described, thereby gaining meaning in social discourse—varies
considerably. As R. Radano and P. V. Bohlman point out, listeners may
now acquire recorded musics, formerly bound up within a racial framework, and give them specific, local, alternative meanings. Nevertheless,
this process takes place "within a global economy that provides, free of
charge, matrices of meaning articulated, if not regulated and controlled,
by the transnational institutions of mass-marketed entertainment."[1]

One such matrix of meaning is the Western historical way of understanding and representing blackness. This primitivist reading of black
culture is contrasted by the African American account of black music and
culture, which arose from 1960s political movements. I will now introduce these two related but very different discourses, both of which link
otherness and black music to one another and both of which represent
important aspects of the 1970s context of funk. I will then conclude with
a discussion of my choice of groove as a primary perspective on funk.

The Primitivist Representation of Black Culture

How, or rather why, has funk taken on the meanings it has within the
Anglo-American field of popular music? A starting point for an answer

to this question is the common opposition of nature and culture, and by extension the West's historical linking of black culture to nature. The representation of African or black culture as barbarian in this sense has been part of the Western understanding of itself for centuries. Over one hundred fifty years ago Hegel, for example, characterized the African as follows: "All our observations of African man show him as living in a state of savagery and barbarism, and he remains in this state to the present day. The negro is an example of animal man in all his savagery and lawlessness, and if we wish to understand him at all, we must put aside all our European attitudes."[2] According to Hegel, the African had not progressed beyond his immediate existence to an awareness of any other substantial and objective existence; he had not yet attained "the recognition of the universal." As a consequence, the African is not even considered to be at an early stage in the development of our civilized world but instead represents a threshold to history: the African becomes a negative limit for what humanity can be.[3] As James Snead has pointed out, the African comes to represent "an absolute alterity to the European"; the African works as an other against whom we define ourselves.[4]

As postcolonial theorizing has brought to the fore, this othering process—characterized by Hayden White as "ostensive self-definition by negation"[5]—has resulted in a very particular lens through which the West has seen others and made them almost the same, regardless of their striking diversity. Others have all, in short, become what we are not. Others—including other places and other times—have been used as a way of identifying ourselves, thus ending up in a metonymic relation with all of the features structurally glued to the other pole of the culture-nature axis, such as (mind-)body, (intellect-)emotions, (complexity-)simplicity, and so on.

The features linked with such a position of otherness have in turn been considered bad (see Hegel) or good. While the former may be characterized as an instance of a modern affirmative primitivism, the latter should be considered as a critique of modernity. In it the same features are attributed to the other, but they now represent a more natural, more authentic—in short, more human—way of life than the alienated modern world. In line with A.-B. Gran (2000), we may paraphrase White and call this turnabout a process of *critical self-definition by negation*.[6] In this version of primitivism, which is often labeled romantic primitivism, nature is good, culture is bad.[7]

The case of blackface minstrelsy in the United States supports the assumption that this *ambivalent attitude* seems to have always characterized white people's encounters with black culture. Blackface roles became increasingly important to minstrel shows during the nineteenth century, representing an image of black people as they were seen and portrayed by whites. Although the stereotypes changed somewhat over the years, the main features of the image remained constant: blacks were strongly infantilized, presented as simple, happy people who were unable to cope with the freedoms and challenges of a modern "adult" world (and consequently best off in the safer world of the slave plantation). According to Christopher Small, blackface minstrelsy was met by a double-sided response in its white audiences, showing how affirmative and romantic primitivism may often be at work simultaneously. On the one hand, there was the envy that the white person, caught up in a formidable work ethic and overarching Puritanism, felt about the black person, who was perceived as irresponsible, sexually potent, and devoted to the pleasures of the moment. But there was also a genuine admiration of certain qualities in the black community, its communality and soul, or "emotional honesty," as Small puts it. It was the need to make sense of this complex of feelings that lay behind the popularity of blackface minstrelsy, according to Small: "The minstrel show articulated with precision these attitudes, being a vehicle for caricature which served to render innocuous the fascinating but dangerous culture of the blacks."[8] In short, blackface minstrelsy answered a need in white culture to sort out these mixed feelings toward blacks and also get in touch with what black culture had to offer, but in a way that kept the attractive otherness of black culture at a distance.[9]

Eric Lott, in his impressive study of minstrelsy entitled *Love and Theft*, also underlines the ambivalence of the white audience's meeting with blackness, and how the minstrel show took the form of a simultaneous drawing up and crossing of racial boundaries. According to Lott, the minstrel show displayed a mixed erotic economy of celebration and exploitation, and minstrelsy was often an attempt, within a context of cross-racial desire, to repress through ridicule the real white interest in black cultural practices. According to Lott, this made blackface minstrelsy a sign less of absolute white power and control than panic, anxiety, terror, and pleasure. He writes, "The minstrel show was less the incarnation of an age-old racism than an emergent social semantic figure highly responsive to the emotional demands and troubled fantasies of its audiences."[10]

As Edward Said has argued with regard to the Orient, such primitivist representations of an othered culture by the dominant culture often have consequences also for the othered culture's understanding of itself. As he states in *Orientalism*, "Like any set of durable ideas, Orientalist notions influenced the people who were called Oriental as well as those called Occidental, European, or Western; in short, Orientalism is better grasped as a set of constraints upon and limitations of thought than it is simply a positive doctrine."[11] This mechanism is also at work in the primitivist representation of black culture, which has influenced black self-representation in certain ways. In some cases it has been adopted without mediation or even comment. In other cases it has been inverted or reproduced with a double message. This may have been the case when, in the last decades of the nineteenth century, black artists entered the minstrel stage, many of them "blacked up" and acting out the same stereotypes as the white minstrels of the previous decades. Surprisingly, blackface minstrelsy by black performers was extremely popular with not only white but black audiences too. So how could this be?

According to Small, there may be several reasons for black artists blacking up. First of all, the minstrel stage was one of the few opportunities for a black performer to earn a living. Second, it meant a chance to display one's theatrical and musical skills. Third, and most important in this context, blackface minstrelsy may be interpreted as an example of an old strategy used by the abused: to take the abusive label, invert its meaning, and wear it as a badge of pride. Small claims that the black minstrel probably had much more to say to the black audience than to the white. And he was probably able to do so, for, as Small reminds us, both the black minstrel and the black audiences were descendants of slaves who had been communicating clandestinely for generations: "And so it was that minstrelsy, which had been a way of affirming the inferiority of black people, became for those same people an avenue of advancement and helped in the creation of a language of self-presentation which was not without importance in the struggle for recognition as people. But . . . there was a price; the minstrel image has haunted blacks ever since."[12]

The double voice of the black minstrel, as well as the ambivalent response of its white audience, suggests preconditions for the exchange between black music and a mixed audience, and it is no less topical today. The outcome of this double-voiced strategy is, however, twofold. On the one hand, it is a form of black power in which black agency links up with white passivity, a situation that may be used by black artists for their own benefit. On the other hand, it is yet another case of black people affirming the role of the exotic other. As such, the double-voiced utterance is both a means of uniqueness and a confirmation of the status quo. Seen from the outside, it affirms the stereotype; seen from the inside, it comments upon it in a process of self-parody or self-reflection.

A parallel situation from contemporary music arises in rap and the black concept of "badness," which signifies a certain way of behavior, a style and attitude, as Cornel West explains:

> For most young black men, power is acquired by stylizing their bodies over space and time in such a way that their bodies reflect their uniqueness and provoke fear in others. To be "bad" is good not simply because it subverts the language of the dominant white culture but also because it imposes a unique kind of order for young black men on their own distinctive chaos and solicits an attention that makes others pull back with some trepidation. This young black male style is a form of self-identification and resistance in a hostile culture.[13]

Badness is both a means of uniqueness and a confirmation of the primitivist representation of black culture. As such, it is attractive to, but out of reach for, whites (and, we should add, black women, who instead suffer from this form of black power).[14] This source of power, however, can also be considered an internalization of the otherness of black culture, one put forward by the dominant white culture. Particularly if we take into consideration the profound inequalities in discursive and economic power, badness may appear to be another example of an oppressed culture adopting the oppressor's representation of itself.

Why, then, is this primitivist representation relevant to a study of funk?

The primitivist account of black culture in our recent history, as wild, irresponsible, closer to nature, out of control—but also more sexually potent—unavoidably influences contemporary relations between blacks and whites on all levels. It does not always sound as baldly colonial as Hegel's quotations, but it is still there in its more or less subtle disguise as an imagined counterpart in the process of Western self-definition: a dream of otherness. This is certainly also the case in the field of music. It is striking how black music has been placed in opposition to European high art musical traditions in the West. In contrast with Western art music's traditional focus on form, harmony, and thematic development, African music, for example, has been identified mainly with rhythm. This has no doubt influenced the study of African music, both regarding what music is chosen and what aspects of it are examined. In short, studies of rhythm, in particular West African drumming, seem to be privileged over vocal traditions and other African music that is more focused on melody and chords, and this selection of music is probably biased according to musical aspects that are constitutive of the music's otherness.

This was addressed by Kofi Agawu in an article entitled "The Invention of 'African Rhythm'" (1995). In a rather harsh critique, Agawu questions the validity of the account of African music given by both Western and African scholars within this field, especially its focus on the complexities of African rhythm. This construction is, according to Agawu, maintained by three errors; the first concerning the claim that African music should constitute a homogenous whole: "The continued use of the phrase 'African music' when one's authority is an African village, town, or region reproduces the metonymic fallacy—the part representing the whole—faced by most writers on Africa."[15] The second error he calls "the retreat from comparison": although the claim about the complexities of African rhythm presupposes a comparative framework, it rarely leads to explicit comparison. He continues: "For such comparisons to have force, we need to do more than casually allude to the other term in the binary framework."[16] The third error has to do with the lack of a critical evaluation of African musical practice, both with regard to whether a performance is good or not and whether informants are reliable.[17]

From Agawu's Foucaultian informed perspective, the construction of the notion "African rhythm" is at the center of a whole discourse that has been—and still is—extremely powerful within the field of black music studies:

> Note that this notion has been promulgated by both Western and African scholars . . . It is therefore not simply a case of westerners (mis)representing African music—although given the political and economic realities that have shaped the construction of the library of African music, and given the blatant asymmetries of power that the colonial encounter has produced, there are solid grounds for indulging in the politics of blame. What we have, rather, are the views of a group of scholars operating within a field of discourse, an intellectual space defined by Euro-American traditions of ordering knowledge. It is difficult to overestimate the determining influence of this scholarly tradition on the representation of African music.[18]

In *Lying Up a Nation: Race and Black Music* (2003), Ronald Radano extends Agawu's critique, arguing that the emphasis on rhythm as the primary defining quality of black music is a modern idea, deeply linked with what he calls "the dialectics of modern racial ideology." According to Radano, the idea emerged in the beginning of the twentieth century in response to a specific historical circumstance, namely the increasing presence of African American popular music in the public sphere. Radano identifies this linking of race and rhythm as a meeting or crossroads of two conceptions of blackness that he names descent and displacement. *Descent* is the search for the origins of black rhythm. Radano, interestingly, traces this line back to theories of cultural and racial difference in early comparative musicology, pointing out how the idea of rhythm as a more natural, more original—that is, a more primitive—form of human behavior took shape as part of the overall processes of "ostensive self-definition by negation" presented above.[19] As we know, rhythm has been placed at the center of the identity of black culture in subsequent discourses, and if we adopt Radano's perspective, this may appear to be an instance of unmediated appropriation of the first position's (white comparative musicology) representation of an othered culture (black music). I will return to a discussion of this toward the end of this chapter.

In addition to this search for origin along the temporal-historical axis, Radano identifies a spatial axis, a conception of blackness as *displacement*, or more precisely as "sounds out of place." As African Americans began to move about the American territory in the postbellum era, they inevitably challenged the boundaries that had once constrained them both physically and socially. As a consequence, black music appeared in public more frequently, becoming, in his words, "a potent blackness 'on the loose.'"[20] He writes: "In black musical production, then, we recognize the emergence of a formidable social expression inextricably related to the creation of American modernism. Its potency derives from its articulation of a radically new conception of racial otherness growing from the spatial dimensions of the crossroads as it intersects temporal affiliations north and south." While earlier conceptions of otherness linked the identity of 'the other' to a certain place, which according to an ethnocentric point of view was conceived of as homogenous and with absolute properties, this new understanding of black music "defined the essential nature of blackness by exceeding place in ways that anticipated other fractured dimensions of modernist art and culture."[21]

According to Radano, this made the new black music and its ragged rhythm uncanny, a magical force that was thought to infect anybody— or rather any *body*—that came in contact with it. In line with this, when "hot rhythm" peaked with the music of the "jazz age" of the 1920s, it was considered almost an epidemical threat. As one contemporary writer put it, hot rhythm could "get into the blood of some of our young folks, and I might add older folks, too."[22]

The parallel to the discourse on rock 'n' roll in the 1950s is indeed striking, and within the Anglo-American field of pop and rock in the 1960s and 1970s we find the same double notion: on one hand the romantic primitivist understanding of black music as origin and nature, and on the other hand the intertwined conception of hot rhythm. On the positive side, we have the communal feeling of the rock concert or the dance floor, and the ideal of honesty in musical expression; on the negative side, we have the aspects of rock culture that are perceived as "dirty"—irresponsibility, sexual freedom, pleasure seeking in the moment—all commonly linked with rock's roots in black musical culture. A twenty-five-year-old text by Simon Frith may serve as an example of how important the primitivist account of black music has been for rock: "Whereas Western dance forms control body movements and sexuality itself with formal rhythms and innocuous tunes, black music expresses the body, hence sexuality, with a directly physical beat and an intense, emotional sound—the sound and beat are felt rather than interpreted via a set of conventions. Black musicians work, indeed, with a highly developed aesthetic of public sexuality."[23] Frith's quotation also seems to describe black music as closer to nature. Significant qualities of the music are understood as unmediated bodily expression and as ineligible for conventional processing and interpretation on the reception side. In short, the artifact nature of black music is denied and the body is reduced to the sexual body alone.[24]

The longing for the "other side" of typical Western values, for keeping a certain distance from the mainstream, is central to the entire history of popular music in the West from the 1950s onward.[25] In line with this, Robert Pattison has interpreted the whole field of rock as a rebellion against rationality and order—the official super-ego of the West, as he calls it. To quote the title of his book, rock is "the triumph of vulgarity."[26] The perceived "black" aspects of popular music, especially its rhythm and its distorted sounds, have been central means for realizing rock's subversive power, as well as its anti-Western values. These aspects have, in short, worked as a carrier of the otherness sought after in this music. In the words of Radano and Bohlman, "The imagic power of 'blackness' appears as a dislocated, fragmentary hypertext of post–World War II American popular sound."[27]

As a genre focused on rhythm or groove, funk has been perceived almost as blackness in its purest form. This musical difference from the "official" musical tradition of the West, art music, has made funk an especially effective means for living out the other side of Western culture. It is, thus, not very surprising that funk has been described as "body music" within the West, and more than this, as the bodily experience par excellence: sexual pleasure. It has been interpreted as a distillation of repetitive rhythm, the aspect of rock commonly regarded as most closely related to sex.

To interrogate this reductive understanding of funk is not to deny this music's striking physical appeal: funk is designed to move the body; it is dance music. Rather, we may begin to introduce a more nuanced understanding of the appeal of funk and the complexities of its grooves. Moreover, the flip side of the primitivist understanding of black music is that the spiritual aspects of the funk experience seem to have completely vanished. It is my claim that these spiritual aspects are as important as its bodily aspects to the white Western fan's fascination with funk and the state of being it offers. Most likely, as I will argue toward the end of this book, they are inseparable.

Black Is Beautiful!—Black Music and Black Struggle

Within American academia, we find a discourse on African American music that is far from the body-and-sex discourse of rock. Historically, it points back to the vital period of black political struggle in the 1960s, when aesthetic aspects of black music were often subordinated to political aims, or, as Henry Louis Gates Jr. writes: "One repeated concern of the Black Aesthetic movement was the nature and function of black literature vis-à-vis the larger political struggle for Black Power. How useful was our literature to be in this centuries-old political struggle, and exactly how was our literature to be useful?"[28]

This program for the Black Arts Movement is highly present in the seminal 1972 anthology *The Black Aesthetic*. In his introduction, Addison Gayle Jr. writes: "The question for the black critic today is not how beautiful a melody, a play, a poem, or a novel, but how much more beautiful has the poem, melody, or novel made the life of a single black man? How far has the work gone in transforming an American Negro into an African-American or black man?"[29]

A main task for the Black Aesthetic Movement was, as one white critic described it, "the act of creation of the self in the face of the self's historic denial by our society."[30] Although this must be said to be a constant aspect of black culture and black political struggle in the United States, the 1960s were characterized by a sharpening of the effort against the white mainstream. A policy of explicit anti-integrationism articulated a rather harsh critique of the black middle class that was ready to fit into the American mainstream. In this era, "American" in fact comes close to meaning the opposite of black: to be American is to be anti-black, or, in the words of Gayle: "The serious black artist of today is at war with the American society as few have been throughout American history."[31] Later he adds, "To be an American is to be opposed to humankind, against the dignity of the individual, and against the striving in man for compassion and tenderness: to be an American is to lose one's humanity."[32]

The backdrop for this confrontational line was no doubt partly the American intervention in Vietnam. However, the double moral standards of liberal white America, as well as an increasing understanding of how the liberal ideology in many respects failed to change the conditions of black America—it often worked instead as a vehicle of repressive tolerance[33]—were also important. According to Gayle, revealing the white liberals as "the modern-day plantation owners they are" should be a primary target for African American critics. The liberal's ideology, he writes, is "a cosmology that allows him to pose as humanitarian on the one hand, while he sets about defining the black man's limitations on the other."[34]

In line with this, one point central to the Black Aesthetic Movement was the encouragement of the black artist to give up working with the white public in mind. The price for becoming an American was too high, Gayle says, because it seemed to mean giving up one's own identity. Or, in Hoyt W. Fuller's words, "[The] black writer has wasted much time and talent . . . seeking an identity that can only do violence to his sense of self."[35] The true black artist should rather speak honestly and avoid pretending or adjusting his mannerisms to the mainstream white audience. According to Gayle, the black artist has simply "given up the futile practice of speaking to whites, and has begun to speak to his brothers."[36]

As a result, the principles for a genuinely black aesthetic were worked out in the different fields of art. Among these, music seemed to have a privileged position. First, it was a cultural expression that presented itself as less "infected" by the Anglo-American West, at least when compared to writing, which was the primary mode of expression for many of the articulate participants in the Black Aesthetic Movement. In the field of writing, it seemed much more complicated to cut off black practice from Western practice. Many black writers were themselves fully aware of the subtleties and complexities characterizing the relation between the white canon and black literature, and they struggled with the dual nature of their heritage. In the domain of music, however, it seemed as if the black tradition were more unequivocally black. At least the terrain was easier to map, because the demarcation line was more striking. In his introduction to an essay on black aesthetics in music, for example, Jimmy Stewart does not hesitate to state that "There have always been two musical traditions: the musical tradition or aesthetic of white people in the West, and the musical tradition of Black people in this country."[37]

Today, such a clear-cut separation is more difficult to maintain; the overlaps and intermingling are striking. Moreover, decades of deconstruction and postcolonial thought have brought about insights into how identity is always part of a relational framework. Nevertheless, even though one might not hold on to an essentialist position, it is not difficult to understand what Stewart means. There are differences that make it easy to distinguish between white and black musical traditions, not least regarding the *approach* to music making. One might, in short, say that black musicking has a different creative focus; it is a *performing art* in the deepest sense. Or, in Stewart's words, "the imperishability of creation is not in what is created, is not in the art product, is *not in the thing* as it exists as an object, *but in the procedure* of its becoming what it is."[38]

As a consequence, in the Black Aesthetic Movement's attempts to identify an especially black literary aesthetics, writing partly took music as a model: "The writers are deliberately striving to invest their work with the distinctive styles and rhythms and colors of the ghetto, with those peculiar qualities which, for example, characterize the music of a John Coltrane or a Charlie Parker or a Ray Charles."[39]

A key theme within the Black Aesthetic Movement was its link to African culture. As a performing art, music is a form of cultural heritage that may be transmitted independent of material resources. It was, therefore, well suited to rebut the claim that an enslaved people was a people of lost culture.[40] Together with storytelling and other oral literary practices, approaches to music making were examples of cultural resources that had traveled from one continent to another with the people and their collective memory, and the approaches could later be applied to the instruments of the new world. This could, then, be linked to the fact that the black treatment of instruments—the piano or the voice, for example—is very different from the Western art music tradition's treatment, and it could further be used as evidence for the existence of a particularly black aesthetic linked with African musical practices. In Stewart's words,

> The instruments didn't come with free lessons and all, like you get at Wurlitzer . . . It was a matter of being left to our own resources to determine how the music was going to be produced on those instruments. This . . . meant that we had to impose on borrowed instruments an aesthetic convention that we obviously possessed even before we acquired them . . . It indicates that a Black aesthetic existed, and that this aesthetic has always governed what we have produced.[41]

While the political aspects of this debate peaked in the late 1960s, it has remained very influential in American scholarship to this day. As Gates writes, "The impetus of the Black Arts movement of the sixties, the literary and aesthetic wing of the Black Power movement, served two functions to which academic critics of the seventies and eighties are heir: the resurrection of 'lost' black texts, and the concomitant need to define the principles of criticism upon which a 'genuinely black' aesthetic could be posited."[42] In line with this, musicological attempts at defining a genuinely black aesthetic have been focused on the African influence on black American music, and on the common approach to musicking, claiming that it is the approaches, rather than the actual sounds that these approaches make, that unite the different black musical traditions.[43] Or, as composer and musicologist Olly Wilson states, "The common core of this Africanness consists of the way of doing something, not simply something that is done."[44] According to Wilson, this influence can be summed up as follows:

- a tendency to create musical structures in which rhythmic clash or disagreement of accents is the ideal;
- a tendency to approach singing or the playing of any instrument in a percussive manner;
- a weakness for a kaleidoscopic range of dramatically contrasting qualities of sound;

- a tendency toward a high density of events within a relatively short time frame; and

- a tendency to create musical forms with antiphonal or call-and-response musical structures.

Furthermore, importance is placed on the tendency to incorporate physical motion as an integral part of the music-making process, and on the social setting: music is a social activity where everybody, in a sense, participates on an improvisatory basis, although within a clearly defined and shared framework.[45]

Given the favorable position of jazz and other African American popular styles with regard to both their aesthetic quality and their popularity, music has been a powerful way of focusing a specific black identity within the larger American society. Music has, moreover, worked as a convincing link to the African past. Not least, much funk fits easily into the characteristics listed by Wilson above, and James Brown's funk in particular is often used to substantiate the linking of African and African American music.[46] In his book on black musical styles from 1950 to 1990, Guthrie P. Ramsey Jr. points to James Brown's production of the 1960s as extremely important for the new nationalism or black consciousness in the same period. According to Ramsey, the 1960s and 1970s should be regarded as the second phase of what he calls "a grand narrative of progress" named "Afro-modernism." This story is connected to the new urbanity of African American communities and the significant sociopolitical progress in black America in the first half of the twentieth century.[47] In this second phase of Afro-modernism, the results of migration patterns in the first part of the century coincides with mass media texts, which African Americans living all over the United States would believe spoke to and about them as a group. According to Ramsey, James Brown epitomized this moment: "James Brown ruled the private and public spaces of black Chicago. You heard him constantly on the radio, at the block party, in roller rinks, homes, clubs, and stores. Everywhere."[48] There were several factors that contributed to this. First, as mentioned previously, his musical language, "the *spontaneity-within-the-pocket* funk approach" that he developed in this period, attracted black cultural nationalists interested in the link to an African past.[49] Second, his lyrics—both his political use of the word "black" and his emphasis on social justice and racial uplift—and his oral style of vocal delivery, which evoked a seemingly on-the-spot communication with an imagined community, combined with his own personal history to make him a reliable spokesman for black communities.

The relation between the music of James Brown, the politicized discourse of the Black Arts Movement, and the specific historical situation of African Americans in the United States in this period illustrates how music, discourse, and sociopolitical circumstances intertwine. In fact, Ramsey's account of the importance of James Brown for this era reminds us of the reciprocal relation of music and social and cultural matters. Contrary to what was often the case in the "older school" of cultural studies and subculture theory, where music was assumed to mirror underlying social structures and relations, the formative role of music in *shaping* such cultural and social matters must also be taken into account. It is exactly when we come to this relation between music and sociocultural identity that we find a severe difference between the discourses discussed in this chapter.

As scholars G. Born and D. Hesmondhalgh point out, music may be used in sociocultural processes in different ways. While it is worth recalling, especially in the context of this study, that music may well be used to *transcend* a certain sociocultural identity, music is also, as the discourse surrounding the funk grooves of the 1960s and 1970s in black America shows, a very effective means of affirming and delimiting the boundaries too: "Against prevailing views that music is primarily a means for the imagining of emergent and labile identities, we stress that music is equally at times a medium for marking and reinforcing the boundaries of existing sociocultural categories and groups."[50] To point out this fact is not to subscribe to an essentialist position, nor to fall back on an old static model of homology. Rather, it is a reminder of the fact that, in Ramsey's words, "All this talk of fluidity, indeed the idea of ethnicity as process and not a static existence, does not prevent our understanding how people experience group identity from a reified, though contested, 'center.'"[51] Keeping this in mind and recalling as well the formative role of music in these processes, both on an individual and a collective level, we may approach the task of understanding how funk, as Western music "with a distinct difference," as Ramsey puts it, came to play different roles in the two different social worlds that meet in the subject matter of this book.[52] Before moving on to the analyses in parts II and III, however, a few comments on this difference, and the related focus on funk as grooves, need to be made.

A Common Source of Otherness?

Both the Black Arts Movement of the 1960s and the African retention arguments put forward by African American musicologists are examples of how important music has been in the process of shaping an African American history and identity in the United States. Within these discourses the features of black music are not seen as part of an interracial relation but rather in isolation from, and sometimes even in opposition to, white culture. In *Lying Up a Nation,* Radano criticizes the essentializing tendency of scholarly research on black music in general, although he credits the major contributions these scholars and writers have made in making the black tradition visible in academic institutions and writings. In Radano's view, the power of black music to enforce the collective "we" of blackness in these works comes forward as a black musical metaphysics emerging from America's own racial imagination, one that responds to the assimilationist intentions of erasure:

> In political terms, the metaphysical claims of black music that became emblematic of the Black Arts Movement challenged a vulnerable white supremacy that could no longer explain away the power and appeal of black musical achievement. As enabling as these racial essentialisms may have been, however, they also constrained the comprehension of black music's more fundamental insurgencies, particularly with reference to the undermining of racial categories.[53]

Radano's claim is that the importance of black music for the black identity project has led to a politics that betrays the underlying interracial relations' role in the understanding of the conceived essence of black music.[54] One consequence of such a politics is that one overlooks the fact that the discourses on blackness discussed in this chapter, although differing severely in important aspects, share some fundamental features. They both rely on the notion of black rhythm as a core characteristic of black music. Moreover, they both separate themselves from the mainstream, understanding blackness as difference. Radano's work shows how the results of the European processes of self-definition by way of negation in the nineteenth century may have blended into the Afro-centric discourse on black music in the United States in the following century, forming "a sturdy basis for defining and redefining difference across the twentieth century."[55] According to Radano, this historic moment, which is characterized by the shift in public perception that reinvented black music as rhythm, represents no less than "a veritable watershed in the formation of black modern music."[56] It was from this common ground that black rhythm spread across the Western world, infiltrating the very core of the experience of being modern on both sides of the color line.

In general, the hybrid character of funk and other black American music, on the production and the reception sides, seems to be under-emphasized in the ethnomusicological discourse on black music. Radano's rendering of how the story of black rhythm as the main identifying feature of black music came to be as part of an interracial relation of black and white is thus both important and convincing. Moreover, it suggests a view of black music that recognizes the significance of blackness and black music for both blacks and whites. In this book, the aim of which is to investigate the meeting of black dance music and a white Northern European audience in the 1970s, such an interracial matrix for understanding black music in fact becomes no less then a fundamental premise.

Funk is commonly regarded as black rhythm music par excellence. As such, funk has served as a consummate example of the blackness of black music. In line with the critique above, one might ask if the focus on rhythm in the study of funk, and in this book, betrays a more correct—in the sense of free of racial inclinations—approach to funk. In my view, however, there are many reasons for keeping a focus on rhythm in the study of funk. First, and this is presumably in great part due to the circumstances focused upon by Radano, the *reception* of funk, on both sides of the color line, has been extremely focused on rhythm. Put differently, the ideological grounding of certain tendencies in the historical reception of funk cannot change the *effect* of black rhythm on its audience as it once was, there and then. Even though one might have wished that the reception turned out to be less inclined to racial categories, the fact that it was may not be revised.

Second, despite the aforementioned ideological construction's disproportionate influence upon the perception of black musicking, rhythm is an important aspect of it. To completely avoid discussing black rhythm when dealing with black music would be to throw out the baby with the bathwater. After the "watershed" described by Radano, black music has to a great extent developed as rhythm music, because the ideology constraining black music to rhythm has influenced its production, especially as commercial distribution has become more and more important. This is also a point made by Radano: "As black per-formers entered into more public circumstances controlled by white au-thority of taste, they were compelled to work within the parameters de-fining the nature of race music. In this, they did not simply perform black music but produced those particular expressions that affirmed ra-cial difference within a broad system of relations and according to a structural logic that was unmistakably ideological."[57] In line with this, it is possible to believe that African American musicians have contin-ued to develop and generate forms that highlight musical blackness, though for the pleasure of an interracial audience. This probably holds true for many popular black forms, like swing, rhythm and blues, bebop, cool, soul, funk, and more. And as West reminds us, this structu-ral logic of racial origin is still at work in our time in what is probably the most widespread and influential contemporary manifestation of blackness: rap.

There is also a final, and perhaps more pragmatic, reason for sticking to a focus on groove in this situation: there is a striking lack of studies of rhythm and groove in musicology, including popular music studies. And as would hopefully be clear by now, this lack is not a coincidence. Rather, it is in itself a product of a racially inclined musicological tradi-tion, which, as Radano suggests, may also be the common ground of the otherness of *both* discourses of blackness presented and discussed in this chapter. As a fulfillment of a black aesthetic on several levels, in-cluding its emphasis on performance in general and performing with "style" in particular, funk may serve as a perfect starting point for cor-recting this imbalance in musicological focus and interest.

II

A Brand New Bag

Analytical Investigations

Despite some telling descriptions of the turn toward funk by James Brown and his band, there are few attempts in the musicological literature to actually trace these changes in songs. A confrontation with the early funk of James Brown as sounding music would probably disturb the clarity of the picture that is typically presented:

> Brown would sing a semi-improvised, loosely organized melody that wandered while the band riffed rhythmically on a single chord, the horns tersely punctuating Brown's declamatory phrases. With no chord changes and precious little melodic variety to sustain listener's interest, rhythm became everything. Brown and his musicians and arrangers began to treat every instrument and voice in the group as if each were a drum. The horns played single-note bursts that were often sprung against the downbeats. The bass lines were broken up into choppy two- or three-note patterns, a procedure common in Latin music since the Forties but unusual in R&B. Brown's rhythm guitarist choked his guitar strings against the instrument's neck so hard that his playing began to sound like a jagged tin can being scraped with a pocketknife. Only occasionally were the horns, organ or backing vocalists allowed to provide a harmonic continuum by holding a chord.
>
> The chugging push-pull of the Brown band's "Brand New Bag" was the wave of the future.[1]

In this text from *The Rolling Stone Illustrated History of Rock & Roll,* we get the impression of a total change from previous musical styles and of all of the features of the new style working comfortably together.

Certainly, many of the songs from this period—from "Papa's Got a Brand New Bag" in 1965 to the more fleshed-out funk tunes of the early 1970s—are more or less funk. They are, however, always something else as well. It is usually different aspects of different songs that point toward the "new style": all of the features listed above—semi-improvised vocals, one-chord "harmony," implied polyrhythm, the rhythmic riffing of the horn section and the guitar, the fragmentation of the bass line, and an overall percussive approach—are relevant, but they are seldom, if ever, present at the same time. The transition from rhythm and blues to funk, the former represented by tunes like "Papa's Got a Brand New Bag" and "I Got You (I Feel Good)" (1965), the latter by "Cold Sweat" (1967), is in many ways rather vague, either because the new features to some extent were already there or the older ones remained present.

Nevertheless, one develops an image of James Brown working deliberately on a "proto-funk." In a fairly short period of time, he introduced almost all of the basic concepts of his new direction, all of the features that in a certain peculiar (and ultimately nonexistent) moment crystallized as a new style and are labeled "funk." So what was this "new style"?

From Songs to Grooves

"Cold Sweat" is often regarded as James Brown's first funk tune.[2] The groove is not very different from a predominantly r&b song such as "Papa's Got a Brand New Bag." Nevertheless, the change is substantial. In "Papa's Got" there is still a song, in the sense that something—a melodic line, a chord sequence—is allowed to spread out on top of the rhythmic foundation. The division of labor is clear: the vocal resides on top, guitar takes care of the middle registers, and drums and bass provide rhythmic drive "down low."

In "Cold Sweat" only fragments remain. All of the instruments, including vocals, work more or less in the same way, forming small but significant rhythmic gestures that are linked in every direction. The groove has become an intricate fabric of sharp percussive sounds in which one sound brings on the next: the texture of the music has changed from horizontally divided layers of sound to a rhythmic patchwork. The decrease in tempo, from 148 beats per minute in, for example, "I Got You" to 116 beats per minute in "Cold Sweat," is an important aspect of this change, because it leaves room for a more detailed shaping of micro-level events as well as the delimitation of each rhythmic gesture.

At the same time, the overall formal scheme of a standard tune with verse and chorus or a blues pattern becomes gradually less pronounced.[3] In earlier r&b-derived songs like "Papa's Got a Brand New Bag" and "I Got You (I Feel Good)," the basic two-bar unit of the groove is part of larger formal divisions on several levels. "I Got You" has, for example, a verse and a chorus. The verse is a twelve-bar blues, while the chorus moves between the same chords in a way that might be said to be quite typical for an r&b song: IV-IV-I-I-IV-IV-V-V.

Also, "Papa's Got a Brand New Bag" contains formal units larger than the two-bar basic unit, namely a twelve-bar blues pattern that, contrary to "I Got You," runs all the way through the song. It is not implemented in a binary structure of verse and chorus and is only interrupted at one point, by a section based on one chord that completes an eight-bar bridge after the second complete blues pattern. This part may in itself point toward the leveling out of song form that was to come with funk. It gives no pronounced feeling of a larger symmetrical formation beyond the hints given by James Brown's lead vocal, which might suggest a grouping in four plus four bars.

Strictly speaking, "Cold Sweat" also has a formal division on a higher level—that is, a binary form of verse and chorus/bridge. However, many aspects give the impression of the absence of overall formal division that is so typical of most funk. One of these aspects is the shift to modal harmony. "Cold Sweat" is the first of many funk tunes by Brown in a Dorian mode, which allows for a more circular or nondirected temporal feel. When it comes to chords, the verse of "Cold Sweat" is completely leveled out— again, the lead vocal is the only part that points toward a regular division into four-bar groups. Moreover, the chorus works more as a bridge, reinforcing the verse as the main harmonic level of the song. In this respect it reminds us of the kinds of departures from the main groove often found in later songs by James Brown—for example, the famous and forcefully launched bridge of "Sex Machine."

Through this weakening of the traditional formal divisions of a song, the groove becomes what everything turns upon. The design of—and play with and within—the eight beats or two measures that are repeated almost endlessly throughout the song becomes the main challenge, for performer and critic alike.

In this part of the book, I will concentrate on the grooves of James Brown and his bands in the golden era, from "Papa's Got a Brand New Bag" (1965) to "The Payback" (1973, released in 1974). As I discussed in part I, the music of James Brown from this period was important to the struggle for a black cultural identity and history as a means of demonstrating an African influence on African American music and culture. In this section, however, my focus is not primarily on the cultural impact of these grooves. I will rather undertake a musicological investigation of the musical events that take place within the basic unit of a funk groove. Chapter 4 will be devoted to identifying some important rhythmic figures in the grooves of James Brown, while chapter 5 focuses on how these grooves are played.

Before turning to actual analyses, however, I will present in chapter 3 a framework for the understanding of grooves. As a part of this framework— even though my ultimate perspective will be different—I will pay a visit to some of the literature on West African music and on the African influence on African American music. The aim is to work out a means for analyzing and understanding "groove-directed" music—or, to use a concept from sociology, to work out an *ideal type* of music structured by and focused on rhythm.[4] As a part of this effort, several texts from the scholarly literature working with concepts such as African music, African rhythm, or the African influence on African American music have proved fruitful.[5] As an ideal type, however, my analytical framework should not be confused either with African music or with African rhythm in all of its empirical diversity. As Max Weber makes clear, an ideal type is by definition reductionist: "In its conceptual purity, this mental construct cannot be found empirically anywhere in reality."[6] Contrary to what is often the case with key concepts in academic discourse, however, an ideal type is a *conscious* reduction, an analytical device or filter that helps us understand and focus on the phenomenon at hand.

3

A Fabric of Rhythm

On Multilinear Rhythm

In *The Music of Africa* (1974), at the start of a chapter called "The Rhythmic Basis of Instrumental Music," Ghanaian musicologist J. H. Kwabena Nketia describes some important features of what might be called the ideal type "African rhythm." First he points out the most basic premise for an ideal type such as this, as well as for a groove, a feature so obvious that one often tends to forget to mention it: "The interrelationship of rhythmic patterns or phrases in strict time is controlled by relating them to a fixed *time span*, which can be broken up into an equal number of segments or pulses of different densities."[1]

In a funk groove, this unit is one or two bars, and I will refer to it as the *basic unit*, while the term *period*—where nothing else is indicated or suggested by way of context—is reserved for the level of grouping found in almost every pop tune except funk tunes and operates in units of four or eight bars.

Put another way, one could say that the rhythmic pattern, which often consists of several layers, has a fixed length in time, and, moreover, that the pattern is repeated. Ethnomusicologist Simha Arom calls this *isoperiodicity:* African rhythm is organized as a repetition of units or—in Arom's words—periods of equal length and with an invariant number of isochronous pulsations.[2] Arom emphasizes that this periodicity occurs through the repetition of an identical or similar unit of musical material and not through giving some beats more weight than others: "The basic temporal principle of rhythm is bringing back a form."[3] He claims that accentuation in isoperiodic music does not form a regular accentual matrix: every pulsation or beat within the period has the same status. As a consequence, there are no intermediate levels between the pulsation and the period and no matrix of strong and weak beats.

Normally, a funk groove is not isoperiodic in the sense offered by Arom, because the beats of the basic unit are weighted and the pattern has an audible beginning. A funk groove is, therefore, a hybrid of traditional Western rhythm, where measure is a significant structural constraint, and Arom's African rhythm, where the unit emerges through repetition of identical or similar materials. Whether the time signature should be considered 4/4, 8/4, or 4/2 varies from groove to groove. Regardless, the time signature is not to be confused with the distribution of weight that is implied in the 4/4-matrix of "classical music." I will shortly return to this.

Nketia divides the basic unit of the groove schematically in two and multiples of two (four, eight, sixteen, and so on; see fig. 1a), or in three and multiples of three (six, twelve, twenty-four, and so on; see fig. 1b). One of the levels in such a scheme of slower and faster pulses may be regarded as the basic pulse.[4] Usually quarter notes—a rather moderate pulse, in other words—regulate performance and are thus pointed to as the *basic pulse*. A pulse with a higher density generally constitutes the basis for the shaping of melodic and percussive rhythms and is thus called the *density referent*.[5] However, if the density referent is at the level of eighth notes, this does not mean that one instrument necessarily plays an audible series of eighth notes. The point is rather that melodic and rhythmic shaping takes place in relation to this unit as the shortest possible duration in the groove.

The basic unit of the groove can be made up of different rhythmic figures, and the basic pattern of rhythm might be described as a stable of separate figures played on top of each other, or perhaps in parallel. Nketia refers to this layered musical texture as *multilinear rhythm*. To find one's way in this weave of rhythm, it is important that every layer is audible, so that it has its own distinct place in the whole. Hence, part of the purpose with this kind of organization is to articulate every thread— ideally, every tiny accent should play a meaningful part.

Nketia further distinguishes between *divisive* and *additive* rhythms, either of which can be related to duple or triple pulse schemes or both. Divisive rhythm is characterized by a symmetrical division of the basic unit, as when twelve beats are grouped as six plus six, or eight beats as four plus four. Additive rhythm is, on the contrary, marked by a natural asymmetrical grouping of the basic unit, for example by splitting

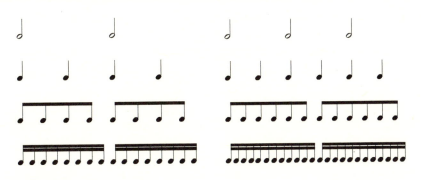

Figures 1a (left) and **1b** (right).

twelve beats into seven plus five, or five plus seven, or eight beats into five plus three. If an additive rhythm is further broken down, its basic components will often be groupings of two or three pulsations.

Nketia's ideal type of African rhythm is, however, not only characterized by the frequent occurrence of combinations of two and three in the longitudinal direction, succeeding each other over time. The combination of two and three is also frequently present in the vertical direction. An important means of differentiation in the fabric of these rhythms is to let the different layers form *cross-rhythms*, which means that rhythms based on different schemes of pulsations are played in parallel. Cross-rhythm is also referred to as polymeter, due to the fact that it can be regarded as an instant of duple and triple meter occurring simultaneously.

As mentioned, it is important to emphasize that in this context the time signature 4/4 does not imply a beat sequence of strong-weak-strong-weak, as is often the rule within classical music. How the beats are weighted varies from genre to genre. The sequence might well be quite the opposite: weak-strong-weak-strong, as in a typical backbeat. Every beat might also be equal in weight, as Arom claims for African rhythm in general, or, as with much funk, the first beat might be the only quarter that stands out as a really heavy beat. It might even be difficult to identify one primary sequence of relative weights, because it will vary according to the figure used as its point of departure.

Another important means for making every layer audible and promoting complementary rhythms is referred to by Nketia as *spacing:* "The rhythmic lines may be organized in such a way that they interlock. In order to achieve this, the parts which interlock are arranged so that they start at different but specified points in time."[6] Similar or identical figures may be phase-displaced in time so that the figures form a rhythm and a counter-rhythm. This inclination to displace figures is in many ways parallel to how Richard Waterman in 1948 described the relation between accompaniment and melody in "hot" African music as *off-beat phrasing:* "Where the accents of European melodies tend to fall either on the thesis or the arsis of the rhythmic foot, the main accents of African melodies—especially those of 'hot' music—fall between the down- and the up-beats. The effect thus produced is that of temporal displacement of the melodic phrase, in its relationship to the percussion phrase, to the extent of a half beat."[7] This temporal displacement makes it possible to distinguish between the different figures. At the same time, the figures are being locked into their positions. They keep each other steady.

A layer might also be given a specific role in the musical interaction through *grading:* "The rhythms . . . must be graded in density or complexity in relation to the role of each part as accompanying, response, or lead instrument. Instruments which perform similar roles may have a similar degree of complexity."[8] The layers might, in other words, be related to different frequencies of pulsation, and layers that have the same grading will often be complementary and/or play similar roles in the musical whole.

Virtuality—Actuality, Figure—Gesture

The different levels of pulsation are commonly referred to by their musical note values as quarters, eighths, sixteenths, and so on. However, it is important to distinguish between levels of pulses within such a theoretical framework and what is actually heard, between quarters as a reference structure and quarters as a sounding rhythmic gesture. Even though a rhythm is often related to a certain level of pulsation, and even though it should be possible to understand it as an externalization of the reference structure, played rhythm is in principal something other than the formal divisions of a metrical framework. Its different levels of pulsation comprise a non-audible reference structure, and not even the basic pulse, which will often concur with the basic beats of the meter, has to be played, even though it is often present as sound in one way or another—for example, in the form of handclaps.

Hence the need for explicating a paradigmatic premise for the analytical work that follows, namely that rhythm is conceived as an interaction of something sounding and something not sounding (the already mentioned reference structure). The latter is always at work *in* the music, and to me it is impossible to understand rhythm without taking it into consideration.

In order to make clear the status of such non-sounding musical events, it seems useful to introduce Gilles Deleuze's notion of *virtuality*. In *Difference and Repetition* (1994), Deleuze discuss the relationship of the actual, the virtual, and the real; according to Deleuze, the virtual is not the opposite of the real but of a different manifestation of reality named the actual. In fact, the virtual is fully real and must be defined as a part of the real object, as though the object resides partly in a virtual domain: "Exactly what Proust said of the states of resonance must be said of the virtual: 'Real without being actual, ideal without being abstract.'"[9] In parallel, we might conceive of musical reference structures as virtual aspects of the real music, while the sounding events are actual manifestations of the same reality. The music has a part of itself in a virtual domain.

Along these lines, structures of reference in funk will be dealt with as a virtual *reality*. Even though the structures of reference at play in a rhythm are not actual sound, they should not be regarded as something abstract or external to the music. Rhythm happens, so to speak, in the midst of actual sound and non-sounding virtual structures of reference (which, moreover, might have to do with the perceptual processes generated in the listener), and the sounding event may play both with and against the virtual structure.[10]

In both poetry and music, this interplay of sounding and non-sounding aspects is traditionally analyzed as a relationship between rhythm and "meter."[11] As regards the grooves here, however, I will discuss them as a relationship between "gesture" and "figure."

Gesture names a demarcated musical utterance within the fabric of a rhythm. It might be a riff or a vocal phrase, or a part of either, or a group of beats, or just one beat, as long as it is perceived as forming an entity, a sounding gestalt. A musical gesture includes in principal every aspect of this entity—that is, the actual as well as the virtual. Even though one parameter often tends to be the primary characteristic aspect of the gesture—it may be shaped by, for example, timbre, rhythm, or melody—the gesture transcends any traditional division into analytical parameters. In the case of funk, the primary shaping aspect is most often rhythm, but timbral shaping is also common, as with James Brown's remarkable shouts.

The figure is a virtual aspect of the gesture and might be conceived of as a proposal or schema for structuring and understanding the gesture. In the following analysis, the figures will be represented by means of the notational system, which is satisfactory in most cases. However, when working at a micro-level, there are also figures in play in the funk grooves that may not be satisfactorily accounted for by traditional notation.[12]

The distinction between figure and gesture is inspired by the Bakhtinian discussion of the difference between a sentence and an utterance. While linguistic studies use the sentence as part of an abstract system, the utterance refers to the sentence as spoken; it is "not a conventional unit, it is a real unit."[13] According to Bakhtin, there has been a tendency within linguistics to overlook the actuality of sentences, to forget the fact that sentences are always being uttered by somebody. Hence, the utterance has been ignored as the fundamental and primary unit of speech: "speech can exist in reality only in the form of concrete utterances of individual speaking people."[14]

This is also at the core of Paul Ricœur's short but instructive discussion of the difference between a linguistics of language and a linguistics of discourse.[15] The distinction comes from Ferdinand de Saussure (*langue* and *parole*) and Louis Hjelmslev (schema and usage). By way of the French linguist Emile Benveniste's linguistics of the sentence ("sentence" here coming close to Bakhtin's "utterance"), Ricœur outlines the difference in a way that, slightly modified, may be used to work out the difference between figure (schema) and gesture (usage) in a groove. First, while gestures are temporally realized and in the present, figures are virtual and transcend time. Second, whereas figures have no subject, in the sense that the question "Who performs?" does not apply at their level, gestures refer immediately back to their speakers. Thirdly, whereas the virtual structure of a figure refers only to other virtual structures within the same system (for example, a metric system), gesture refers to a world, inner or outer, that it is supposed to describe, express, or represent. Although gestures are not necessarily *about* something in the traditional sense of a discourse, they have particular histories and mean something to the listener. Finally, whereas figure is no more than a preliminary condition for musical performance, gesture is music performed, tacitly understood for someone, for an other.[16]

According to Bakhtin, the two poles are mutually dependent. He does not describe the connection between the actual utterance and the virtual sentence as an opposition but as a mutual realization. The structural or virtual sentence of linguistics comes into being as far as an actual utterance is spoken, and the other way around. An utterance is not to be regarded as an actualization of a structure existing independently of the utterance, either before or afterward.

Through his insistence on the utterance as the primary object for the study of language, Bakhtin also underlines the social aspects of language. As touched upon in the introduction, for Bakhtin this is far more radical than to say, for example, that one has to interpret a text or an utterance "in light of context," or that "context has to be taken into consideration," and so on, implicitly understanding reality as something external to language. Bakhtin instead emphasizes how the social aspects of language, its context, are aspects of the utterance. The context can neither be removed nor supplied from the outside. Hence, the utterance is dialogical in its essence. It is always already directed toward an other. This situatedness, the fact that an utterance is always spoken by someone with regard to some other, also marks the musical gesture, a point to which I will return.

For Bakhtin, the model for the delimiting of one utterance is an actual change of speaking subject as experienced in the dialogues of everyday life. However, the dialogical aspect of what Bakhtin calls "secondary speech genres"—where several voices occur within one actual utterance, as for example in a novel—is also ascribed to the real dialogue of everyday life: "these phenomena are nothing other than a conventional playing out of speech communication and primary speech genres."[17]

Along these lines, it is probably relevant to equate the dialogue of musical gestures as heard, a *fictional* dialogue, to the musical dialogue as it takes place in a band. However, it should be emphasized that dialogue between musicians and fictional dialogue experienced by the listener are different things. Even though one might make use of one's own performing experience when analyzing the music from the perspective of listening or dancing, a difference remains. From the perspective of a listener or a dancer, one musician, for instance the drummer, may be involved in the design of several gestures, both simultaneously and in succession. Moreover, several musicians may contribute to one gesture, for example the downbeat. Due to a tiny little difference in time between the beat of the kick drum and the sounding of the bass, a downbeat may be stretched out. The actual dialogue of two musicians on the side of the musical production may, in other words, contribute to the shaping of one gesture on the side of reception.[18]

The distinction between figure and gesture is important in order to focus on how patterns of rhythm are shaped in time. At the level of figure, one rhythm might be identical to another, while at the level of gesture, they may be different. That rhythmic gestures may be related to different figures and thereby to different pulses and levels of pulses is, moreover, a way to describe how differentiation takes place within the complex, multilayered structure of rhythm. Both spacing and cross-rhythms may have different grading, and when all of these separate, simple principles are adopted at once, if two runs against three—both simultaneously and in succession—and the figures are displaced and everything happens at several levels at once, the result might be quite complex and rather immense.

The strategy on the part of the performers lies in a strict division of labor, in what has been called *apart-playing:* each performer concentrates on her own part and its immediate surroundings.[19] An inexperienced participant should avoid absorbing too much in one go, instead entering the fabric at a certain place and working her way from there. However, the precondition for such a strategy is, again, that every single layer—every single gesture in the weave—is audible. Not only do the gestures have to reside in different places in time, but they have to occupy different positions in the virtual sound box.

The Heterogeneous Sound Ideal

According to Olly Wilson, African American music is characterized by a general inclination toward percussive sounds and a certain type of texture—the *heterogeneous* sound—where timbral contrasts are preferred to timbral unity. He explains: "By this term, I mean that there exists a common approach to music making in which a kaleidoscopic range of dramatically contrasting qualities of sound (timbre) is sought after in both vocal and instrumental music. The desirable musical sound texture is one that contains a combination of diverse timbres."[20] It is important to emphasize that the contrasts at stake are more dramatic than normal moderate variation within a predominantly homophonic sound (at least in somebody's ears). It is a question of extremes, regarding both dynamics and timbre.

According to Wilson, the heterogeneous sound ideal is reflected in musical practice in at least two ways. First, it appears in the form of extreme variation within one voice or single "line," as Wilson prefers to call it.[21] A singer may, for example, move through a dramatic range of timbres within a fairly short period of time. And as he points out, "This is particularly true when the single line is the principal point of musical interest as, for example, in an unaccompanied part for voice or instrument, or the solo line of an accompanied piece."[22] Second, the heterogeneous sound ideal is characteristic of musical ensembles where several instruments play together at the same time. Contrary to a string quartet, where the timbral qualities of the instruments are cognate—in some cases to such an extent that it is difficult to separate one from another—an ensemble or band within the African American tradition will probably consist of instruments with contrasting timbral qualities, preferably with percussive properties that make them audibly distinct. Such differences in pitch and timbre contribute to differentiating the threads in the fabric of rhythm. Nketia writes:

> In multilinear organization, the use of instruments of different pitches and timbres enables each one to be distinctly heard. It enables their cross rhythms to stand out clearly in the form of little "tunes." Hence, although rhythm is the primary focus in drumming, some attention is paid to pitch level, for the aesthetic appeal of drumming lies in the organization of the rhythmic and melodic elements.
>
> It is for similar reasons of design that attempts are made to utilize sonority contrasts wherever possible . . . contrasts which can be exploited in the formation of rhythmic patterns.[23]

In other words, the prejudice in favor of timbral and dynamic contrasts has consequences both for the spatial dimension—simultaneous instruments are articulated as single voices through differences in timbre and pitch—and for time. One voice, for instance a lead vocal, often presents an enormous range of different sounds regarding timbre, pitch, and dynamics within a rather short period of time.

In order to grasp this spatial differentiation, it seems useful to think of the music not only as a process in time but as a virtual *room* of sound. The organization of the many layers in a multilinear rhythmic structure may be imagined as a set of different positions in this three-dimensional sound box. Left to right might refer to a stereo mix and constitutes one axis (x), while two other axes indicate height (y) and depth (z), respectively.

High to low (y) is linked to pitch and frequencies, while front to rear (z) depends on timbre and dynamics, or, in other words, close/distant and strong/weak.[24] Viewed this way, rhythmic figures characterized by light timbre and/or high pitch, as for instance a bell or hi-hat cymbals, are placed in the upper parts of the sound box, while those characterized by dark timbre and/or low pitch are placed in the lower parts. Weak sounds with low volume and/or a minute presence of high frequencies, as well as a less pronounced attack segment, will end up at the rear, while sounds with high volume and/or much treble will be in the front.

In a drum ensemble, or in groove-directed music more generally, the depth of the sound box is limited, because all of the sounds are more or less percussive. Due to a marked attack, they will mainly unfold up front, leaving the space behind them empty. The sound will only fill up the space backward insofar as an instrument also offers sonorous richness, as is the case with a large drum. Deep drums fill up more space, so dense rhythmic figures will be played by instruments with a small, less spatial sound, while instruments with a broad sound are reduced to playing less dense figures. As a consequence, there is room for more, as well as more dense, figures in the upper parts of the sound box than in the bottom.

As Olly Wilson points out, within this type of music we find a tendency to fill up the whole sound box: "There is a tendency to create a high density of events within a relatively short time frame—a tendency to fill up all of the musical space."[25] This is related to the fact that all "expansion," all development of the rhythmic patterns, has to take place within the limits of the basic unit. Increased complexity does not lead to more extensive formats—the patterns do not expand into more measures—but to a higher density.

The Conversational Mode

Striving for differentiation among parts becomes increasingly significant as the number of layers and figures increases. One aspect of this differentiation is *grouping*. Figures are organized as rhythmic dialogues: the performance of a figure does not take place in relation to all of the other figures in the weave, but as part of a dialogue with one other, usually complementary figure. Both grading and spacing are means for the grouping of voices in rhythmic dialogues: voices can be related to the same level of density, or they can be similar figures that are displaced in time.

Traditional forms of call-and-response are in many ways clear-cut versions of this general tendency to make "antiphonal musical structures," as Wilson calls them.[26] In fact, the dialogic approach is fundamental on all levels of the fabric of rhythm. According to John Miller Chernoff, to play one single rhythm in an African context is quite unthinkable.[27] There are always at least two rhythms going at the same time, and in a certain sense one rhythm defines the other: "In short, musicians must keep their time steady by perceiving rhythmic relationships rather than by following a stressed beat . . . Only through the combined rhythms does the music emerge, and the only way to hear the music properly, to find the beat, and to develop and exercise 'metronome sense,' is to listen to at least two rhythms at once."[28] The complementary rhythm is, among other things, important for steady time: steady time is not achieved by following an accentuated beat or by playing exactly (on) the beats, but rather through being part of a rhythmic relation.

Chernoff opposes this way of relating to rhythm to what might be called a Western way, where the ideal is to "keep time": "We can think about this difference in sensibilities as the difference between perceiving a rhythm as something to 'get with' or as something to 'respond to.'"[29] This is illustrated by Chernoff's account of an attempt to teach some African drumming to a cousin in the United States who was trained as a classical pianist. Alone, she manages well after having learned the pattern by way of counting. However, when being forced to relate to another, complementary rhythm, in this case Chernoff's off-beats, she loses her own beat: "I asked her to beat a steady rhythm on a table top, and she of course did so quite well until I added the off-beats between her beats. She became so erratic in her beating, speeding up and slowing down, that she accused me, incorrectly, I would think, of deliberately syncopating my beats in an effort to confuse her.[30] The classically trained pianist is confused by the conversation with another rhythmic layer. Chernoff's African drum teacher Ibrahim, on the contrary, gets lost when playing alone: "Ibrahim felt that his isolated beating was meaningless without a second rhythm, but more than that, he could not even think of the full range of stylistic variations he might play without the beating of a second drum. There was no *conversation*."[31]

Nketia is also concerned with the grouping of voices into pairs and the fact that the phrasing of each voice is fundamentally shaped by the resultant pattern: "Contrasts in the tones of the interlocking parts . . . form a pattern heard as resultant, which is, in effect, the realization of a preconceived figure, theme, or tune. Hence, it is this resultant that forms the basis of the initial organization of the parts."[32] A perfect shaping of a rhythmic gesture is, in other words, dependent on a relation to another gesture. Every rhythm is, first and foremost, understood and performed as part of a larger whole. A rhythm becomes an event of interest through dialogue.[33]

In a dialogue the attention goes in both directions. In line with this, Chernoff claims that an African drummer is as much concerned with what is not played as with what is: "A good drummer restrains himself from emphasizing his rhythm in order that he may be heard better. Just as the beat of an ensemble is made interesting by the master drummer, so a rhythm is interesting in terms of its potential to be affected by other rhythms."[34] One might give similar emphasis to a rhythm by playing *lower* rather than louder. Removing a rhythm from the common fabric might actually give the rhythm heightened attention, but at the same time, it is a way to shift focus to another complementary rhythm: "A drum in an African ensemble derives its power and becomes meaningful not only as it cuts and focuses the other drums but also as it is cut and called into focus by them."[35]

In groove music in particular, the space between the notes seems very important. It is as if the silence creates a tension that locks the groove: the gaps between the sounds create the groove as much as the sounds themselves do. The gaps almost represent a field of power, making the gestures stick to their positions—in other words, where and how the sound is ended is as much a part of the gesture as where and how the sound starts. Similarly, Chernoff suggests that it might be fruitful to study music as a pattern of open spaces: "*The music is perhaps best considered as an arrangement of gaps where one may add a rhythm, rather than as a dense pattern of sound.*"[36] At the same time, in principal it seems odd to consider the negative to be more important than the positive. The reciprocal relationship between figure and non-figure renders a preference for one or the other meaningless; their relation is better viewed as fundamentally complementary.

Even though a rhythm is primarily shaped through a dialogue with another complementary rhythm, this "local" dialogue always takes place among other rhythmic conversations. One's own rhythm is always indirectly tied to the rest through this weave of rhythmic dialogues. When the density of the sound box increases, it might, as mentioned above, become very difficult to relate to the totality of rhythms. One tends to direct oneself according to the immediate surrounding soundscape, relating only to the closest gestures and leaving the rest of them to themselves.

It is also necessary to stick to one rhythm without too much deviation, which might disturb the balance of the construction as a whole, as
Chernoff states:

> If a drummer stays too far from his rhythm, he will misaccentuate or over-
> emphasize the beat and thus ruin the intriguing balance, and if he moves
> into too close a synchrony with another drum, he negates the potential ef-
> fect of both rhythms. The rhythms must be clearly distinguishable from
> each other because one rhythm determines the way we can apprehend an-
> other rhythm. Changing the part of one drum in a composition, therefore,
> would alter the effect of the total rhythmic fabric.[37]

In other words, the design of the rhythmic fabric calls for discipline,
precision, and temperance. The division of labor is clear and highly respected: some voices stand firm (the *support* drums), repeating the same
pattern throughout the piece, while only the master drummer supplies
variation and directs changes. When she or he improvises, it is also
about making the others sound better, not displaying personal virtuosity. The ideal is a gentle improvisation.

On Internal Beat

Even when it is comprised of only a single rhythm, the rhythmic gesture is still part of a rhythmic dialogue, though only one side of the
dialogue is heard. In a groove, the rhythm triggers an underlying
basic pulse, an internal beat that also forms the basis for how the gesture is in turn played. This internal beat is fundamental for playing,
dancing, and listening—in short, for understanding the groove.
However, it does not need to be articulated as a part of the sounding
music, or as Chernoff says about African music, "The rhythm that
might be considered the main beat of the music is not emphasized.
We can say that the musicians play 'around' the beat, or that they
play on the off-beat, but actually it is precisely the ability to identify
the beat that enables someone to appreciate the music. We begin to
'understand' African music by being able to maintain in our minds or
our bodies, an additional rhythm to the ones we hear."[38]
    Dancing, handclapping, and stomping are, as a rule, externalizations
of this internal beat. In the African music studied by Chernoff, however,
supplying the basic pulse can be difficult for an inexperienced listener,

who may have problems finding a pulse that is shared among the performers.[39] The rhythms may not seem to meet at any point, and the pattern has no beginning or end. Rather than trying to identify a starting point and then count the way to the correct position, one needs to locate oneself in relation to other voices through a dialogue with the other rhythms.

In a classic article, Richard Waterman calls this ability to connect to a shared pulse "the metronome sense."[40] This term might, however, be slightly misguiding, because the internal beat does not have to be a steady or isochronous pulse; it is instead culturally shaped. Supplying the right rhythm, the main beat, is more than identifying the smallest common multiple of the pulse according to a metronome. Even in those cases where there is little doubt regarding where the pulse is, the beats might be phrased in different ways and have different weights.

In fact, the basic pulse does not need to be played or expressed in any way at all. According to Waterman and Chernoff, however, in an African context the listener or dancer will almost always take active part in the musicking, supplying the main beat by moving the body, without or with sound, for example by means of rattles attached to the feet. Chernoff actually goes so far as to invert the relationship here, claiming that the drums accompany the dance rather than the dancers the drums. The music is "a-music-to-find-the-beat-by,"[41] or, as Waterman puts it, "African music, with few exceptions, is to be regarded as music for the dance, although the 'dance' involved may be entirely a mental one."[42]

Along these lines, we may say that the rhythmic fabric is not a dense mass of sound but rather an open weave whose in-between spaces, comprising the negative of the weave's pattern, are as important as the sounding events. Ideally, there is always room for another voice. In Chernoff's words, "A good rhythm, if it is to enhance itself, should both fill a gap in the other rhythms and create an emptiness that may be similarly filled."[43] The successful performer, through mind or body, manages to fill in the right rhythm.

Genre and Individuality—The Art of Signifyin(g)

Just as a stable, repetitive rhythmic framework makes it possible for the tiniest variations to emerge, conventional modes of expression and various standard formulas are means for elucidating a personal touch. According to Chernoff, it is common in Africa to use stylized and conventionalized social forms to achieve "interpersonal intimacy": "Africans impose a formal institutional or social framework on their affairs in order to personalize their behavior and expressions against a specifically limited context of meaning. From an African perspective, once you have brought a structure to bear on your involvements, and made your peace with it, the distinctive gestures and deviant idiosyncrasies of personality can stand out with clarity."[44]

In his book *The Signifying Monkey*, Henry Louis Gates Jr. claims that the play with standard patterns or conventionalized formulas is also a significant and striking aspect of African American language and culture.[45] With the stories of the trickster Signifying Monkey[46] as a point of departure, as well as the common use of the verb "to signify" in black English, Gates describes how verbal meaning is created through so-called tropological revision, through an exchange between the levels of literal and figural meaning. Signifyin(g) turns out to be repetition and revision in one and the same maneuver—to signify upon something is "to repeat with a difference":[47] "It is as if a received structure of crucial elements provides a basis for poeisis, and the narrator's technique, his or her craft, is to be gauged by the creative (re)placement of these expected or anticipated formulaic phrases and formulaic events, rendered anew in unexpected ways."[48] Gates claims that rhetorical skills tied to this kind of "repeating with a difference" are highly regarded in African American communities: "The name 'Signifying Monkey' shows the hero to be a trickster, 'signifying' being the language of trickery, that set of words or gestures which arrives at 'direction through indirection.'"[49]

Gates himself points out the parallel in music, where jazz tunes such as those of Count Basie and Oscar Peterson bearing the titles "Signify" and "Signifying" are built around the processes of revising something already well known that is never played, only implied: "Because the form is self-evident to the musician, both he and his well-trained audience are playing and listening with expectation. Signifyin(g) . . . creates a dialogue between what the listener expects and what the artist plays. Whereas younger, less mature musicians accentuate the beat, more accomplished musicians do not have to do so. They feel free to imply it."[50]

Gates uses the term intertextuality for this form of indirect inclusion of something absent through repetition and revision, and the parallel to intertextuality in the sense of Kristeva and Barthes is fairly striking. According to Barthes, every text is an intertext. Other texts—bygone or contemporary—are present within it in more or less recognizable forms, and as a condition for every text, intertextuality cannot be reduced to a question of sources or influences. The intertext is a general field of anonymous formulations that can rarely be traced back to an origin. The quotations are unconscious or automatic—they are without quotation marks.[51]

The main difference between Gates's signifying and Barthes's and Kristeva's notion of intertextuality is that the latter concept is tied to an aesthetic universe where the new has been—and still is—a far more attractive label than the already known or old. Because nonrepetition is the norm, repetition and revision are rarely intended or explicit but rather something one prefers to ignore or perhaps even suppress. To focus on intertextuality, then, is to reveal the "hidden" traces of other texts.

However, when half of the point *is* repetition, and the other half, revision, basically relies upon it, intertextuality—if it is still to be called by that name—is so evident and so obvious that it becomes almost transparent. In this case the texts of the tradition should rather be considered different realizations of the same material and the same rules, though this "same" does not exist in pure form in time or space. As Gates points out regarding the stories of the Signifying Monkey, even though the material and the rules for the tale are shared and well known, there is no authorized original. The many stories about the monkey do not exist as one fixed text but as "a play of differences."[52]

As a consequence, notions like pastiche, quotation, and cliché miss the point because they presuppose a norm of nonrepetition. A funk riff is *not* a quotation without quotation marks; it belongs to its actual song as well as to the similar riffs that preceded it and those that are to come. It is in the nature of funk that the same riff has been played many times before, and that it will be played again. Actually, pastiche, quotations, and clichés simply describe the particular cases where intertextuality comes forward as a certain theme. They name those instances where it becomes necessary—for one reason or another—to point out what is going on all the time. As Gates puts it, "Tradition is the process of formal revision. Pastiche is literary history naming itself, pronouncing its surface to be the displaced content of intertextual relations themselves, the announcement of ostensibly concealed revision."[53] Generally, one might say that the interplay of manner and matter in an oral tradition is often about exploring old material in a new way. Rather than inventing new material, it is important to generate something special within a stable framework—in Small's words, to focus on "original creation within the framework of the idiom and of the given material."[54]

This process will always take place in a field between two poles: genre, or tradition in its broadest sense, and individual style. The relation between genre and individual style is one of mutual presupposition: the material, formulas, and rules of a genre do not exist apart from the individuals who practice it. Pure genre only exists in the form of nonexistence, as convention, like virtual figures making themselves known through sounding actualization. On the other hand, there is no individual signature independent of the collective genre. Every time there is a musical utterance, there is also a genre being exhibited; to use Bakhtin's words, "We learn to cast our speech in generic forms and, when hearing others' speech, we guess its genre from the very first words; we predict a certain length . . . and a certain compositional structure."[55] That is to say, genre is nothing that comes to the music from outside; rather, it is announced by the music: every time a funk groove is realized, the genre "funk" is manifested at the same time that it is changed.

However, this relation might also be turned upside down: confidence with the rules of the genre is a necessary presupposition for a funk groove to be manifested, for the utterance to have effect, and for the musical gesture to work as a gesture, as an entity having an address. According to Paul Ricœur, genre is what mediates between production and reception by way of a dynamic ensuring that both take place according to prevailing rules: genre makes the discourse—or groove—into a public object, ready for memorization, able to be written down. The role of the genre is not only to protect communication with regard to the first utterance; it also contributes to the fact that the message survives the initial situation of discourse, that the utterance survives its own death with a potential for revival. Ricœur describes this as follows: "The genre establishes the first contextualization, but, being at the same time a virtual decontextualization of discourse, it makes subsequent recontextualization of the message possible."[56]

The interplay of genre and individuality is nothing special for funk, Chernoff's African rhythms, or Gates's African American play with words. The point is rather that the individual solution within these traditions tends to consist of manner and not matter; as Gates says regarding the stories of the Signifying Monkey, "Precisely because the concepts represented in the poem are shared, repeated, and familiar to the poet's audience, meaning is devalued, while the signifier is valorized.

Value, in this art of poeisis, lies in its foregrounding rather than in the invention of a novel signified."[57] Within a cultural universe like this, clichés take back their proper role as that which gives form, becoming a presupposition for the individual to appear. The formal becomes the springboard for the personal: familiarity with a figure makes it easier to distinguish a special touch. The lack of innovation on the level of material or matter is not to be understood as an overwrought respect for tradition or as an interest in repetition as such. Rather, the stable repetitive structures and modest modification of tradition reveal the artist's need to indulge at the level where the artistic challenge is located. The new manner, the tiny variations that make the same into something different, has to be able to emerge.

4

Rhythm and Counter-Rhythm

That was James' formula in its purest form, because none
of those parts really go together.
—Fred Wesley on *Get on the Good Foot*

When Bootsy Collins demonstrates funk in the BBC series *Dancing in the Street*, he plays a determined, unsyncopated first beat followed by several broken, syncopated gestures.[1] What is it about these lines that evokes "funk"? How is it possible to summarize a style by means of a few notes on a bass?

In my view, even though the funk bass is an icon of the genre, funk is not primarily about bass. On closer inspection, the funk canon exhibits a wide spectrum of bass figures. Bass playing can be simple and straightforward, as in many James Brown tunes. It can be syncopated but at the same time full of wide open spaces, as in the Parliament song "We Want the Funk." Or it can be the main ingredient in a dense weave of syncopated notes, as in Graham Central Station's "The Jam." In other words, a tune can be classic funk without the typical funk bass. Nevertheless, the latter is exactly as Bootsy Collins plays it: besides the heavy first beat, it is broken, almost fragmented, and in parts very syncopated.

For the present, I will leave the heavy first beat, the alleged *One*, at that, and focus on its surroundings, the syncopated rhythms. If funk is this closely tied to this kind of bass playing, it is probably because the bass takes care of an important rhythmic function: its small, fragmented gestures work against and break up the more or less articulated 4/4 pulse. But how are these gestures organized? Do they form certain patterns?

Simple Syncopation or Secondary Rag?

In his article entitled "The Significance of the Relationship between Afro-American Music and West African Music" (1974), Olly Wilson introduces a distinction between *simple syncopation*—singular deviations from a basic pulse—and more complex patterns of syncopation, which according to Wilson ought to be considered instances of polyrhythm. He traces this distinction back to the difference between primary and secondary rag in ragtime, where primary rag (simple syncopation) is identified as the "momentary displacement of the regular accent implied by the metrical framework," while secondary rag is "the superimposition of one, two, three upon the basic one, two, three, four."[2]

Wilson argues that a clear-cut separation between syncopation and polyrhythm must be avoided, and that it is always necessary to consider the different roles and total interaction of the layers in the fabric of rhythm: "If the foreground rhythm (i.e., basic metrical pulse) is not displaced or is displaced only momentarily, the result will be syncopation, but if the foreground rhythm is displaced . . . or a lesser rhythmic level is displaced over a long time span, the effect of polyrhythm will occur."[3] Whether one understands a rhythmic gesture as a layering of cross-rhythms or as a syncopated figure depends upon the cross-rhythm's ability to attract attention. As Wilson points out, how long the competing rhythmic layer is present—how long the counter-rhythm is allowed to play before it is adjusted in accordance with the main rhythm—is very important. If a regular pattern of syncopation appears in the music for a long time, sooner or later it ceases to be heard as deviation from the main pulse: it ends up forming an independent and equally relevant layer of pulses. However, this change also depends upon how self-reliant the competing rhythmic gesture is and how clearly the figure is articulated.

A Tendency of Cross-Rhythm

The funk and funk-related songs of James Brown contain many asymmetrical rhythmic figures, often organized as a grouping of eight eighths into 3+3+2 or sixteen sixteenths into 3+3+3+3+4. If one takes the view that syncopated notes are not deviations from a basic pulse but rather comprise a regular pulse of their own, they may be considered hints of a cross-rhythmic layer or, more precisely, a counter-rhythm with a tendency toward cross-rhythm.[4]

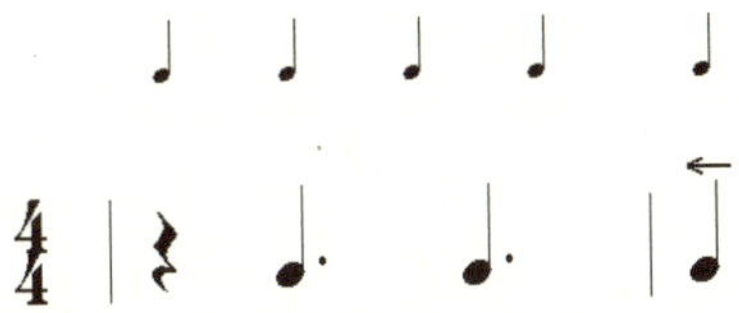

Figure 2. Counter-rhythmic pattern in "Cold Sweat."

On this point, a shift from r&b tunes to early funk is clear. In tunes like "Papa's Got a Brand New Bag" and "I Got You (I Feel Good)," there is no tendency toward cross-rhythm in the sense given above. All of the instruments support the prevailing meter and relate to its basic pulse of quarters or duple multiples. Syncopation represents only solitary departures from the main beat—a "primary rag," to use Wilson's term.

In "Cold Sweat," however, there is a different basic feeling. The rolling quarters are replaced by a vertical swing. On top of all of the layers of different subdivisions of the basic meter (4/4), there is an asymmetrically grouped figure stepping forward through the interplay of snare drum and bass guitar/bass drum. This counter-rhythm is subject to spacing: it is displaced by one quarter and starts on the second beat of the 4/4 bar. It ends on the first beat of bar two, which comprises the third main beat of a virtual cross-rhythmic pulse (see fig. 2).

In this tune, the counter-rhythmic layer is not very noticeable; it is very short and quickly returns to the main rhythm. In later songs, a counter-rhythm can be much more striking. In "The Payback" (1974) it is both more obvious and more unambiguous: the first four strokes of the guitar riff form a figure of four against three in relation to the three first quarters of the main pulse (see fig. 3a). Similar to this, in "Stoned to the Bone" (1973) one guitar plays a pattern that groups the eighths of the bars in an asymmetrical figure of 3+3+2 (see fig. 3b). This figure is commonly used in Latin American dance music and is referred to as "rumba rhythm."[5] It is also common in r&b and soul music, and I will refer to it as the "standard pattern," since it may be viewed as a simplified duple time version of the so-called standard pattern of African music.[6]

In these tunes, the counter-rhythmic figures are clearly drawn up and carried out in their pure forms, without veiling. Both of these grooves, then, convey a play between a main rhythm and a counter-rhythm with competing basic pulses: they carry *a tendency toward cross-rhythm.* In fact, figures 3a and 3b are closely related, in that the figure of

Figure 3. a) "Stoned to the Bone" (left) **b)** "The Payback" (right)
Counter-rhythmic figures in "Stoned to the Bone" and "The Payback," standard pattern and four against three (4:3), respectively.

four against three can be understood as the beginning of an asymmetrical grouping of 3+3+2, where every note is divided and played in two parts, as in the following table: 3+3+2=(3+3)+(3+3)+(2+2)/2.

In earlier songs like "Hot Pants" and "Make It Funky," both from 1971, one finds a subtler variant of the same tendency toward cross-rhythm. In both songs the counter-rhythm is established as a pattern of accents within a subdivision of sixteenths (see fig. 4). The matrix of accents is, however, similar to the figure of four against three in "The Payback." The first four accents form a figure of four against the first three beats of the bar. On the fourth beat, the figure is adjusted to the main rhythm. In "Hot Pants" the counter-rhythm is merged with the main rhythm through a "triple" beat of sixteenths placed surprisingly far up front in the sound box. However, it is competed with by a tambourine with the same grading, relating to the same pulse level. The tambourine is played as a subdivision of sixteenths but with accents that emphasize the main basic pulse.

Also, the guitar of "Make It Funky" is centered around a figure of four against three with a final double stroke on the fourth quarter note. The figure becomes clearer after a while, and from 1:30 (elapsed time) to the bridge it comes through as a pattern of accents in the played subdivision of sixteenths. The chopping of the guitar is harder and more rough-edged than in "Hot Pants," but the gesture as a whole is further behind in the sound. All in all, the counter-rhythmic function of the guitar is not as pronounced here. Many of the elements in the groove pull clearly in the direction of the main pulse and subordinate the effect of the counter-rhythm. This is especially so with the unusually steady eighths, played on half-open hi-hat cymbals, that underline the duple rhythm.

However, it is not only the elements *surrounding* the cross-rhythmic layer that pull the entire rhythm in the direction of the main beat. There are also mediating aspects *within* the counter-rhythmic layer, because the subdivision of sixteenths tends to blur the pattern of cross-rhythm. In fact, the sixteenths work almost like a common denominator, articulating the connection between the main rhythm and the counter-rhythm. Hence, the counter-rhythmic layer also supports and confirms the basic meter. The counter-rhythm does not represent a competing alternative basic pulse but instead animates from *within* the main rhythm, both fortifying it and keeping it together, like an element of tension keeping things in place.

Even though there are obvious shared characteristics between the "pure" version of the cross-rhythm layer and the one that is integrated into a subdivision of sixteenths, the latter is a more typical funk riff. The riffs of "The Payback" and "Stoned to the Bone" are almost too tidy to be funk. They are too distinct, too unambiguous, too verging on schematic: they lack the extra refinement that characterizes the riffs of "Hot Pants" and "Make It Funky," which makes the latter appear to be elaborations of the former. However, "Hot Pants" and "Make It Funky" came first!

The third and "funkiest" version of this tendency toward cross-rhythm in the songs of James Brown adds still more to this chronological confusion. The guitar riff of "Soul Power" is closer to the fully realized funk riff of many P-Funk tunes and the more polished funk of the late 1970s. However, "Soul Power" originates even further back in time, with the JBs of 1970, the band in which the brothers Catfish and Bootsy Collins made short if astonishing appearances on guitar and bass, respectively.

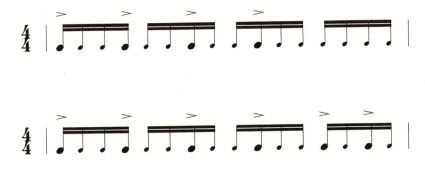

Figure 4. a) "Hot Pants" (top) **b)** "Make it Funky" (bottom)
Counter-rhythmic figures as accents in a subdivision of sixteenths.

Figure 5. Counter-rhythm in "Soul Power."

In "Soul Power" there is no subdivision of sixteenths running throughout, nor is the counter-rhythm as clear-cut as in "The Payback." The single and double sixteenths instead only hint at an underlying cross-rhythmic pulse. Even though the counter-rhythm in this case is more fragmented, an incomplete version of the four against three figure is present in both parts of the repeated musical period. The onset of the figure is displaced: it starts on the second beat and ends by opening out toward the fourth (see fig. 5). This variant may be described as a further development of the straightforward and somewhat cruder cross-rhythmic strokes of "The Payback." It might, however, also be understood as a chopped-up-version of the accentuated layer of sixteenths from "Hot Pants" and "Make It Funky." More importantly, in "Soul Power" it becomes even more striking how the funk riff, while carrying a potential for cross-rhythm, instead animates and breaks up the primary meter by challenging the regular beat. The funk riff does not set up a separate layer of counter-rhythm, nor does it compete with the main beat. It plays with the main beat by being played around it.

Limitation, Concealment, Fragmentation—On the Perfectly Imperfect Balance

In his description of African drumming, Chernoff emphasizes that the drumming should be balanced so that the cross-rhythm appears clearly. To sustain both duple and triple pulse, one has to avoid moving too far from the actual beat: "A musician should deliver not too many and not too few off-beat accents because people can get thrown off the beat, and at a certain point either their orientation to the rhythms will shift or they will begin hearing the separate rhythms as a single rhythm. In either case, the tension has been lost and the music becomes dull. The lead drummer, however, balances his beating so that the cross rhythms will remain distinct."[7] In other words, in the African ideal type *both* basic pulses are clearly present. They are almost equal, not only with regard to analysis but as sounded.

In funk, the pulse of the counter-rhythm is, as a rule, not sufficiently stated to make the music appear to be the product of two different basic pulse schemes. The groove *is* to sound like "a single rhythm": there is no equality between rhythm and counter-rhythm, and the latter is to be clearly subordinated to the former. To achieve this (right) "wrong" or "unjust" balance of rhythm and counter-rhythm is extremely important to the funk sound. The counter-rhythm should destabilize the main meter without being so articulated as to threaten to take it over.[8]

This balanced imbalance may be taken care of in different ways. It can be solved by a difference in volume, as in the James Brown tune "Get Up, Get Into It and Get Involved" (1970). In this song there is an ongoing cross-rhythmic effect on the level of sixteenths, yet it is never strikingly audible in the totality of sounds. The guitar is playing straight duple sixteenths, while the congas and bass operate by swung sixteenths. However, due to the guitar's placement toward the back of the sound, no collision emerges.

As seen in the preceding analysis, it is also important to note whether the counter-rhythm is allowed to form a continuous pattern and how long the pulse of the counter-rhythm is left loose before being adjusted to the main beat. The influence of the counter-rhythm may, in other words, be controlled through a *limitation in time.* If the counter-rhythm is clearly articulated, it has to be ended before the *pulse* of the counter-rhythm is established as such. Because the competing pulse might become too obvious compared to the pulse of the main beat, a regular pattern of syncopation cannot be allowed to continue for too long.

In all of the songs examined above, the polyrhythmic figures are all concluded before establishing themselves as unambiguous layers of cross-rhythms. In the standard pattern of "Stoned to the Bone" (see fig. 3a), the basic pulse is picked up at the start of every bar: the first beat of the basic two-bar unit cuts the last eighth of the third stroke in the counter-rhythm, reinforcing the meter of 4/4. In "The Payback" (see fig. 3b), where the guitars are organized as a call and response, the first gesture in the pattern of the call guitar is finished by a straight double stroke on the two last eighth notes, almost to make sure that the main pulse does not get lost, as if it needs a moment of reinstatement before the polyrhythm restarts in the next bar. From the same time period there is also a tune containing a clear-cut figure of triplets on top of a duple rhythm. In this song, called "Doing It to Death" (1973), the adjustment takes place as early as the third beat of the bar, probably because the feeling of triplets in the first part of the bar is so strong that the total rhythmic feel of the song is challenged. Due to this, the 4/4 pulse has to be reinforced by an emphatic duple, almost strong-weak, gesture right on the two last quarter notes of the bar.

When it comes to songs like "Hot Pants" and "Make It Funky," the influence of the cross-rhythmic layer is also restricted through a limitation in time. However, cross-rhythm is also hidden in the subdivision of sixteenths—in other words, the *concealment* of the cross-rhythm is there as a part of the counter-rhythm itself. As I mentioned earlier, in both of these songs the layer of counter-rhythm establishes, by itself, the important connection to the main meter through articulating the common denominator of the two basic pulses: the unit that makes the figure divisible by both two and three. Along with a tendency toward cross-rhythm, the counter-rhythmic layer also contains a counterweight to cross-rhythm. Since part of the energy is already channeled in the direction of the main meter, the effect of cross-rhythm is therefore moderated. The correct (im)balance is partly secured within the counter-rhythm itself.

In "Soul Power" the cross-rhythmic layer is also regulated by a limitation in time. Furthermore, the strokes are performed most discreetly; they announce themselves only in the form of a small, distracting flutter, as a careful disorder in the main 4/4 pulse; they are so quick and elusive, so light, that one has almost forgotten the first when the second arrives. One part of the riff does not point toward the next, as it might when integrated into a subdivision of sixteenths. The counter-rhythmic layer is more *fragmented*, less continuous—in short, too much of a gathering of solitary syncopated notes to represent a real threat to the 4/4 pulse. The main rhythm is left undisturbed, while the counter-rhythm sneaks around in the gaps.

This is partly due to the fact that the phrasing of the counter-rhythm is somewhat overruled by the main rhythm. However, tunes like "The Payback," where the figure of the counter-rhythm is more articulated, are also characterized by a balance tilted away from the phrasing of the counter-rhythm. While the main rhythm is almost unaffected by the counter-rhythm, this is not the case in reverse. Even though the counter-rhythm in these songs appears to be the more clearly drawn, independent figure, it does not push the main rhythm significantly. In "The

Payback," the quarter notes in bass drum and snare drum seem to be fairly insensitive to the polyrhythmic riff of the guitar. Their deviation from an isochronal position is rather the result of an inner dialogue between bass drum and snare drum that is characterized by the snare's small but not unusual hesitation: in relation to the distinct pulse triggered by the bass drum, the snare drum is a little late.

While this dialogue seems to be rather uninfluenced by the guitar's counter-rhythm, the opposite is not true: the guitar riff carrying the figure of four against three is considerably influenced by the 4/4 rhythm. In relation to the underlying pulse, the 4:3 figure is notably stretched at the end of the two-bar basic unit. The last part almost develops as a negotiation between the cross-rhythmic pulse of the 4:3 figure and the fact of this figure's incompletion; the phrasing attempts to hide the disagreement between its eventual resumption and the injunction of adapting to the new beginning.

The balance of rhythm and counter-rhythm is not solely about limiting the influence of the cross-rhythm on the whole. It has another side as well: one has to avoid a basic pulse that is *too* authoritarian, or the fabric of rhythm as a whole might end up too ordered or straightforward. Due to this, the primary 4/4 meter and its subdivisions should not become too evident. This is particularly important regarding higher duple subdivisions (eighths and above). If the layer that represents the common denominator for both rhythm and counter-rhythm, say the sixteenths, is very distinct, the counter-rhythm will soon appear to be simply a province of the main meter. For example, straight sixteenths with accents on the main beats, as in a standard disco groove, will have too much of an ordering effect. They tidy up every counter-rhythmic tendency and tame possible deviations due to a potentially cross-rhythmic pulse. Nor can counter-rhythm be absent from the sound for too long. When the counter-rhythm fades, there is no more funk; when funk's characteristic rhythmic ambivalence is destroyed, it abandons the groove to an unequivocal 4/4 rhythm.

This also holds good the other way around: the main rhythm has to be present in one form or another. A counter-rhythm must counter something, because a strongly syncopated figure is not funk as such. However, it will most probably trigger an internal beat in the listener. In other words, the listener may herself balance out the counter-rhythm, adding the basic pulse by dancing, clapping, or simply thinking it.

When it comes to the common figures of cross-rhythm in funk—four against three, or the standard pattern—their phrasing will probably reveal their origin against a basic pulse of 4/4 and through this convention trigger a counterweight to the cross-rhythmic pattern in the confident listener. The internal beat on the production side is manifested in the sound in a way that makes it more easily activated on the reception side.

Viewed this way, one might say that the 4/4 beats are likely to always be there, but the counter-rhythm might not. The pulse of 4/4 goes with the counter-rhythm as an internal beat, as the basis that gives syncopated figures their full meaning. On the contrary, we do not automatically supply an alternative basic pulse: the counter-rhythm has to be present in the rhythmic fabric, either as sound or as an echo of sound.

Rhythm and Counter-Rhythm—A Metrical Romance

So far, at the level of structure, it seems to be typical for the funk groove to carry a layer with a tendency toward cross-rhythms. There is a tension between the basic pulse and its alternative, between rhythm and counter-rhythm. Even if the latter is subordinated to the main basic pulse of 4/4 and does not appear as a continuous rhythmic layer, it has to be present as a destabilizer of the main rhythm, as a possible but unarticulated alternative. At the same time, in funk one is not supposed to hear cross-rhythms as cross-rhythms. The basic pulse is the reference for the other or alternative basic pulse: one layer of pulses—that is, one rhythm—is primary and puts considerably more stress on the secondary layer than the other way around.

This imbalance seems to be essential. Contrary to the equality Chernoff describes in African music, it is as if the funk groove draws much of its power from this borderland between syncopation and cross-rhythm. This is probably also why it is so important to avoid articulating the higher levels of pulses, eighth notes and above, too clearly: the smaller the units, the more urgent the need for obscuring exact positions. Even on the level of eighths (if the regular beat is in quarters), a duple pattern that is too accurately played can cause trouble. On the level of sixteenths the balance becomes even more precarious: this level can only be hinted at as a discreet subdivision of a rhythmic pattern, and/or be swung to a greater or lesser degree.[9]

The funk groove thus seems to be distinguished by a certain uncertainty regarding metrical positions, by a feeling that the groove pulls in several directions at once. However, this ambivalence can probably also be traced to a limited part of the rhythmic pattern: solitary rhythmic gestures. In "The Payback," where the figure of four against three is rather straightforward, the ambivalence is at the end of the figure, where the competing layer of pulses is forced back into the main rhythm. It is precisely in this phase—when the pulse of the counter-rhythm starts to swell, when the phrasing gets dull and obviously laid back and the figure starts losing its contours—that the groove is at its most funky.

In other words, the most interesting polyrhythmic relation in funk is probably not where a clear-cut rhythm is combined with an equally clear-cut counter-rhythm. Rather, it appears when a layer of potential cross-rhythm is used to create small stretches in time that fall between a dominant basic pulse and hint at its virtual alternative. Perhaps the point of funk is to establish these small spaces, which can then be manipulated or played with. Perhaps it is only against such a fabric of cross-rhythms that funk's many small and specifically funky musical gestures can be (per)formed as early or late, as (almost) on the beat and (almost) on another as well.

This is why the cross-rhythmic gestures and their built-in ambivalence are so satisfying: the strokes of the counter-rhythm both comprise and do not comprise a competing layer of pulses, the riff suggesting a subdivision of the main meter while relating through its accents to a different pulse. This may also be why the borderland of duple and triple subdivision, coupled with a tendency to swing the sixteenths that is almost always present at higher pulse levels, so successfully creates the lack of clarity proper to the funk groove. The point is not to combine a basic rhythm with the "right" portion of independent counter-rhythm but to "deform" those figures so as to make them both one and the other, both rhythm and counter-rhythm at the same time.

Both the production and the reception of music made within such an aesthetic framework require sensitivity to the small-scale musical gesture, to displacements and variations on a micro-level. It is therefore time for a closer inspection of the basic units of the grooves, with our ears aimed not only at larger rhythmic figures and patterns on a traditional structural level but also at regularities on a level that in many cases would be regarded as an absolute microcosm. As the following analyses will show, this is where much of the creative work in funk takes place. Dealing with minimal differences and seemingly insignificant nuances, the funk player concentrates on giving her rhythmic figures exactly the right shape in time and space. Now we must increase the resolution and focus our senses on the barely audible, on aspects of funk that might, in fact, only be felt.

5

"The Downbeat, in Anticipation"

It had its own sound: the music on one-and-three, the
downbeat, in anticipation.
—James Brown on
"Papa's Got a Brand New Bag"[1]

As suggested in the previous chapter, the *manner* of funk—how things are done—is very important. This is what James Brown hints at when he claims that it all started with "Papa's Got a Brand New Bag," with its characteristic light, early accent on an expected strong beat. This is most striking in the horns: the groove is set with a short toot, a marked attack played as if it were a little early in relation to the basic pulse implied by the rest of the rhythmic fabric. This manner also appears in the guitar part, which is played almost exactly on beats two and four and is marked by the same extremely snappy phrasing of each stroke. Then, at the end of every blues sequence (on the first beat of bar ten), the bass and the guitar make a similar gesture in unison, an off-stroke before the vocal line "Papa's got a brand new bag" and the following "shangalang" riff on the guitar.

In the BBC program where Bootsy Collins demonstrates funk on the bass, drummer Jabo Starks refers to the One as an especially important beat.[2] The One is on top of the basic unit; it is the first beat of the pattern and as such a focal point of the groove. James Brown's slogan "the rhythm on One" also points to the importance of handling this aspect of the funk groove in the right way. As part of this, however, the One should also be *played* in the right way. And as Starks's demonstration clearly shows, this means that the One should be played on top, or, in other words, as a *downbeat in anticipation*.[3]

In "I Got You (I Feel Good)" the special effect of this downbeat in anticipation is clearly audible in positions other than the first beat of the bar. In the riff performed by the horn section between the turns, for example, the horns play two short "syncopations" on the beats. Then they play them off the beat, using exactly the same phrasing, and with no pulse being marked by hi-hat or any other instrument. It is striking how, by means of a few strokes, the riff manages to halt the groove's forward progress and disturb the stability of the underlying pulse. And, though we might expect that the offbeats would clear up the situation by being closed precisely on the following strong beats, they are also made too short, so that nothing really lines up. Schematically, they are sixteenths being played in the place of eighths (see fig. 6).

However, neither "Papa's Got a Brand New Bag" nor "I Got You (I Feel Good)" from 1965 are actually funk. As discussed earlier, they are rather examples of James Brown's repertoire of r&b. The song that is commonly regarded as the first funk tune from James Brown's hand, "Cold Sweat," was made two years later, in 1967. The fact that it sounds so different from the first two mentioned is due to, among other things, the unique approaches of the drummers involved. Melvin Parker's playing ("Papa's Got") is distinguished by a laid-back, cool attitude that makes the groove float, while Clyde Stubblefield ("Cold Sweat") uses accents, syncopations, and ghost strokes to cut up the drumming into a number of smaller components.[4] These are woven together with the rest of the band rather than formed into an independent layer of drums, which gives "Cold Sweat" a more fragmented, chopped-up sound than the earlier r&b tunes.[5] It is as if Stubblefield's sixteenths emerge as the new density referent, the smallest possible unit in the rhythmic fabric.

Change of Density Referent

In "Papa's Got a Brand New Bag" the density referent is at the level of eighth notes. Much of the rhythmic play in the song is concerned with the relation between this level and the basic pulse of quarter notes, implicated among other places in the dialogue between bass drum and snare drum. Moreover, the tune is characterized by a faster tempo than "Cold Sweat," and by an obvious backbeat. Against this rhythm, which revolves around the main beats, stand figures related to the level above the basic pulse, represented by slightly swung eighth notes in the bass or simply the hi-hat. The only element that pulls in the direction of a

($\quad$ = 148)

Figure 6. The rhythm of the break played by the horn section in "I Got You (I Feel Good)"

pulse level above the eighths is the "undersized" phrasing in horns and guitar mentioned above: the downbeat in anticipation.

Nor is the main subdivision in "Cold Sweat" to be found at the level of sixteenths, because the hi-hat plays only eighths. However, so many of the rhythmic strokes and phrase endings are so short that the song must be said to show a highly developed ambivalence toward its smallest rhythmic unit. The drumming is cut up into pieces by means of ghost strokes on the snare drum. The clean guitar riff, which is rather heavily performed in the lower part of the register, pushes against the strong beats, but every note seems to be clipped in a very snappy manner. Also, the phrasing of the riff played by the horn section points toward a density referent on the level above the main subdivision in eighths (see fig. 7). Later on, the ambivalence is clearly demonstrated in the solo section. The saxophone plays in accordance with a density referent on the level of sixteenths, while the bass, at least most of the time, does not (this becomes obvious in the section with drums and bass).

The emerging non-fit of subdivision and phrasing—subdivision implying one density referent and phrasing another—is a feature of "Cold Sweat" that is extremely funky. The certain effect of the downbeat in anticipation might also be explained within such a framework: what is wrong, or exactly right, with the downbeat played by the horn section in "Papa's Got" is the way it is too short in relation to the main subdivision in the song. The phrasing does not relate to the ruling density referent but suggests a density referent on the level above eighth notes.

Viewed this way, the downbeat in anticipation is something more than a local phenomenon tied to particular positions in the fabric of rhythm. It is rather a way of phrasing that eventually comes to characterize figures of rhythm in general and then spreads to whole layers of rhythm. It might have started in the form of an attack from the horn section, but it ends up as a standard feature of counter-rhythmic and/ or cross-rhythmic gestures, especially guitar riffs. This is clear from the prototype tune of Brown's "brand new funk": "Sex Machine."

Figure 7. Basic groove in "Cold Sweat" (standard pattern indicated by circles).

"Sex Machine"

According to James Brown's former road manager Alan Leeds, "Sex Machine" (1970) resulted from an attempt to revive "Give It Up or Turnit A Loose" in a radically new arrangement during a tour with the new JBs that included Bootsy and Catfish Collins.

> We were on our way to Starday-King's newly refurbished studio for the first recording session with Brown's new band. Too nervous to be tired, the fellas anxiously ran through the only tune they'd record that night. Sure enough, there were the licks I'd heard in "Give it Up." Only this time, the song was named "Get Up, I Feel Like Being a Sex Machine."
>
> Brown called for a take, but stopped when he stumbled over a phrase. On the second take a mysterious metamorphosis took place. We witnessed an instinctive musical genius that magically bypassed the normal thought process, evoking a vocalese from deep inside. When it was over, Brown broke into a wide grin.
>
> He was ecstatic. He had transformed a simple groove into a piece of gold.[6]

According to Leeds, the arrangement was completely focused on the interaction of the Collins brothers and drummer John "Jabo" Starks. Starks played a pretty simple groove with a subdivision in eighths, pushing forward toward the offbeat strokes on the snare drum. The snare drum is extremely well placed in the sound box and cracks like a whip, thanks to Starks's technique and his further sharpening of the sound through the simultaneous closing of the previous beat on open hi-hat. His drumming is not fragmented; it includes a few slightly swung sixteenths but not the scarce, shortened type that chop up the groove. Rather, he continuously pushes forward.

Against this, Bootsy Collins places his distinctive short but very soft sequence of sixteenths. He never settles on the beats, instead nestling up to them (beat three) or distributing their weight in the form of a series of short notes (beats two and four).[7] The combination of the soft sound, smooth phrasing, and clearly drawn sixteenths is extraordinary and fits extremely well with Starks's dynamic drumming: the groove is full of small, well-articulated gestures completing one another in a floating curtain of smoothly accented straight sixteenths.

On top of this is Catfish Collins's guitar, which articulates quite another approach. Catfish plays sharply cut, percussive strokes on the beats. The first two have hardly any extension in time, while the third lasts all the way to its ending on an early fourth beat.

Figure 8. Basic groove in "Sex Machine."

The fourth beat is in fact the only counter-rhythmic indication that really stands out from the groove. It is a typical example of the snappy phrasing that also characterizes the downbeat in anticipation: the note is both early and too short.

At first glance this last stroke seems to be no more than a single syncopation; it appears as primary and not secondary rag, to use Wilson's distinction. However, if one relates the early four to the previous stroke right on the third beat, one might see the contours of the first two strokes of a figure of four against three. The third is often completed by James Brown, for example by way of the recurring vocal phrase "Get up!" (see fig. 9).

"Sex Machine" is a good example of the perfectly imperfect balance of rhythm and counter-rhythm mentioned above, which makes it almost irrelevant to identify a sounding counter-rhythmic layer. Among other things, this is due to the highly ambiguous last stroke of the guitar, which arrives a little before, yet *almost* on, the fourth beat. The end of the guitar riff is so ambivalent, so influenced by the main pulse and pulled toward its beat, that it could possibly be both on and off the one and the other: both an early and an accurate beat.

This highly accurate inaccuracy makes it possible for one and the same gesture to form a part of several figures, in this case an articulation of the main beat and the previously described counter-rhythmic pattern in the second half of the bar. In addition to this ambivalence regarding which figure—and pulse scheme—this rhythmic indication is a virtual part of, its ambiguous timing throws doubt upon the authority of both pulse schemes. Starting with the alternative scheme, the early fourth beat has to be there to get the counter-rhythmic pulse started. At the same time, it is obviously also bringing about a destabilizing effect by being slightly too late for the position that has to be confirmed to trigger such an alternative pulse. The stroke is, in other words, off the pulse scheme that is partly constituted by the stroke itself. The scheme is confirmed and cancelled in one and the same move.

This form of uncertainty also brings into focus the way the main basic pulse of a funk groove needs to be constantly disturbed. Even though the main rhythm overrides the counter-rhythm and pulls the timing of the latter in "dubious" directions, the main basic pulse of quarters is not one of rest. Also regarding the main pulse, the anticipation of the fourth beat is characterized by aiming at a double communication: the tiny but sharp rhythmic gesture both is and is not the fourth beat. It obscures the "correct" fourth, occupying the space of a fourth

Figure 9. Counter-rhythmic pattern in "Sex Machine" (indicated by circles).

beat without being one. Actually—or perhaps virtually—it disturbs the fourth in a way that makes an accurately positioned fourth no longer possible.

On and Off—On Displacement, Offbeat Phrasing, and the Way to Treat Strong Beats

The dynamic relation between the syncopation and the beat—the syncopated guitar stroke being pulled toward the beat but never touching it—also illustrates how a beat can be made more dynamic and less settled by stretching it out in time.[8] As mentioned, the last stroke of the guitar riff in "Sex Machine" is so late that the off stroke virtually coincides with the beat on the snare drum that it is intended to anticipate. Rather than forming a syncopation, the closing of the guitar riff acts as an extension of the attack of the snare drum, which thereby is moved a little earlier in time: it stretches the limits of how early an attack can be without losing contact with the strong beat, and it increases the tension before the beat, adding more power to it.[9] Viewed this way, the strong beat is no longer simply a position but a rhythmic gesture in and of itself, unfolding in time and space. The correct location—the core of the beat—becomes more a center of gravity or concentration of energy than a fixed point in a metrical framework.

In general, avoiding a clear placement of strong beats seems to be a central theme in James Brown's funk, especially during the period when Bootsy Collins was a member of the JBs. In "Sex Machine" it is most striking in the bass playing. The bass line never settles down on the strong beats, spreading its energy instead both before and after them: the strong beats are thus "muted" by preceding small notes, or their energy is rolled out after the beat in sequences of sixteenths. The bass line points to the positions of the 4/4 pulses but never marks out exactly where they are. In this way, the gestures of small notes surrounding heavy beats are able to ground the groove without making the strong beats too articulated; the energy is always led away by afterbeats.

Moreover, on closer examination all of the strong beats in the groove of "Sex Machine" are extended by played upbeats. None of them is as strikingly full of tension in relation to the following strong beat as the offstroke of the guitar riff. However, all of these pick-ups to the beats have a similar effect, in that they keep the groove in motion through the positions where musical forces are pulling "downward." They point out the significant beats of the pulse without accentuating them. When the various riffs arrive at a main beat, it has in a sense already passed. One is already heading for new (pre)beats.

Schematically, the pattern of pick-up gestures in "Sex Machine," understood as the overarching movement from upbeat to a more or less heavy main beat, can be represented as in figure 10. Drums (a ghost stroke on the snare drum anticipates the kick drum) and bass guitar play the first pick-up, bass alone the second. Then this heavy rhythmic constellation pauses while the pick-up to the third main beat occurs as a swung sixteenth on the hi-hat. With the pause in drums and bass, this layer of the groove is inverted. For a while, drums and bass take on a counter-rhythmic (but not cross-rhythmic) function: the rhythm is displaced by one eighth and starts with an upbeat to "three-and." The guitar then plays the already thoroughly discussed early four beat while the bass completes the figure of drums and bass on its own with a pick-up to "four-and." Then drums and bass turn their rhythm back, starting over again with an upbeat to the main beat one (see fig. 10).

This displacement of the pattern in drums and bass might be understood as an instance of what Nketia calls "spacing." When displaced, the pattern becomes complementary to the basic pulse, which is still running: one fills in the gaps of the other. As discussed earlier, Waterman describes this phenomenon as "off-beat phrasing," because the displacement—from his point of view—leads to a relocation of accents and rhythmic strokes. While "normally" falling on the beats, they are now being placed between them, on the offbeats. Another and more

Figure 10. Pattern of pick-up gestures in "Sex Machine" (indicated by circles).

obvious version of this is found in the guitar riff of the bridge of "Sex Machine" (see fig. 11). In this pattern the rhythm is also inverted between the first and second parts of the bar, but here the strokes in the second part are placed earlier than expected. The pattern is also less displaced. In the first part of the pattern, the guitar is playing double sixteenths *on* the beat. In the second, the onset is moved one sixteenth ahead. The guitar does not play double strokes as in the first part, but the single sounding sixteenth is almost automatically supplied with a second, due to the subsequent stressed beat.

According to Waterman, in offbeat phrasing the displacement is usually ahead, so that the melodic beat anticipates the percussion stroke.[10] In this respect, the displacement of the guitar in the second part of the pattern in the bridge of "Sex Machine" is typical. However, a closer look at the first part of the pattern reveals that this might also be understood as an instance of offbeat phrasing in Waterman's sense. Instead of ending the double stroke on the next eighth, on the note that according to a pulse on eighth notes would have been the next regular beat, the chords are played on the offbeats of the eighth notes, thereby anticipating the following strong beats (that is, the "one-and" and "two-and," from a 4/4 point of view).

Seen this way, there is a fairly close relationship between Waterman's offbeat phrasing and the gesture named the downbeat in anticipation. When the displacement is ahead, it is almost as if the latter is to be regarded as a "singular" instance of the former. The relation is perhaps somewhat clarified by the following tautology: an anticipated

$(\decrescendo = 106)$

Figure 11. The guitar riff of the bridge of "Sex Machine."

downbeat is a singular instance of offbeat phrasing, while offbeat phrasing moves the stress from the downbeats to the offbeats before the downbeats—or, in other words, in anticipation of the downbeats. However, there might well be a difference in accent between the two descriptions: while offbeat phrasing lays out the phenomenon as if the very figure or pattern is moved from on to off, the downbeat in anticipation takes as a starting point that the figure is unchanged (the downbeat), though the manner is different (in anticipation). I will return to this distinction, or rather connection, of matter and manner later on. However, before doing so, we must look closer at the singer James Brown and his role in the fabric of rhythm, in terms of matter, manner, and both at once.

More on Manner—James Brown as Vocal Percussionist

As discussed earlier, the guitar riff in "Sex Machine" is clearly inflected by the snappy phrasing characterizing the downbeat in anticipation. However, even the vocals are by and large marked by a shortening of phrase endings. Because the voice's rhythmic function may be less obvious than the other instruments', it is probably easy to underestimate the significance of the vocals for a song like this.[11] In "Sex Machine," James Brown is the "master drummer" in several ways. First of all, he is the one who varies his part and gives cues for the different sections, like the piano riff and the bridge. Furthermore, the voice is the instrument that suggests a grouping of the bars in four and four, or eight and eight, while at the same time overriding these attempts at grouping by introducing new beginnings at the most unexpected points in time.[12] Last, but not least, it is the voice that more than any other instrument provides the downbeats in anticipation, which appear to be everywhere in this groove. "Sex Machine" would not have been the same song without a vocalist like James Brown, without the precision and concentrated energy that distinguish his vocal attacks.

Even though the vocal line is varied all the way through, it is in no way free improvisation (if such a thing is even possible). The voice is so integrated into the rest of the fabric that it has to be perceived within the fixed patterns of the accompaniment. This is particularly true with regard to some specific places in the repeated basic unit that are treated more or less the same throughout the song. One of these is the upbeat to the basic unit. In almost every bar possible (except the piano riff, the bridge, the cueing before the bridge, the end, and so on) this is modeled on some variant of the same figure. The first—the "Get up!" gesture— occurs fully twenty-eight times in the course of the song's five-minute duration. The gesture starts at "four-and" and ends almost on, but not exactly on, the first beat of the basic unit. The sixteenth in the middle of the gesture (between four-and and one) is, moreover, only suggested as a little swing in the sentence melody.

Both the beginning and the ending of Brown's gesture form a part of several of the significant repeated patterns in the song. As discussed earlier, the attack of the "Get up!" gesture might be considered the third indication of a figure of four against three starting on the third beat of the bar. Probably even more important is how this stretches out the significant first beat of the basic unit: the closing of the "Get up!" gesture is a typical downbeat in anticipation, and the fast consonant that ends it is extremely short and perhaps also a little early.

Brown's "Get up!" gesture is commonly answered by the phrase "Get on up!," sung by band member Bobby Byrd. As a response to the "Get up" call, Byrd's phrase is also regular enough to form a part of the rhythmic fabric. However, regarded as rhythm, it is not as accurately articulated as Brown's call. The phrase always leads up to the third beat of the bar, but Byrd is not consistent in ending the gesture as a downbeat in anticipation. Sometimes he shapes the "p" much in the same manner as Brown's downbeats in anticipation, but sometimes he places the "p" straight on the beat, neutralizing the effect of the shortened ending.

Brown's second variant of the upbeat to the basic unit occurs rather frequently as well but has a slightly different design. It can be found in rhythmically similar combinations of words like "the scene," "machine," "right on," and so on. Schematically speaking, the energy of this gesture is also concentrated around the last two sixteenths before the subsequent beat one. It starts on either the first or the second sixteenth but is always in contact with the latter before its landing on the first beat. This ending also tends to be a little early but is not as snappily phrased as the "Get up!" gesture. In general, the entire gesture is more forward directed: it is pumping toward the first beat and has much in common, in its rolling salsa effect, with the prebeat and afterbeat playing of the bass.

The offbeat phrasing and the underlying stress on sixteenths of the two gestures described above pull the song in the direction of a density referent of sixteenths or perhaps even smaller note values. In general, the vocal line is so snappy, so light and frenetic, that not even sounds with a longer duration are allowed to die away comfortably. Even the lasting notes have to be broken up by a light accentuation of their underlying short notes. The snappy phrasing and the somewhat "manic" mood of the singing require a very high precision, and it cannot flag. Every little lapse—a somewhat lazy ending, an imprecise onset, a slack phrase without the same energetic core, any decrease in energy level or precision—stands out. With just a little slip-up, the singing seems to lose its nerve.

In other words, in these surroundings, a high level of energy in the singing does not necessarily result in magnified or extravagant gestures. With such a high density referent, the margins in time are very small, and this requires attention to minute time spaces and their accurate pacing. There is no room for expressive swelling. Making too much of a rhythm—a heavy syncopation, a dwelling on a potentially virtuosic detail, an overdone ornament—will immediately lead to the next one beginning too late. Nothing can lose contour.

Perhaps this is the reason why "Sex Machine" gives an impression of extraordinary suppression and control. It is almost as if James Brown provides himself with an inner resistance that has to be forced while he—almost literally speaking—squeezes out the sound. He never lets the sound loose but instead improvises in a style of focused restraint. He presumably requires this self-chosen asceticism to control the rhythmic aspects of his singing. It allows the onsets and phrase endings to be sufficiently accurate; the vocal utterances to be properly placed in time; and the attacks to be short and distinct, with a strain of fortepiano.[13] This is how he can solve the simple yet difficult task he measures out for himself: to be in place in time, with a surplus of energy and a voice always at the ready.

Disturbing the Internal Beat

One of the interesting things regarding this particular way of phrasing and the downbeat in anticipation is that, strictly speaking, it is an open question as to whether a note is actually "early" or not. Regarding its position in time, the note is probably placed in such a way that it could be heard as completely in time if in a different timbral shaping. In other words, the note is experienced as early here, partly because it is phrased as being early. Instead of reinforcing the downbeat, this gesture suspends the ideal or correct downbeat by taking the place of the downbeat without playing its part.

Again, it is important to point out that the "correct" location of the beat here does not imply a chronometrical division of the time span into, for example, eight beats. It follows from the underlying pulse as it is *experienced* or implied by the pattern of rhythm as a whole. In funk it is rather easy to catch this basic pulse, due to the unmistakable metrical framework of the music. At the same time, on closer examination the actual location of the beat remains quite unclear. The beat appears as rather dynamic, and this is probably due to aesthetic strategies such as the downbeat in anticipation, which seems to aim at a destabilization of the main basic pulse. Put simply, the rhythm as a whole points to one location of the main basic pulse, while a certain part of the groove, the downbeat in anticipation, denies it. The groove as a whole refers the pulse to the beats, while the downbeat in anticipation hides them: what is anticipated never arrives; there is no orderly, unambiguous downbeat. The accurate beat is thereby suspended, because one has already passed the beat that was expected to come. The downbeat in anticipation is, in other words, not equal to a real downbeat that is played too early. The anticipation is played too late to form a syncopation—as such, it never completes its own movement. The closing, which is as significant for its shaping as the beginning, never occurs: the anticipation never ends on an alternative strong beat. It only overshadows the beat that is supposed to be there—or, alternatively, it stretches the beat out in time.

Even the tendency to surround strong beats with small notes might be understood as an instance of stretching the strong beat out in time, although in a slightly different manner than the downbeat in anticipation. In cases such as the pick-ups to the strong beats and also the rolling bass lines of sixteenths typical of Bootsy Collins's playing, one might rather think of what happens as an offbeat-based pulse of sixteenths being triggered around the beat, working as a magnet both before and after it and thereby absorbing some of its energy. This is probably not as threatening to the basic pulse as is the downbeat in anticipation, but it has a similar effect: a reinforcement or reinstallment

James Brown. MICHAEL OCHS ARCHIVES.COM

The JB's. MICHAEL OCHS ARCHIVES.COM

James Brown. MICHAEL OCHS ARCHIVES.COM

Album cover of *Sex Machine* (1970). © UNIVERSAL

Album cover of *The Payback* (1974). © UNIVERSAL

of another pulse scheme—for example, the sixteenths immediately before and after the strong beat—takes some of the attention from what, on the other hand, has to be a center of force.

The Pulse of the Rhythm and the Pulse of the Counter-Rhythm

As mentioned, the downbeat in anticipation might be understood as an emerging misfit of the dominant subdivision and the localized phrasing of one or more rhythmic gestures. However, by and by, this tendency to throw doubt on the density referent by animating the groove with some snappy phrase endings seems to spread to the whole groove, and these hints of a faster pulse, combined with an increased difference in timbre between the slower and the faster layers—the slower getting deeper and more dull, the faster becoming even more high-pitched and percussive—seem to result in an increased distance between the upper and lower parts of the sound box.

As discussed earlier, this phenomenon is already present in "Cold Sweat," which may be heard as an emerging disparity between upper and lower layers in the groove. In the main groove of "Sex Machine," however, the snappy phrasing and connected doubling of the density referent are even more striking. The distance to the lower layers has also increased here, because the main basic pulse becomes half as fast due to the extra weight added to beats one and three. In fact, the characteristically funky guitar riff may alone be said to contain this tension between the fastest and the slowest pulse scheme in the song. On one hand, the guitar contributes to suggesting a slow pulse on the half notes through an unequal distribution of weight on the four quarter notes; on the other hand, it contributes to suggesting a density referent of very short units through the snappy closing of the riff almost before the fourth beat, one that does not in any way match the slowest basic pulse.

The first groove of the song "Soul Power" is also characterized by guitar strokes of this type, and the snappy phrasing is highly responsible for the earlier mentioned fragmentation of the cross-rhythmic layer of four against three. The phrase endings of the bass also consequently relate to a density referent on the level of sixteenths, while the main elements in the drumming, bass drum and snare drum, clearly prepare a density referent on eighths. The span from the slowest basic pulse to the fastest is, in other words, considerable and to some degree threatening for the pattern as a whole: the upper and the lower layers of the groove seem always about to part.[14]

As James Brown's protofunk moves in the direction of funk, this incongruity becomes more and more conspicuous. In the live recording of "Ain't It Funky Now,"[15] the move from the foregoing song "Brother Rapp" to "Ain't It Funky Now" is characterized by the basic pulse and the density referent going in opposite directions. In "Ain't It Funky Now" the tempo (that is, the basic pulse) goes down. Instead of continuing in the breathless up-tempo feeling of the previous song, the drums lean backward, grounding the groove, while the typical funk riff of the guitar pushes forward against a pulse twice as fast as the basic pulse.

The snappy phrasing and the growing incongruity of the basic pulse and the density referent contribute greatly to the vertical swinging motion that distinguishes funk. As we shall see, this span from top to bottom, and from the fast to the slow, is even more striking in the somewhat over-mature P-Funk grooves. However, it is important to point out that this process is about more than moving the density referent from the alleged natural subdivision of the basic pulse to a level above that. The effect of this way of phrasing depends at least partly on the fact that these notes are *too* short. Put another way, it arises from the absence of a regular structure of pulses that can be used to schematize it. If an accent falls completely on a scheduled position—for example, due to an unambiguous, regular density referent on sixteenths, as in disco— the effect is different.

Moreover, on closer examination it becomes clear that this snappy phrasing very often appears in connection with a counter-rhythmic layer. In "Sex Machine," to take one example, the coupling of the fast set of pulses and the counter-rhythm is obviously present in the guitar riff of the main groove. As discussed earlier, the combination of the two last strokes of the guitar riff and the vocal onset on "four-and" may be understood as a counter-rhythmic pattern of four against three that begins on beat three. This is also the figure that locates the two most striking instants of the way of phrasing that characterizes the downbeat in anticipation, the syncopated fourth beat in the guitar and the vocal phrase "Get up!"

Furthermore, if one considers the pattern of four against three as a counter-rhythm to eighths, not quarters—that is, as a standard pattern working against a tacit alternative doubled basic pulse—then not only does a faster density referent appear in connection with the counter-rhythm but also a basic pulse that is twice as fast as the main regulative beat.[16] Viewed this way, it may seem that, in the figure of four against three, the expanded distance between basic pulse and density referent is part of the very structure of the figure itself. As funk develops, this is also the version of cross-rhythm that becomes typical for the style.

In other words, the exchange between main rhythm and counter-rhythm might entail more than an "unnaturally" distant relation between basic pulse and density referent. The very point might be to let the questions regarding both density referent and basic pulse remain unresolved to some extent. The excitement might once again lie in the ambivalence: the snappy way of phrasing and the counter-rhythmic figure have an effect because, while the rhythm rests on the main beat, the counter-rhythm has a beat of its own.

Ants and Downstrokes

If the tension between the upper and lower layers in the groove is essential, and part of this tension is created by a snappy way of phrasing, the downbeat in anticipation, it may be reasonable to agree with James Brown: perhaps it all started with "Papa's Got a Brand New Bag," with an early toot of the horns that later on spread to other layers and other positions in the groove. After a while it became a manner, a way of phrasing that could be named after a song where it is highly cultivated, in fact to such an extent and in such a one-sided manner as to hardly count as funk: "I Got Ants in My Pants" (1971).

"Cold Sweat," "Sex Machine," the first groove of "Soul Power," and "Ain't It Funky Now," to mention only a few, are fundamentally marked by this typically funky way of phrasing. However, contrary to "I Got Ants in My Pants," these songs are based on a slow pulse. In other words, the feeling of being constantly a little on top in the funk groove is balanced by the feeling of being constantly laid back or completely grounded in the lower layers of the groove. In relation to how short the short actually is in "Sex Machine," it seems as though the lower layers still have some capacity left for increasing the discrepancy between the heavy, rich-sounding bottom and the snappy, fast layers on top. The slow pulse is heavy, but not *that* heavy. The strong beats are stretched in time—by pick-ups, by the cross-rhythmic tendency of the last part of the guitar riff, by the diverse early strokes in the faster layers—but not to the breaking point. Even though the discrepancy between the upper and lower layers is there, the groove is actually quite moderate in relation to the grooves yet to come. The incongruity of density referent and basic pulse is not yet that aggravating, and the figures are still fairly clearly drawn; they are not completely overwhelmed by manner.

Nonetheless, analysis supports the claim that those features of the rhythmic fabric that become so obvious later on are already there, just on a smaller scale. In "Sex Machine" the process has not yet gone that far: important features of the funk groove do not yet comprise musical structure in the traditional sense. They are still a manner, a way of doing things. What is not yet quite there, among other things, is a really heavy first beat. Even though the first beat of the basic unit in "Sex Machine" is given weight and clearly works as the focal point of the groove, it lacks the all-embracing groundedness, the threat against the motion forward, that appears in later heavy funk grooves—for example, those of Parliament.

So, even though James Brown and his bands in most ways fulfill the style tentatively summed up in *The New Rolling Stone Encyclopedia of Rock*'s attempt at a "definition" of funk—"bass-driven, percussive, polyrhythmic black dance music, with minimal melody and maximum syncopation"[17]—there might be a higher order than the alphabetical one at work when the next definition to appear is "Funkadelic: See George Clinton."

III

Funk in the Crossover Era

6

A Brand(ed) New Fad

Now when we finish with this session, they'll know where
funk come from. Every time I look, listen at the radio, I
hear, I hear JBs. I hear James Brown. Can't even say,
"Good God." But that's alright, I don't care. They don't
never give me no royalties, and when they get on the
different shows they say, "Yeah, I put it all together
by myself." Listen to James Brown, that's all they got
to ask me. But that's alright, I can take that, yeah, cause
I'm sayin' it loud. But we gonna get on down, 'cause
reality don't ever lie.

—James Brown in *Dead On It* (1975)[1]

Social Change and the Era of Crossover

Despite riots in the inner cities, increasing drug-related problems in the streets, and the leadership vacuum following the assassination of Martin Luther King Jr. in 1968, the 1960s were a vital period for black America both culturally and politically. It is moreover appropriate to regard the activity of James Brown and his bands from the late 1960s and early 1970s as a cultural counterpart to this time. This music became important to the process of identifying a specifically black culture, and Brown's undeniable success as a black entrepreneur in the powerful American music industry made him almost an icon of progress and self-consciousness, of consolidation, hope, and pride. Brown had succeeded in spite of a terrible start in life and seemingly without making musical compromises.

But times changed. The 1970s became a decade of increasing inequality and class divisions within black America. Conditions in the inner cities got worse, and there was a growing despair and disillusion among poor blacks. At the same time, as a consequence of the economic growth of the 1960s, an economic integration had taken place and a new black middle class had emerged. One of the consequences of the processes of upward social mobility was a growing ambivalence among middle-class blacks toward their own history and culture. In Nelson George's words: "The struggle to overcome the overt apartheid of America had given blacks an energy, a motivating dream, that inspired the music's makers. By the mid-seventies, a segment of black America had beaten the odds, leaped over the barricade, and now lived in parts of the country they would have been lynched in a decade before. It struck many of them as time to remove the modifying adjective 'black' from their lives."[2]

This new atmosphere affected the music business in several ways. While the 1960s had proved that a black music market could support a black recording industry, the 1970s was a time when the term "crossover" came to dominate all discussion of black music. Traditionally, crossover refers to the process whereby a record or an artist becomes successful on a chart after having initially succeeded on a different chart. Most commonly this implies a movement from the periphery to the center of the popular music markets, or, in Reebee Garofalo's words, from "a 'secondary' marketing category like country and western, Latin or rhythm and blues" to "the mainstream or 'pop' market."[3] One obvious reason for aiming at the mainstream market was the increase in profits. It was lucrative to have artists succeed in different markets at the same time. However, success on the pop chart in the 1970s meant more than success in two or more specialized markets. As both Garofalo and Jason Toynbee point out, the pop mainstream was the hegemonic market of popular music. David Brackett also emphasizes the relational character of the mainstream, and how "the concept of the mainstream retains its currency through its ability to provide a 'center' for other 'marginal' or 'alternative' genres."[4] Along these lines, he approaches the mainstream as "an ever-shifting hierarchical assemblage of genres that form the mainstream 'supra-genre' during that period. While the mainstream may be heterogeneous, not all genres have the same status within it."[5]

According to Brackett, the genres coded as "African American" have been marginal in relation to the formation of the mainstream, working almost as a "colony, a source from which the mainstream may draw periodically to replenish itself in times of scarcity."[6] Nevertheless, the significance of the instances when the mainstream has "replenished" itself by means of black music cannot be understated. In an article on the influence of black music on the popular music mainstream, Garofalo identifies three periods in this interaction that led to a change in the relation itself. The first was the Tin Pan Alley era of the 1930s and 1940s. According to Garofalo, popular culture emerges as dominant at this time, involving "an awareness of African American influences, but these are safely incorporated into European stylistic patterns."[7] In the next period, the rock 'n' roll era, African American cultural sensibilities become dominant, but the presence of African American artists on the pop chart was still quite marginal. According to Toynbee, this is when we see the emergence of what he calls the second popular mainstream, labeled rock, which lasts from the 1950s throughout the 1970s.[8] The crossover of black dance music in the late 1970s came, in other words, at the dawn of an era deeply influenced by black musical traditions, but still, as Garofalo puts it, "with a need for white interpreters."[9] This goes well with the fact that few black artists and bands actually succeeded on the pop charts in the late 1970s. According to Brackett, the late 1970s was a period of notably few successes for black crossover in the traditional sense.[10]

I have nevertheless chosen to label the late 1970s an era of crossover, for two reasons. First, as has been described by Nelson George, it seems like the urge to cross over in this period was so strong that it affected the core structures of the black music industry. I will soon return to this. Second, the late 1970s was no doubt an era of crossover at the level of style. Similar to how rhythm and blues influenced the rock 'n' roll mainstream in the 1950s, musical styles associated with black musical traditions such as funk and disco moved in the 1970s from the margins to the mainstream—in the terminology of Brackett, new sub-genres came to influence the supra-genre in a profound way. This became especially obvious on the pop charts toward the end of the decade—that is, after the release of the soundtrack of *Saturday Night Fever*.

The music that crossed over to the international pop and rock audiences in the late 1970s had a softer sound. It was highly danceable funk, but it was lighter and lacked the edges of James Brown. In many cases, the music was produced and marketed directly to the mainstream market, and in this respect the late 1970s crossovers appear to anticipate the formidable mainstream successes of Michael Jackson and Prince that were to come. These crossovers may be accounted for in different ways. According to one perspective, they represented the demise of segregated markets and a sign of how influential black music culture had come to be.[11] From another perspective, they represented the very end of the black music industry.

According to Nelson George, a writer deeply concerned with the consequences of crossover for the black music business, the crossover music displayed a calculated, ingratiating hipness that he links to the fact that a considerable percentage of the audience of the new black FM stations was either college educated or comfortable with the values a college education suggested. For these people, identifying with stylish black music was a way of achieving status among the trendsetters. As George writes about Crocker's station WBLS-FM, "In New York, the desire to be hip, to be part of the city's trendsetting class, runs deep, and Crocker tapped into this yearning with a psychologist's skill."[12]

While funk was surfacing as a new, hot style in Western popular music, the crossover mentality that governed artists as well as the major record companies guided the fates of the many black artists who left the black record companies and signed to the majors. At the majors there was more pressure for black artists to seek white sales, and as a consequence many black artists devoted too much energy to a crossover hit. Very few succeeded, and if they did, they often failed to follow up. The single was often chosen primarily for its crossover potential, while the album, which was usually held back until the single was established, would contain a more traditional mix of different black styles. For many of the soul singers of the old era, this strategy proved a disaster, because their traditional followers in the black audience were lost along the way. In George's words, "Black radio emphatically rejected many of their 'pop' efforts or, in some cases, simply didn't like the first single. With no album cuts to play in its place, these acts were left with no airplay for long periods of time."[13] After a while the artist usually lost his or her contract altogether.

Casualties of the crossover era included not only the big stars of the world of soul but also the crucial networks of the black music industry: its independent record labels, traditional r&b radio, concert venues, and retail stores in black neighborhoods. It took several years before the next wave of black music with a clearly black identity, namely hip-hop, managed to reinvigorate the idea of a black music business.

Hot, Hot, Hot . . . ?—James Brown at Polydor

The new cultural situation, with its spirit of assimilation and crossover within the field of black music, affected James Brown in several ways. In 1971 he signed to German-based Polydor, and in his autobiography, Brown claims that this destroyed his music and his sound:

> I'd mix a song until I thought—until I knew—it was right, but they [Polydor executives] would want their machines to say whether it was right or not. I had to register certain numbers on the machines. It didn't matter whether the track was alive and moved, all that mattered was the numbers. I had a warmth in my sound I was trying to preserve, and I wanted the track to be an instrumental before I put any words to it. It's like having a good bedspread but wondering if the mattress is comfortable. They wanted a pretty bedspread. I wanted to make the mattress comfortable.
>
> In the early years with them I was hitting the singles charts in spite of the company. The songs were hits because I forced them through the company and made them hits myself. I was supposed to have creative control, but they started remixing my records. I mixed them, but when they came out they didn't sound like what I'd mixed. The company didn't want the funk in there too heavy. They'd take the feeling out of the record. They didn't want James Brown to be raw. Eventually, they destroyed my sound.
>
> Whatever King Records had been about, Polydor was the opposite. Every King act was individual; Polydor tried to make all their acts the same . . . But they paid me; I can't get away from that. They gave me more money than anybody ever gave me. Mr. Nathan [the director of King] didn't pay me. Polydor would pay me, but they wouldn't give me the freedom Mr. Nathan did.[14]

During the first years of the Polydor era, it is indeed striking how the edgy, energetic style of Brown's earlier songs gradually vanished. Gaining ground was an inclination toward both a more polished sound and toward the more grandiose dramaturgy and rich "live" sound that characterized many of the other funk and party bands of the 1970s, with powerful riffs played in unison by a large horn section, orchestral transitions from section to section, and big band–influenced arranging. In this period James Brown also felt compelled to remind people that there was funk before white critics and their followers

Figure 12. The basic groove of the intro of "My Thang" (handclaps on beats 2 and 4).

"discovered" it. The intro of the song "My Thang" (1973, released 1974) is a quick lesson in how to make "that brand new funk" (see fig. 12). The few bars comprise everything necessary for a funk groove. There is a short bass riff doubled by the guitar, which plays a few eighth notes before finishing off with a heavy One. It is answered by a counter-rhythmic guitar, which plays a displaced 4:3 figure, phrased in the chopped-up, funky manner. Moreover, there is a small but characteristic pick-up to the bass drum before the third beat, while overall an uncomplicated, open drum beat with snare and bass drum alternates in the usual rock manner; the typical quarters on half-open hi-hat link the slow layers of bass and drums to the double-tempo guitar. As a whole, however, the song lacks vitality. The edge—the usual internal dynamics of a James Brown groove—is not there. Everything is just middle of the road, and this song may serve as an example of the standardization of funk for the crossover market that seems to have taken place in this period.

On "Funky President," however, a Polydor release from 1974, James Brown is back to his funk fundamentals, with a bone-dry sound and short, accurate rhythmic gestures. Moreover, the feeling of attending a school lesson has gone. While the intro to "My Thang" sounds like a recipe for funk, "Funky President" realizes it again as music. It is playful and cheeky. The first groove mixes several complementary rhythmic patterns, and the combination of the different patterns gives the song a tendency toward cross-rhythm. The groove has an underlying feel of four against the three first beats of the bar (it is most obvious in the first bar of the two-bar basic unit) (see fig. 13).

In the B section (groove 2), the bass plays the four against three, only occasionally receiving some support from the accentuation in the wah-wah guitar, which treats the swung sixteenths in a rather choppy way (see fig. 14).

In both grooves, there is a pattern of upbeats stretching the strong beats. Even though the pattern changes from groove 1 to groove 2, the same beats are extended: the One begins at the preceding eighth note, while two, three and three-and are anticipated by a sixteenth (see fig. 15).

Even though the groove of each rhythmic layer changes, the total impression is of one groove running throughout the song. The most striking change from groove 1 to groove 2 is that the almost too-straight sixteenths in groove 1 disappear from the overall sound. These sixteenths, which are either too straight or too prominent in the sound, are also almost too definite, rigid, and ordered to take place in the upper parts of the sound box. Viewed this way, groove 2 appears to be an easing of this tension.

"Funky President" was, with one exception, the 1976 discofunk single "Get Up Offa That Thing," the last song to reach a high position (fourth) on the *Billboard* r&b list. It succeeded three number-one singles from the successful *Payback* album (released in 1974), but the streak was

Figure 13. Cross-rhythmic tendency in "Funky President," groove 1 (indicated by circles).

Figure 14. Cross-rhythmic tendency in "Funky President," groove 2 (indicated by circles).

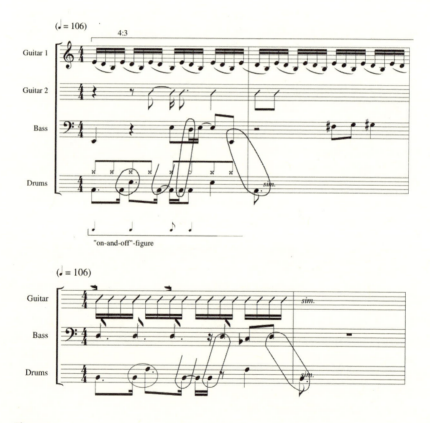

Figure 15.
(top) Pick-up gestures in "Funky President," groove 1 (indicated by circles).
(bottom) Pick-up gestures in "Funky President," groove 2 (indicated by circles).

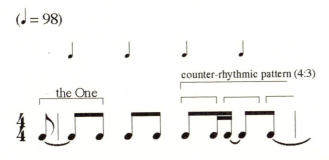

Figure 16. Counter-rhythm and the extended One in "Hot (I Need To Be Loved, Loved, Loved)."

over: more than ten years would pass before James Brown reentered the top ten.[15] Brown still made some honest efforts at producing his "brand new funk," but, perhaps due to the intervention by Polydor described above, his trademark edgy sound and energetic drive are gone. "Hot (I Need to Be Loved, Loved, Loved)" is an example of this. It is probably as close as James Brown gets to the *Rolling Stone Illustrated Music History* definition of funk: "Like a ketchup-laden cheese steak plopped down at a staid dinner party, funk was rude, greasy and unwanted."[16] The gestures are expansive and the funk groove has a more typical laid-back character, but the song was not able to compete with the slickness of contemporaneous crossover funk. Besides, it lacked the feeling conveyed by so many of the grooves discussed in the previous chapters, the feeling of James Brown and his band hitting on something really unique.

"Hot" may be read as a sign of how the funk gestures created by Brown and his bands, among others, were about to become conventional. The guitar riff is extremely typical for the style: a counter-rhythmic single-string riff with "shortened" phrasing that moves between the minor and major seventh. The cross-rhythmic tendency appears at the end of each bar in the form of a figure of four against three, and the last stroke on four-and anticipates the one, almost as an early attack (see fig. 16). The one has, as a gesture, been considerably extended—it has become the One. Its attack is very early and is followed by a traditional one played by bass drum and a very heavy and deep bass guitar, ringing almost without beginning and end and therefore working as pure grounding. In fact, one might say that the end of the counter-rhythmic guitar riff acts as the true start of the (extended) One. Taking this into consideration,

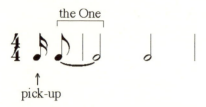

the One

↑
pick-up

Figure 17. The One and its pick-up in "Hot."

the pick-up played by the bass drum as early as the first sixteenth after the fourth beat makes more sense. The pick-up is supported by the closing stroke of the response riff played by the fuzzed guitar, because the riff hangs on the same syncopated note (see fig. 17).

"Hot" is no doubt a funk groove. When it comes to form, however, this song leads out of the groove-focused style to which Brown himself contributed. A traditional song structure of verse and chorus is now about to reenter the music. The A section works like a verse and moves between two similar but varying grooves. The first groove (a) is described above, and the second is a variant (a') where bass takes over the guitar's cross-rhythmic function. The guitar starts again with a distinctive shriek before continuing with a more typical response, a riff after the fashion of "The Payback." After this section (A), consisting of two two-bar units with the a-groove followed by four bars with the a'-groove, there occurs what might be called a chorus (B) (see fig. 18). Over an a-groove the backing vocals regularly enter the song with the phrase "Gimme, gimme, gimme some lovin'." Moreover, in this section, the whole melodic and harmonic complex occasionally moves up a fourth, adding to the song a touch of blues or r&b.

After a while, the contours of this section, which is supposed to be the chorus, are weakened, because it appears to be almost never ending. The backing vocals fail to tail off. Simultaneously, it seems that Brown himself starts on a new verse. The situation remains unclear all the way down to what is, beyond doubt, a new section (C). This section acts as a kind of bridge. The bass disappears and the electric piano takes over the cross-rhythmic function with a typically funky counter-rhythmic riff. After a while, the bass rejoins the accompaniment. The dividing line against the bridge is never drawn clearly. In the end, the overall form appears to be a kind of ABA, with the bridge (C) acting as a middle section.

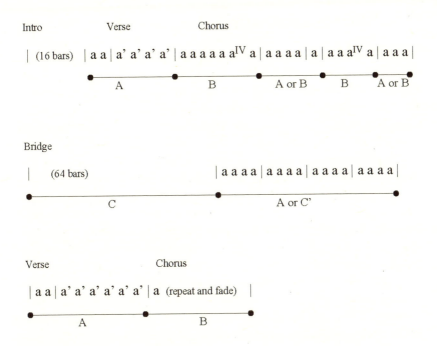

Figure 18. Schematic outline of form in "Hot" (a=2 bars).

"Hot" points to some of the features characterizing funk in the crossover era, including its polished sound and laid-back attitude. Another feature, the process of secularization of black music, will be discussed below.

In the context of this study, however, we must also remark upon the tendency toward a relaunching of the traditional format of Anglo-American pop and rock, the *song*. Even though a binary structure of verse and chorus is still not too apparent, one clearly gets the impression of a structural grouping at a level above the basic unit of the groove. The re-entrance of the traditional song format may point toward the crossover audience's ambivalent response to music with groove as the primary overall structuring principle. More than the edgy sound, the energetic drive, and the percussive attitude to musicking, it was probably the lack of a traditional melody, and of verse and chorus—in short, the lack of a traditional "song"—that mainly prevented the "old" funk of James Brown from really conquering the crossover market for black music. This meeting between funk as a primarily groove-based music and an audience accustomed to something quite different is discussed in part IV.

. . . And Beyond—The Despiritualization of Funk

As we have seen, James Brown's musical production in the period discussed in the previous chapters, from "Papa's Got a Brand New Bag" (1965) to "The Payback" (recorded 1973, released 1974), shares many of the features that are commonly used to identify an African musical heritage in African American music. However, as I discussed in part I, the importance of the process of identifying a specifically black musical tradition was more profound than what can be accounted for at the level of stylistic traits. What was at stake was the uniqueness of the black experience: black styles could be appropriated by a non-black person, but the black *experience* was not understandable for an outsider. At such a level, the question of black aesthetics dealt with a search for a new spirituality—or, as many saw it, the recapture of the old one, "lost and buried deep in our African past."[17]

During the 1970s this link between funk and the struggle for a black history and identity weakened. At this point, however, it should be mentioned that for the mainstream pop and rock audiences that became familiar with black dance music toward the end of the 1970s, the story is different. These audiences never related to this historical link in the first place. We barely knew that it existed, as we barely knew that there was funk before the crossover funk that reached us. In other words, the fact that funk crossed over was not necessarily experienced as a transformation of funk, either musically or culturally, for the target audience of the crossover process. For the white pop and rock audiences thrilled by the new black dance music, the story of funk in one sense starts with the 1970s—with a cultural situation in which funk for the most part connoted hip dance music and hedonism.

From the point of view of black America, however, the crossover era represented a change of focus that was part of a general secularization of black music. Cornel West links this to the emergence of a new nihilism within black America, a loss of hope and an absence of meaning: "As hope remains and meaning is preserved, the possibility of overcoming oppression stays alive. The self-fulfilling prophecy of the nihilistic threat is that without hope there can be no future, that without meaning there can be no struggle."[18]

According to West, the black religious and civic institutions that sustained familial and communal networks were barriers against this threat. During the decades following the 1960s, these barriers had been gradually weakened, and in the essay "Nihilism in Black America"

(1994), West asks: "What has changed? What went wrong? The bitter irony of integration? The cumulative effects of a genocidal conspiracy? The virtual collapse of rising expectations after the optimistic sixties? None of us fully understands why the cultural structures that once sustained black life in America are no longer able to fend off the nihilistic threat."[19]

In addition to a general crisis in black leadership, West points to the saturation of market forces and market moralities in black life as a possible reason for this development. The weakening of the "human infrastructure" of black communities coincided with a general turn in the Western world toward an ideology celebrating the market and private enterprise at the cost of public solutions to social needs. The freedom to choose on an individual level became more important than the need for securing common access to social services. Against this background, it may not be very surprising that, during the same period, the utopian dimension of black musicking, and an important aspect of "the Afro-American spiritual-blues impulse," faded.[20] The ideological change described above distanced many members of the black audience, as well as many of the new funk acts, from the spiritual aspects of black dance music.

The crossover success of black musical styles may be regarded as both a cause and an effect in this process of secularization. On the one hand, a change toward a more secular focus on bodily pleasure probably was a premise for success in the crossover markets, because it made funk more useful for the identity purposes of the new groups of (white) listeners, who did not immediately relate to, or perhaps even recognize, the spiritual dimension of black musicking. As discussed in part I, the mind-centered Western tradition of religion and thought has resulted in a culture hostile to, scared by, and deeply fascinated with both bodily pleasure and the possibility of losing control. In line with this, the bodily appeal and dance floor experience of funk offered a refuge from this overriding need for control and self-presence. It made funk a means of subversion: funk was almost irresistible as a way of identifying with anti-Western values and detaching oneself from the rationality and order of the official culture of the core territories of Western popular music, the Anglo-American world. Within the Western dualistic worldview and its subsequent polarized discourse on the relation of body and mind, the funk experience became not only body music but anti-mind music. Conversely, in an atmosphere deeply prejudiced by the great numbers of "black" crossover successes—that is, of music influenced by black musical idioms—the fact that it was a de-spiritualized version of funk that appealed to the white pop and rock audiences may in itself have worked to move black dance music in the direction of a secular focus.[21]

Due to these forces, funk largely developed into a music highly resonant with, in West's words, "the hedonistic stage of late capitalist U.S. society."[22] As will be discussed in the last chapters of this book, this change does not mean, however, that the dance floor did not have a spiritual aspect in the late 1970s, only that the discourse and understanding of funk, on the production as well as the reception sides, had changed.

The despiritualization of funk also affected James Brown's production in these years. The change in function of his lyrics may, for example, be better understood with the new cultural situation in mind. In Brown's pre-crossover funk, the lyrics acted first of all as part of the groove and/or as comments on the qualities of the groove. On the level of semantic meaning, the texts were rather fragmented, ambiguous, and, not least, allusive of *both* bodily pleasure and spiritual transcendence by way of their highly figurative language. In the songs from the crossover era, however, the allusions to sex are more straightforward, and the words signify in a more traditional, literal sense. In "Hot," for instance, the text deals with a rather earthly desire and is given the form of a story: "I woke up this morning . . ." The reason for Brown's "hot" condition is no longer allowed to float ambiguously in the space between bodily pleasure and the transcendent qualities of the groove. Rather, the funky feeling is explicated in words in a way that makes it almost impossible to misunderstand the bottom line. James Brown "needs to be loved, loved, loved . . ." in a far more tangible way than what is actually the case with "Sex Machine," despite its more suggestive title.

All in all, "Hot" achieved a certain slick, macho attitude that at this time had become more of a program for an entire wing of funk acts. When James Brown introduced songs like "Hot" and "Body Heat," it may have been in response to the general vogue of slickness and hedonism flourishing in this period. However, he cannot quite match the artificial and overtly glam-influenced pornification of the genre in a fresh way. He is not able to announce the message "funk equals sex" as a smooth blending of soft porn and parody—as when a band such as the Ohio Players made their album covers according to the themes "honey" or "fire," the latter realized by means of a woman dressed in a highly form-fitting fire jacket, helmet, and boots with pretty unsuitable heels, at least for firefighting purposes—and, of course, with her hands fitted around a remarkable fire hose, pointing in a slightly upward direction.

The Influence of Disco

During the crossover era, the meaning of funk changed. Funk developed into a trendy musical style and became hot also within the Anglo-American world of popular music. The word "funky" was no longer just an adjective in the African American repertoire of slang, denoting a certain deep, soulful feeling, nor was funk an exclusive sound in the rhythmic laboratory of James Brown and other musical pioneers. Funk had become a fad, a label many artists, white as well as black, wanted to stick on their music. Last, but not least, it had become the thing everybody claimed to have invented last week, all on their own.

As James Brown himself more than hinted at, funk did not come into being in the mid-1970s, but for the record-buying public at large—or, to be more accurate, for the white pop and rock mainstream audiences—this was when funk reached the surface, not only as music but as lifestyle, as fashion, and as a rather freaky, hippie-type approach to life in general. Paradoxically—or typically—it was exactly when funk came to the forefront of the white music industry that James Brown, according to sales figures and journalistic-historical accounts, started to lose his grip.[23] From the viewpoint of the general public, it might seem as if James Brown simply went "underground." According to White and Weinger's liner notes to the *Star Time* anthology (1991), however, it is rather that James Brown started following instead of leading the way:

> JB was caught between two musical trends. He was considered too raw for disco, and yet not heavy or freaky enough for the Parliament-Funkadelic crowd.
>
> Brown himself was for the first time showing signs of weariness and insecurity. He'd been breaking his back for 20 years, running the whole show. Most men attempting half as much would have dropped dead years past. He was the most successful African-American musician of the 20th Century, an internationally renowned superstar—but he hadn't yet been given establishment respect at home.

Brown witnessed acts that he'd inspired break through with more publicity, bigger advances and far greater opportunities than he'd ever enjoyed. His relationship with Polydor soured. Troubles with the IRS began.

His personal problems were reflected in his recordings; Brown started following trends instead of leading them.[24]

One of these trends was the wave of disco that swept over the international pop scene at the end of the seventies. The "pseudosophistication" and theatricality of the disco world was not compatible with the world of soul, funk, and r&b as James Brown knew it. After the commercial breakthrough of disco in 1977, however, when the soundtrack from the movie *Saturday Night Fever* had sold nineteen million copies, it may have seemed almost impossible to ignore the new beat.[25] Many of the songs from the years following "The Payback" are obviously influenced by disco. In "Get Up Offa That Thing" (1976) the depth and ambivalence of a funk groove is gone, even though the riff is arch-funky— it is light, it is danceable, all the beats are equally heavy, the subdivision of the beats is crystal clear, handclaps are dashing around at beats two and four. The only thing that reminds us of funk in the old sense is the middle section (at around 3:40 elapsed time), when the explicated quarter notes take a break and leave room for the bass to circle around the basic beat without articulating it.

The song "Body Heat" is another example of the move toward disco-funk, although it also has many intact funk gestures, among them a classic riff on guitar (see fig. 19). Also pointing toward funk are the snappy phrasing, the cross-rhythmic tendency in the last part of the riff, and the feeling of a double tempo in relation to bass and drums—or, in other words, a difference in density referent between the upper and lower layers of the groove. Moreover, the crisp, light "shangalang" in guitar, with its open voicing in the upper register, is one of several prototypical funk variants for guitar, and there is a pattern of four against three in the second part of the bass riff. All the same, it is the falling line of the bass, combined with a bass drum supplying four steady beats all the way through, that contributes to the song being stylistically beyond the funk idiom. The short, accurate marking of the quarter notes gives the groove a highly articulated pulse and leaves no room for ambivalence.

In the intro of "It's Too Funky in Here" (1979), it is even easier to recognize that funk's time has passed. The disco effect of the bass drum is

Figure 19. Guitar riff in "Body Heat."

beyond doubt. Furthermore, it is supported by various special effects from the disco era, like floating synthesizers and sensual, feminine vocal backing. The intro also includes an unaccentuated "shangalang" guitar in the background, playing all the sixteenths, without any signs of a counter-rhythmic pattern. When the main groove begins, it becomes slightly more funky, with a backdrop of complementary polyrhythmic figures (two rhythm guitars, keyboards, percussion, and so on) as well as a less evenhanded marking of the four main beats. However, even though the bass drum is no longer pumping out 120 beats per minute, the main pulse is considerably more defined—steady and striking, it is more of an ordering aspect than it was in songs made some years before.

If this is funk, as James Brown claims, not only have its spiritual dimensions disappeared, but its musical content has changed as well. Funk has become slick, polished dance music, glam-influenced images, a hedonistic, freaky lifestyle, and, in many cases, a rather macho attitude. In this new situation, James Brown is supplanted by competitors more in accordance with the spirit of the time. His attitude is suddenly wrong. His trademark does not fit in with the new regime: the old sound is too raw for the crossover mentality, too ascetic for the fusion era, too groovy for the disco people, and not "shabby" enough for the P-funk followers. And his attempts to catch up fail him. The new mentality of crossover required less an "anti-American sound," as was prescribed by the Black Arts Movement, than a sound without racial constraints. Music characterized by signs of blackness—by the features that had been identified as a specifically *black* aesthetic, such as a heterogeneous sound, an inclination toward treating every instrument as percussion, a primary focus on the fabric of rhythm—was probably too bound up with connotations of black America, and too far from the average Philly soul–inspired fad of dance music to go well with the new times.[26]

As a consequence, just a decade after James Brown cut "Say it Loud, I'm Black and I'm Proud," black artists were once again caught in a situation where they had to avoid being too black. George writes, "Millie Jackson and Cameo: too black. The phrase echoed with the sound of self-hate: Too black. A retreat from the beauty of blackness. Too black. The sound of the death of R&B."[27]

7

"Some Say It's Funk after Death"

> Funk upon a time, in the days of the Funkapuss, the
> concept of specially designed Afronauts, capable of
> funkatizing galaxies, was first laid on Man Child, but was
> later repossessed and placed among the secrets of the
> pyramids until a more positive attitude towards this most
> sacred phenomenon, Clone Funk, could be acquired.
> There in these terrestrial projects it would wait along with
> its co-inhabitants, the Kings and the Pharaohs, like
> sleeping beauties, for the kiss that will release them to
> multiply in the image of the Chosen One, Dr. Funkenstein.
> And funk is its own reward. May I frighten you?
> —George Clinton

P-Funk as Black Consolidation

By the mid-1970s, black music's emphasis on black experiences and black values was weakened. According to the critical voices, black music had turned beige. In addition, the wave of disco was about to make its mark on the music business. The new cultural situation encouraged a sound and a music free of associations to race and to the sociopolitical situatedness that were sticking to the conventional signs of musical blackness. Lastly, the focus on the big stars of the world of r&b, soul, and funk in the old musical and spiritual meaning of the word was gone.[1]

The most important response to this new cultural situation from the point of view of black America probably occurred in 1975, when George Clinton, Bootsy Collins, and their collaborators in Parliament released two albums: *Chocolate City* and *Mothership Connection*.[2] The albums were loaded with utopian imagery and surrealistic humor, but taken together they formed part of a deeply critical response to the racial aspects of the increasing inequality of power and resources among the different members of American society.[3] Parliament's musical and visual world typically combined central features of blackness with the futuristic worldview and psychedelic humor of much popular music of the 1970s. Their performances were realized in oversized settings (and with a considerable surplus of coolness) and as such captured the spirit of the day. At the same time, their music could easily be interpreted as a determined continuation of the Black Aesthetic doctrine. Instead of struggling with the world within the world, however, Clinton moved the struggle into a zone in which "fantasy is reality in the world today."[4]

The cover of the first Parliament album, *Chocolate City*, portrayed Washington, D.C.'s Lincoln Memorial, Washington Memorial, Capitol Building, and White House melting, presumably, "under the heat of black technofunk and the increasing 'chocolate' character of the nation's capital."[5] Parliament presented a rather psychedelic version of the mantra "Black and Proud," and they invited their listeners, especially the dwellers of "Chocolate cities" and, to a lesser extent, those in the "Vanilla suburbs," to enter the "Fourth World"—a world, according to West, of "black funk and star wars, black orality, bodily sensuality, technical virtuosity and electronic adroitness."[6] In this world, George Clinton resided as the otherworldly Dr. Funkenstein, leading an army of followers and believers in preaching funk as a blessing. Clinton explains, "Once we did Chocolate City—putting black people in situations they have never been in, and it worked—I knew I had to find another place for black people to be. And space was that place."[7]

The extraterrestrial world of Dr. Funkenstein was a utopian place where the power structures and suppressing mechanisms of the first, second, and third worlds did not come into play. Parliament staged this vision in spectacular live shows that brought a lot of attention to the band. When Dr. Funkenstein landed on stage in the Mothership Connection Spaceship, it was no doubt great entertainment. However, the show also displayed a striking social critique. The whole P-Funk cosmology may be regarded as a way of commenting on the marginalization of black culture and the sociopolitical setbacks of the 1970s. In such a political and cultural situation, it probably made sense to imagine any hope for a better future as situated beyond the earthly world, because it would only have caused hopelessness and disillusion to try to imagine it realized as a part of this life.

What might appear at first sight as a rather escapist, psychedelic project can therefore be interpreted as a political project in touch with the spirit of the black struggle of the 1960s. In line with this, West describes Parliament's music as a creative encounter between the "Afro-American spiritual-blues impulse" and highly sophisticated technological instruments, strategies, and effects, interpreting the P-Funk project as an attempt at black consolidation in the face of the increasing class division within black America:

> Ironically, the appeal of black technofunk was not a class-specific phenomenon. Technofunk invigorated the "new" politicized black middle class undergoing deep identity-crisis, the stable black working class fresh out of the blues-ridden ghettos, the poor black working class hungry for escapist modes of transcendence, and the hustling black underclass permeated by drug culture. Black technofunk articulated black middle-class anxieties toward yet fascination with U.S. "hi-tech" capitalist society, black working class frustration of marginal inclusion within and ineffective protest against this society, and black underclass self-destructive dispositions owing to outright exclusion from this society.[8]

At the core of the whole project was the funk gospel of Dr. Funkenstein, which, regardless of the psychedelic clouds surrounding Clinton's appearance, was a clear attempt to revive black music's strong ability to uplift. According to Clinton, the funk grooves were nothing less than a means of arriving at a spiritual focus while also providing bodily release to an afflicted audience.

After exploring the grooves of Parliament in more detail, I will introduce an issue more thoroughly discussed in the next chapter of this book, namely how the musical features of a funk groove may be connected to what I have labeled "the state of being in funk." Or in the words of Clinton: how and why can funk work to fulfill the prophecies of the chosen one, Dr. Funkenstein? Why is funk its own reward?

The Rhythm on One

With P-Funk the sound of funk has gone through a severe dislocation: the distance from top to bottom has become even larger than in the

Parliament. MICHAEL OCHS ARCHIVES.COM

George Clinton. MICHAEL OCHS ARCHIVES.COM

The Mothership Connection Spaceship landing on stage. MICHAEL OCHS ARCHIVES.COM

Promo material for *The Mothership Connection* (1975). FROM THE AUTHOR'S COLLECTION

Promo material for *The Clones of Dr. Funkenstein* (1976). FROM THE AUTHOR'S COLLECTION

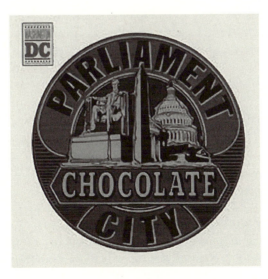

Album cover of Parliament's *Chocolate City* (1975)
© UNIVERSAL

grooves of James Brown. However, this distance has not dissolved the grooves themselves, which are now, if anything, easier to follow. This may be due to a reordering of the sonic material into single gestures: P-Funk seems to have taken the rhythmic layers of James Brown, chopped them up into pieces, mixed the pieces, and then replayed them under orders to obtain the absolute maximum jolt out of every sixteenth. Some are left to smear the syncopation in the bass line, while others are cropped both front and rear into the jumpy short strokes of a piano or guitar riff.

Has the short become even shorter than it was with James Brown, or does it only seem so because the long endures for so long?

In the P-Funk grooves, the One starts to swell. It is heavier and more unifying than the other heavy beats, to such an extent that it is about to become *the* heavy beat—that is, the only one that really matters. The tempo, as a result, has slowed. The Parliament grooves from this period (1974 through 1976) are as a rule somewhat slower than the grooves of Brown and his bands, ranging from 96 beats per minute ("Up for the Downstroke" and "P-Funk [Wants to get Funked Up]") to 108 beats per minute ("Give Up the Funk [Tear the Roof Off The Sucker]"). This leaves considerable room for the beats to swell out in all directions.

"Up for the Downstroke" (1974) is perfectly typical of this new trend. In the main groove of this song, the push forward almost disappears at certain points, as if the first heavy beat temporarily paralyzes the groove. It remains this way until the bass starts moving again, along with the next kick of the bass drum—that is, around beat three in a pulse of quarter notes. Even though the snare drum and handclaps strike beat two in the meantime, the traditional accentuation of beat two and four is so weak and cluster-like that it cannot be said to contend with the heavy downbeats of bass drum and bass guitar. Heard this way, the other half note, where bass moves down a third and starts playing its upward-moving line, becomes the true answer to the heavy One. Just like the stroke on the snare drum traditionally completes the one of the bass drum, the upward-moving bass line in this case becomes the limit of the first heavy downbeat.

The third half note is not answered in the same way on its own pulse level, because the fourth half note is left out, leaving the lower layers of the sound empty. The "pause" after the third heavy half note is spent on completing the faster layers of the song, which are thereby exposed in a novel way: they fill in the rest of their eighth-note and quarter-note patterns without being overshadowed by the heavy, slow beat.

Figure 20. Double set of pulses in "Up for the Downstroke" (groove 1).

The effect is that the song, in addition to its basic pulse on quarters, has a basic pulse on half notes too. The slow pulse is further stressed by a crash cymbal, which marks the first and third half notes (see fig. 20) . Groove 1 in "Up for the Downstroke" may also be said to have two alternative density referents. The hi-hat represents a subdivision of eighth notes, while the sixteenths before the second and fourth half notes of the bass suggest another.

In the B-section (groove 2), the basic pulse is unambiguous, and the density referent is also more clearly located on the level of sixteenths. Both are mainly due to the three fast, syncopated sixteenths in the bass drum, played immediately before the one and three of the slow pulse on half notes (see fig. 21). This gesture accentuates the One by spreading it out as a series of offbeats located immediately before the unplayed but, all the same, heavy working first beat. Simultaneously, this gesture destabilizes the One, establishing a counter-rhythmic (but not cross-rhythmic) offbeat layer of short sixteenths. The latter runs almost throughout the pattern, because the sixteenths trigger a pulse, or rather an expectation of a pulse, on the offbeats (of the eighths), working far beyond the sounding presence of the offbeats actually performed.

This pulse of fast offbeats is at work, for example, when the same bass drum plays its second and fourth stroke unambiguously *on* the beat, underlined by clear-cut pick-ups on the preceding sixteenth. These indications of the basic pulse are actually made more interesting

Figure 21. The bass drum figure in groove 2 of "Up for the Downstroke."

due to how the pulse of the syncopated sixteenths has spread across the bar as a kind of counter-rhythmic echo. For the sake of the organization here, however, one might point out that the dependence is no less when viewed the other way around: the syncopated sixteenths are equally parasitic to the main beat. The intended tickling effect is very dependent upon the presence of a virtual or actual main beat.

Groove 2 in "Up for the Downstroke" is not as heavy as groove 1 and appears tighter, probably because it follows groove 1. The tightening of the territory around the One, and the shift in timing and feeling from extremely late and lazy to rather early, short, and tight is, however, perhaps necessary to revive the effect of groove 1, insofar as groove 1 represents the normal state of affairs. After a while, the heavier groove 1 is experienced as more sluggish than remarkable. In any case, groove 2 makes the return to groove 1 and its rather loose feeling more effective. The drop into the open spaces between the beats becomes deeper and longer, just as it also becomes more focused and relaxed.

The overall groove of "P-Funk (Wants to Get Funked Up)" (1975) is in many ways tailored to the same pattern as groove 1 of "Up for the Downstroke." However, it is more successful: the feelings of tight and accurate on the one hand and loose and lazy on the other are more integrated into one and the same groove. The song moves between "floating" parts and sticky, groovy ones, the latter characterized by a wah-wah bass guitar sound that is both snappy and unmistakably grounded. The beats contain so much mass that they almost overwhelm themselves; each note moves gradually beyond its own limits, spreading slowly into the open spaces.

The effect is most pronounced when the groove returns after one of the sections where the song loses its weight farther down: it is almost lifted up from the ground, floating freely underneath George Clinton's musings on life as an extraterrestrial brother and on the essence of funk in general. The effect is also striking after the passage defined by the ethereal, jazzy trumpet part. At the end of this improvisation, when the song has been without anchor for several minutes and is about to disintegrate, a fully weighted One suddenly catches hold of the listener, right after Clinton's somewhat abrupt "Well alright!" The groove is back, moving slowly forward on a foundation of vague but heavy gestures that stick to one's body. The bass playing is by now far behind and almost stumbling over itself, creating the impression of having lost any constancy and cohesion: its syncopated notes slide into the open spaces, filling up the holes in the fabric of rhythm with a sticky sound.

The significance of the One and the shaping of the dynamic aspects of this gesture were, according to James Brown, things that Bootsy Collins learned from his time with the JBs: "I think Bootsy learned a lot from me. When I met him he was playing a lot of bass—the ifs, the ands, and the buts. I got him to see the importance of the *one* in funk—the downbeat at the beginning of every bar. I got him to key in on *the dynamic parts of the one* instead of playing all around it. Then he could do all his other stuff in the right places—*after* the one."[9] After playing with James Brown, Bootsy Collins moved on to the P-Funk camp, shaping many of their big hits. In a song like "Give Up the Funk (Tear the Roof off the Sucker)" (1975), Bootsy is still sneaking around on the sixteenths, curling the syncopated notes up to the beats or the beats up to his syncopation, all without losing hold of the crucial power surrounding the One.

Even more clearly than the grooves of James Brown, the melody-riff "We want the funk" from this song demonstrates how Brown's doctrine may sound in practice, and how the One is created by getting the band to "key in on the dynamic parts of the one instead of playing all around it." The riff runs through most of the song, starting with a heavy One, which is in fact set on the preceding four, and lasting all the way to the second beat of a basic pulse of half notes. The phrase's ending is a typical downbeat in anticipation, both a little ahead of, as well as on, the third quarter note (or, alternatively, the second half note) (see fig. 22).

The gesture may be characterized as polyphonic, since bass and vocal split up on beats two and three (of the basic pulse on quarters) in an intricate but also very dynamic division of labor: the syncopated sixteenth after beat two is almost to be understood as the attack of the following note on two-and. However, even though the bass lands on this two-and for a moment, the gesture as such is not allowed to come to a stop, because the two-and in the vocal line is a pick-up to the next

Figure 22. The One (gesture a) in "Give Up the Funk."

anticipated downbeat. This effect is again created by a certain cooperation between vocals and bass: it begins with the vocals syncopating beat three and ends with a soft three played on the bass. The latter works like an almost unnoticed extension of the vocals' onset; it becomes the sustain following the vocals' attack.

A similar interplay of bass and vocals is found in the onset of the entire gesture: the vocals start almost straight on beat four of bar two, while the bass sidles up to the beat on the following sixteenth, extending the attack of the gesture by ending it with a soft beginning of its own.

Extended Ambiguity—"The Ifs, the Ands, and the Buts . . ."

In a song like "Give Up the Funk" it becomes almost too clear that the One is not a single point but a gesture stretching out in time. However, "Give Up the Funk" is also an excellent example of how "all the other stuff"—the small syncopated notes, "the ifs, the ands, and the buts"—have to be "in the right places after the one."

The main groove of this song is organized into a pattern of four bars, or two strongly related basic units.[10] If one compares the shaping of the riff of the first part of the first basic unit (bar 1)—a gesture that might be called "the extended One"—with its second part (bar 2), there are many similarities but also some important differences. First, the cross-rhythmic tendency implicit in the vocals of bar 1 (from beat two onward) comes to the surface due to an adjustment in the patterns of bass and guitar: in bar 2, they play in unison with the vocals. Second, considerable weight is taken off the One and to some extent moved to beat two, which is emphasized with a pick-up on the previous eighth note. Furthermore, the early three is a more clearly articulated and more straightforwardly syncopated sixteenth note; it is not pulled toward the third beat in the same way as the anticipation/extension of beat three in bar 1 (see fig. 23).

Seen in isolation, the vocals could be said to represent a cross-rhythmic tendency in bar 1, but one that is not made explicit until bar 2. The vocal contribution to gesture *a* is overruled by the creation of the One: the complementary part played by bass and guitar neutralizes any cross-rhythmic effect. In bar 2, however, this complementary part disappears, allowing the cross-rhythmic pattern to get to work. This time it has a greater effect also because the one of bar 2 is almost without weight—or, put another way, because the real One is a thing of the past. The first indication of a cross-rhythmic pulse, beat two, now becomes clearer, and the syncopated sixteenth ahead of beat three is directed into the counter-rhythmic pattern at the expense of the succeeding beat three.

In addition to gesture *a* and *b*, there is a third variant, gesture *c*, that is played in the second part of the second basic unit as a response to gesture *a*2.[11]

Nor does the one have any weight in gesture *c*, and even though the cross-rhythmic tendency is much weaker than in gesture *b*, it is perhaps a little more present. In many ways, gesture *c* is a hybrid of gestures *a* and *b*, and the special feature of gesture *c* is probably how it installs sixteenths as a subdivision instead of eighths. Gesture *c* promotes the presence of a faster set of pulses than the one represented by a basic pulse on half notes with the main subdivision on eighths. This faster set of pulses is, however, to some extent already suggested by gesture *b* through the cross-rhythmic figure. As a counter-rhythm it might, at least virtually, also play up the rhythm it is counter to, namely a basic pulse on quarters (see fig. 24).

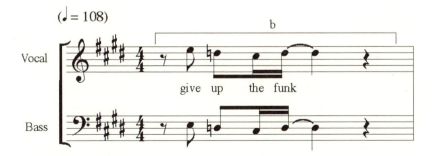

Figure 23. Cross-rhythmic gesture (gesture *b*) in "Give Up the Funk."

Figure 24. Second basic unit (gestures *a2* and *c*) of "Give Up the Funk."

The role of the quarters as an alternative basic pulse is also strengthened as beat two becomes more equal to beat one. In other words, while gesture *b* gives the groove a small push in the direction of a faster basic pulse, this is followed up by gesture *c* in the form of a corresponding faster subdivision. However, when this faster set of pulses is at its strongest, or, rather, its least weak—that is, toward the end of gesture *c*—the One occurs, brushing it all aside, almost as if to make sure that nothing is able to settle.

Gesture *c* is not allowed to work for more than four turns of the riff, after which the accompaniment continues without vocals. In this part of the song the cross-rhythmic pattern is more obvious, with gesture *c* sounding almost like gesture *b*.

Summing up, the riff of "Give Up the Funk" is constructed as a dialogue among a few gestures in which each addresses important functions in the groove. Gesture *a* is a heavy extended One with a (too) early attack, an inarticulate weight connected to the first beat of the bar, and a snappy ending on the second beat of the slow basic pulse of the rhythm, which is in this case measured in half notes. Gesture *b* is not particularly heavy and explicates the cross-rhythmic tendency of the riff. The cross-rhythmic counter-rhythm implies an internal beat of quarter notes—that is, twice as fast as the main basic pulse of the rhythm. The third variant, gesture *c*, supports this faster basic pulse by also suggesting a faster subdivision on sixteenths. However, all of these gestures contribute to the certain uncertainty regarding the density referent by way of the typical funky phrasing. All of the gestures also carry the counter-rhythmic pattern in one way or another, but gesture *b* is the only place where it is allowed to reach the surface, and even then not for long. The counter-rhythm is interrupted almost before it starts working when the third stroke more or less implodes in the field of gravity surrounding the next One.

In spite of this division of labor, the gestures are closely related; in many ways, they are three realizations of the same thing. It is only with attention to very small adjustments that they can be tied to some function in the groove. Actually, or perhaps virtually, all of the gestures are involved in each other's main tasks: even though a counter-rhythm is clear only in gesture *b*, it is also there, if only in a feeble form, in gestures *a* and *c*. The same thing can be said about the alternative, faster set of pulses: the implicit doubt concerning density referent and basic pulse runs throughout the riff. Only the heavy One of gesture *a* is not gathering support from the other gestures.

So, even though there is a certain division of labor among the gestures of "Give Up the Funk," they continuously support and prepare for each other's work. It is almost as if the different main figures of the three gestures are given some nourishment also in those parts of the groove where they are overruled by other concerns: all the necessary underlying structures of reference are nursed along throughout, and on a virtual level they are probably never completely absent. The effect of this is that one particular figure or another may be actualized with a minimum of effort. It takes only a very small accent, or a slightly displaced emphasis, to bring forth any given aspect of this gestural constellation.

The Funk Riff

In many cases, a P-Funk tune is equal to a good riff, and in those parts of "Give Up the Funk" where the main groove is running, it is as if all of the rhythmic parts are concerned with realizing the riff, which becomes, in one sense, the whole song. Bass, guitar, and vocals perform the riff itself, while drums contribute to the riff while insuring that the underlying basic pulse is running. However, in the recorded version of the song, every now and again the distinct riff has to give way for the prophetic-visionary message of George Clinton. And this is quite often the case with P-Funk. In "Chocolate City" (1975), the music acts almost as a backdrop for George Clinton's musings on a possible black takeover of the White House. The riff is not really the main focus of attention, but it is present enough to give the whole event an underlying black funk feel.

In album versions of P-Funk songs, the groove is seldom left unchanged for a long time. It is therefore easier to get in touch with the energy of the P-Funk grooves on a live recording. *P-Funk All-Stars Live* (at

Figure 25. The piano riff in "Chocolate City" (live version).

the Beverly Theater in Hollywood; 1990) successfully documents the grandiosity of a P-Funk event. As a concert recording it has an uncommon mixture of live energy and good playing that transcends the event's immediacy, and it does not fall apart when listened to out of context.[12]

The two first tracks work as a medley of their many distinguished riffs, including the riff from "Chocolate City," played on the piano by Bernie Worrell with an unmistakably funky timing. The phrasing of the riff stumbles along in short steps so that not even the steady handclaps of the audience on beats two and four are able to anchor it to a stable pulse.

Looking closer at the riff, its syncopated short notes form a pattern of four against three in the first and third bars, but the strokes are so closely cropped and so "misplaced" that the underlying figure is almost overwhelmed by the manner of performance (see fig. 25). The riff never falls completely into place, due both to the extraordinary phrasing and to the fact that there is no real One. The weird syncopation acts almost as a teaser for the vertical swinging movement that is to come.

The audience, however, knows what is about to begin: the riff of "P-Funk (Wants to Get Funked Up)." It also comes on the piano, with a similarly extreme manner of phrasing, as if all of its syncopated sixteenth notes have become thirty-seconds. In the "P-Funk" riff, there is a pattern of four against three from beat two onward. It is adjusted to accord with the main pulse on the fourth beat but seems to recommence in the second bar. However, on the second stroke of bar 2, the figure is twisted into the same offbeat phrasing as we saw in the bridge of "Sex Machine." The double stroke in sixteenths on "one-and" is not the second stroke of a 4:3 pattern but rather an upbeat to the first in a series of offbeats (see fig. 26).

The series of offbeats in bar 2 of this riff pulls in the direction of a faster subdivision for the groove, but this is not otherwise obviously the case. The syncopated sixteenths seem too suspended—they are too late, too "inaccurately" played—to really introduce an underlying pulse *scheme* of sixteenths. However, this is exactly what makes it possible for them to be part of several figures. The early indication of three-and in bar 1 is a typical downbeat in anticipation. It is almost exactly similar to the closing of the "Get up!" gesture in "Sex Machine" and might easily be reinterpreted as the preceding sixteenth. And this is actually what happens in bar 2, when the figure, this time starting at the first beat, is twisted from a 4:3 pattern into offbeat strokes on an early two-and.[13]

In other words, in this song the two gestures are also pretty close to being identical. While the ambiguity of "Give Up the Funk" is shaped through various combinations of parts pointing in different directions, the ambiguity of "P-Funk (Wants to Get Funked Up)" lies in small-scale adjustments to the same homophonic gesture, which can be written equally well as one or the other. If the early three-and of bar 1 is transcribed as a syncopated sixteenth, it looks exactly the same as the offbeat pattern of bar 2 (see fig. 27).

In fact, the second sixteenth of beat two of gesture *b* is placed only a little earlier than the corresponding stroke of gesture *a*, introducing the possibility that it is part of a 4:3 pattern played heavily on top, as in the "Chocolate City" riff mentioned above. The fact that gesture *b* ends up as a series of offbeats is thus not clear until the figure is concluded through the last offbeat stroke ("up"). At that point there is, at least for the moment, no more doubt about it.

This does not last for long. With the next gesture *a*, the ambivalence returns, this time inverted. The series of offbeats is still there, offering a virtual alternative. Even gesture *a* is, in actuality, almost midway between a 4:3 pattern and an emerging series of offbeats. It is perhaps

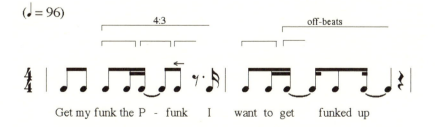

Get my funk the P - funk   I   want to get   funked up

Figure 26. The first phrase of the melody-riff of "P-Funk" (live version).

($\downarrow = 96$)

Figure 27. The first phrase of the melody-riff of "P-Funk" in alternative notation.

only the emphasis on "P" in the syncopation of beat three that saves the gesture from ending up as a series of offbeats. The third beat of the 4:3 pattern ("funk") is obscure; it can be pinned down as both the one sixteenth and the other.

After some time the audience chants along the melody-riff from "P-Funk," to some extent leveling it out. Three-and in the first bar ends up straight on the eighth, and the two last offbeat strokes in the second bar end up straight on their following eighths rather than slightly ahead of them. When the piano takes a break, letting the audience continue on their own, the rhythm moves in the direction of a football chant, but not completely. The early three of the first bar, and the early two of the second, are actually snappy enough to retain a funk feel, although the gesture becomes considerably more distinct and less ambivalent. The offbeat figure is lost, while the 4:3 figure, with its cross-rhythmic effect, remains. This is also the case, at least to some extent, with the ambivalence surrounding the density referent, since the two syncopated notes keep their snappy phrasing, although it is far less extreme than when the riff was played by Worrell.

The close of this "warming-up" leads to the introduction of the band (track 2). The tempo increases and the new piano riff is tighter than the preceding ones. At last it turns out to be fragments of the riff from "Do That Stuff." After eight repetitions it attains the right melody and is played in unison by the bass and a fuzz guitar (see fig. 28). Compared to the complete versions of the riff (a/c), the piano version (b) is stripped down. Its melodic aspects are absent: the contour is leveled out, and the rhythmic strokes that allowed for a smooth melody and the passing tones in sixteenths have also been removed. The piano version appears to be almost a rhythmic skeleton of the riff.

Interestingly enough, this riff is also composed of three closely related gestures. The riff opens with a typical One gesture, starting with a marked early attack, immediately followed by a swelling around and after the metrical one. The gesture is finished off by way of a short and accurate whiplike stroke on beat two, which nevertheless occurs a little bit late in regard to a metrically correct position. The gesture is, in other words, allowed to swell at either end.

Beat two of this first gesture works as a link to the second main ingredient in the riff. Schematically, this is a 4:3 pattern that starts on the third beat and ends on a syncopated fourth beat. Because beat three is a typical downbeat in anticipation, and beat two is a little bit late, the counter-rhythmic pulse is probably already running by the time it reaches beat three. The space between these two beats is closer to the distance between beat three and the syncopated fourth beat than in the impression given in the transcription above. Viewed this way, it might

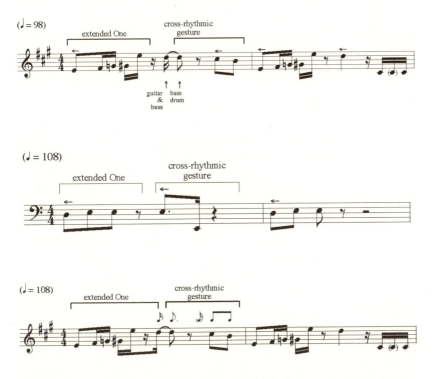

Figure 28. Counter-rhythmic riff of "Do That Stuff": (a) album version (top), (b) stripped-down live version (piano) (middle), (c) complete live version (bass and fuzz-guitar) (bottom).

Figure 29. Stripped-down riff of "Do That Stuff" with thirty-second notes as the density referent.

be more accurate to represent the counter-rhythmic pulse with a period of 7/32 (see fig. 29) and not 3/16 as in fig. 28b.

In the album version of the riff, it is even more obvious that the counter-rhythmic pulse starts on the second beat, not the third. First, there is no cross-rhythmic pattern starting on the third beat. Second, the latter is so accurately syncopated in guitar and bass that the beginning of the 4:3 pattern, almost after the fact, is placed on beat two (it is not very obvious when it happens). In this version, the cross-rhythmic pattern is also interrupted earlier: the two strokes on four- and rather unequivocally relate to the main basic pulse and its duple subdivision.

Even in this riff, the gestures are closely related. This is perhaps most obvious in the stripped-down live version, where the rhythmic ambiguity is taken to the extreme and where the counter-rhythmic pulse seems to be running already at beat two. However, by this time, it seems as though the pulse started even earlier—more precisely, in the obscure circumstances preceding beat two. If one looks closer at details in the One gesture, it becomes clear that it might also be understood as supporting the counter-rhythmic pulse in gesture *b*. The one is always played too early, and the two is always too late, and this might—with some room for adjustments of the period— allow for a coupling with the counter-rhythmic pulse (see fig. 30). Even though the One as a gesture is primarily directed toward the dynamic aspects of the one, the gesture also seems to prepare and prolong the counter-rhythmic pulse.

Again, this riff is an example of how a thoroughgoing and extended ambiguity is realized by means of phrasing and minimal variations in timing. As discussed above, this ambiguity might also be achieved in other ways, but it seems to always be there, either as the polyphonically realized ambiguity of the pick-up gesture—as in the album version, where there is a combination of bass/guitar on an early three and bass drum straight on the beat—or as the homophonic downbeats in antici-pation found in the stripped-down version. Or, in the accomplished live version, as both of these.

In the stripped-down version of "Do That Stuff," there is a point at which the continuity of the groove seems to be threatened in a very special manner quite typical for the style. This happens every time the groove approaches a (new) One. It is most striking in bar 2 but is usually also present in bar 1. It is as if the groove stretches itself to the limit, or almost beyond it, by creating the feeling of the One always being late despite the fact that it is actually early. If we use the alter-native counter-rhythmic pulse scheme as its basis, however, this event becomes less paradoxical. With the counter-rhythmic pulse as a starting point, one might assume that an expectation of a new indica-tion of the pulse is triggered at least two thirty-seconds before the syncopated One actually arrives (see fig. 31). The counter-rhythmic pulse is probably pulling the expected position of the syncopated note away from the beat. When the syncopation actually occurs not only a little bit late but two thirty-seconds after the expected posi-tion, one has a strong feeling of the One being delayed, as when a heavy beat is "syncopated" by being played on the following six-teenth note.

In the stretch of time when something is expected—the whole musi-cal system seems to seek the emerging resistance of firm ground—noth-ing happens. The cross-rhythmic pulse, which by this time has endured for so long that it appears about to override the main pulse, has most likely gone too far. The continuity breaks down: one is not able to con-nect the last indication of the pulse with the next one. With reference to this alternative counter-rhythmic framework, there is a moment of total indetermination, almost a freefall. One has leapt outward but does not

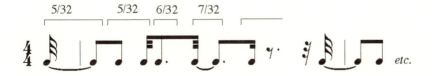

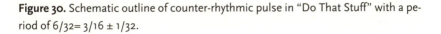

Figure 30. Schematic outline of counter-rhythmic pulse in "Do That Stuff" with a pe-riod of 6/32= 3/16 ± 1/32.

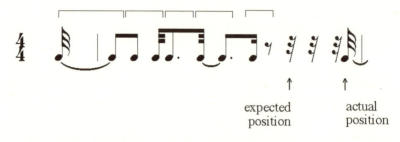

Figure 31. Expected and actual One in "Do That Stuff," with the counter-rhythmic pulse indicated by brackets (period = 3/16 ± 1/32).

land until the framework returns to the main basic pulse of the rhythm, until the primary One finally arrives, bigger, more surprising, more confident.

Perhaps this is a moment of transition, when nothing rules—a moment of virtual chaos. The little delay, with the little threat of discontinuity, is enough to suspend the counter-rhythmic pulse for a moment. It makes space for the gesture that needs space (but preferably also as little attention as possible in advance), the gesture that always shows up but that probably had been somewhat eclipsed for a moment: one gets up for the downstroke, for the rhythm of the One.

Grounded Ambiguity—On the Stable Unstable

In P-Funk's music, the classic funk riff becomes a small groove in itself. As a consequence, it no longer seems fruitful to treat the One in isolation. The One becomes more and more a part of the riff, together with almost everything that is needed to make up a funk groove. The entire fabric of rhythm has melted down to one single, polynomial gesture. Everything is directed toward the realization of one motion; the groove *is* almost equal to the riff. The groove is still marked by a continuous tension between different figures—between rhythm and counter-rhythm, between a very slow and a not so slow basic pulse, between a "natural" subdivision and a phrasing that appears far too short. These various tensions, however, seem to have moved into every single gesture; each contains an aspect of every task carried out by the different rhythmic layers in the grooves of James Brown. Moreover, the gestures seem reminiscent of each other, both in the active and in the passive sense of the word. Instead of a multilayered structure, where one layer, voice, or part actualizes one aspect of the groove all the way through in tandem with others, every link of the P-Funk riff is directly or indirectly involved in all of its aspects—perhaps with one exception: the One, which, due to natural causes by virtue of its weight, is neither able nor allowed to run throughout. The different subsections of the riff have their main function, but they are also supporting and preparing each other's performance almost continuously. By means of tiny little adjustments in phrasing or timing, one gesture is first tilted to the one, then to the other. This holds true whether the ambiguity is due to one stroke being phrased as both the one and the other (a typical downbeat in anticipation) or whether it is due to a combination of two strokes, namely a downbeat *and* an anticipation. The latter is a typical Bootsy Collins maneuver that is found in the many pick-up gestures in James Brown's "Sex Machine" and in the polyphonically realized riff of Parliament's "Give Up the Funk."

When the funk riff is almost the whole groove, as in the P-Funk grooves, it is even more striking how the fundamental ambiguity of these gestures is cultivated. However, close readings of the grooves of James Brown pointed in this direction as well; this ambiguity was also present in his repertoire in the form of an ambivalence, though one realized somewhat differently. In contrast to the P-Funk tunes, a tune like "The Payback" has a more or less multilinear structure, in the sense that every layer in the fabric of rhythm seems to play a certain figure. Other tunes, like "Cold Sweat," rely upon a patchwork fabric of rhythm. The central figures of this song are to be identified across a number of parts and layers. One figure no longer has its own corresponding gesture. In a song like "Sex Machine," however, the groove is more open and easier to grasp. The main gestures, for example the guitar riff, are clearly outlined. Moreover, several of the gestures embody the tensions also found in the P-Funk riffs. One and the same gesture relates to several figures at once, containing both rhythmic and counter-rhythmic aspects and playing up both primary and secondary pulse schemes at the same time.

In other words, even in the funk grooves of James Brown the relation between rhythm and counter-rhythm is not primarily interesting as a relation between a clearly articulated rhythm and an equally clear cross-rhythmic counter-rhythm. The point is rather to be found in a certain uncertainty regarding metrical positions. Only in this way is it possible to explain why the counter-rhythmic gestures of "Sex Machine"— where the ambivalence is to be found within one single gesture, and where the counter-rhythmic strokes both are and are not a competing layer of pulses—are so extraordinarily interesting.

This may also explain why the borderland of duple and triple subdivision is so crucial, actualized by the more or less swung sixteenths that are almost always present in a funk groove. The point seems to be to "deform" the figures so that they can be both rhythm and counter-rhythm at the same time. It also becomes clear that the tendencies toward an "unnaturally" fast density referent have to be about something more than schematically moving the density referent one step upward. The effect of the "early-short" way of phrasing arises especially from the fact that it is *too* short. Rather than presenting new answers to the central questions regarding basic pulse, subdivision, and density referent, the main point of the secondary set of pulses is to obscure the dominant replies.

In other words, despite significant differences—in sound, textures, and how the fabric of the rhythm is designed—regarding how the grooves are realized, there are striking points of resemblance between the prototypical funk grooves of James Brown and the more overmature riff-based P-Funk grooves. What might be described as "tendencies" in the funk grooves of James Brown have become central themes of the P-Funk riffs; in the latter, for example, it seems no longer relevant to speak of ambivalence. The ambivalence has become almost internalized: the doubt has moved in with the gesture, which has become a stable instability. The gestures have almost become independent, in the sense that the underlying virtual structures of reference are, literally speaking, no longer so close.

On the other hand, the riffs may be exactly like this because they are located safely more or less in the middle of two competing figures of reference—that is, because the gestures on the level of figures are both the one and the other. Perhaps the gestures themselves produce a basis of reference essential for their shaping, playing up more than one framework so that the sounding events can be kept firmly in a double grasp. Perhaps the gestures take form exactly in this span from one figure to the other; perhaps they are completely dependent on both sides to stay in place in time.

Following from this, the dialogical timing described earlier as the "conversational mode" is in the case of P-Funk more than a dialogue involving sounding gestures or a sounding gesture and an underlying structure of reference. It seems that the P-Funk riffs can only take shape through a two-way virtual conversation, one that is never heard as such. The double dialogue with underlying virtual figures works on the level of gestures—on the level of actual sound—almost like the space of rhythmic tolerance mentioned earlier. It confines the space that the gesture may use without losing power or precision, without ceding the space that the gesture has to stay within to remain itself. However, taking into consideration a virtual level as well, the structures of reference might be exactly the other rhythm that stabilizes the first one: they are "something to respond to."[14] As such, they are probably required to orient the phrasing in one way or another, making it possible to move a gesture closer to one figure at the expense of the other. The remarkably stable but rather extreme phrasing of the P-Funk riffs—they are always deformed in the same way—is made more comprehensible by means of such a notion of an underlying double-sided dialogical process. In short, the stabilization of such an extreme realization of a figure is probably only possible by way of a relation to another figure.

As discussed earlier, many of the central gestures of funk are distinguished by this particular ambiguity: they may trigger and then maintain several virtual structures at once. At the same time, they have the ability to destabilize those same structures. The aim of this destabilization is, however, perhaps not primarily to create uncertainty as to which virtual structures are in charge: there is no doubt, for example, that funk is in 4/4. (It might, however, be somewhat more difficult to establish exactly when the four beats take place.) Nor does this destabilization sincerely threaten the figures at play: it is not very difficult to identify parts of the riff as forming a 4:3 pattern or a series of offbeats. The point is rather that the destabilization veils the figures so that they never become truly evident or fully actualized.

In line with this, one might say that rather than making the stable unstable, the point is to place the stable under a constant pressure so as to make it a stable unstable. The aim of destabilization is not to loosen the groove's grip but to make it even more powerful by bringing the tensions of the groove to the limit, but not beyond.

One Nation under a Groove!—The Gospel of Dr. Funkenstein

Though it is easy to recognize when funk becomes funk historically, it is also true that just about when this happened, music was already on to something else. This is, as discussed in the previous chapter, the case with the post-"Payback" funk tunes of James Brown from the mid-1970s.

Their attempt to hold on to a certain historical moment makes them always-already passé, as if there is a strain of something unmistakably old-fashioned sticking to these tunes—not because they are reusing older material but rather because they are marked by a certain drive to keep up with the times.

Nor does the funk of the P-Funk congregation often coincide with a historical notion of pure funk. Even though P-Funk is no doubt funk, there are some aspects of their music that from the very beginning pointed far beyond the style. Parliament strongly echoes 1970s rock and psychedelia, and the group also favored the large performance formats quite typical for the end of that decade: they joined the group of bands that changed the concert into music theater, that broke out of the three-minute radio-formatted hit song concept in order to make more anarchistic, free-floating statements. It is also striking with regard to their album formats how much P-Funk belongs to another time. While James Brown's recordings often give the impression of a documentary of the golden moments of a jam session, Parliament's songs are clearly made for the recorded medium.

One aspect of P-Funk's musical product, however, that clearly differs from a lot of other psychedelic music of that time is its social commitment. While many white hippie-influenced bands made a kind of introverted psychedelia, Parliament was eager to get their message out. In several songs George Clinton explicitly deals with the changing times, more precisely with black powerlessness in a white world, worshipping the hope for change through the creation of a black utopia: the extraterrestrial world where black is the primary position, the positive, the first, the normal—in short, where black has conquered the White House. This will to communicate in a nonmusical sense also influences the music. For long periods the words dominate, while the music primarily provides a basis for the prophecies of Dr. Funkenstein.

With regard to musical form, this leads P-Funk out of funk. The music of Parliament does not obey the inner logic of dance music, as do the grooves of James Brown, which go on and on and are made for dancing. At least this is so on P-Funk albums, where several songs, although still far from the traditional binary verse-chorus arrangement, have different sections, a format commonly used in the new wave of black crossover music. In other words, a P-Funk tune is in the album version often closer to a song in the traditional sense, and thereby also closer to the format dominating the white world of popular music at that time.

At the level of groove, however, P-Funk clearly was a forceful response to the threat to musical blackness represented by both crossover funk and disco. The music was, as West has pointed out, an instance of the Africanization of African American popular music (in the sense that it was linked more closely with a notion of black identity) at a time when musical blackness and black values in general were devalued. P-Funk is music that stresses the groove and focuses on the riff as a primary musical entity in a particular way that constitutes blackness. Its rhythmic design cultivates a micro-rhythmic level and is in this respect almost to be regarded as an anti-crossover demonstration: the One rules; there is no sign of the equally weighed 4/4 rhythm of disco (at least not until 1977, when the songs "Bop Gun" and "Flash Light" show some signs of influence from the new fad); there is a total absence of a straight layer of even sixteenths, and the grooves are heavy, almost "anti-light."

Last but not least, the P-Funk grooves seem to be designed to seduce the listener or dancer to stay in the present. An important aspect of this is how the riff creates a circular feel. As will be discussed in the next chapter, however, the heavy One and the sophistication and ambivalence at the micro-rhythmic level also contribute heavily to keeping the listener and/or dancer busy with the groove, transforming the experience of a funk groove into a whole state of being.

Especially live, George Clinton and his P-Funk crowd cultivated this potentially meditative character of the groove to the extreme, celebrating the idea of a transcendent musical experience and using the funk groove as a means of achieving it. From the point of view of black America, therefore, P-Funk was probably the most potent response to the situation facing the black music business after its crossover to white markets. It was a pronounced response to the contemporary challenges for black America, and a forceful reply to the changes that put an end to funk in the old musical and spiritual meaning of the word: after all, there was funk after death. Funk was still a blessing simply because the uplifted character of the funk experience gave strength. On one level, thus, the message from Dr. Funkenstein was no more, or no less, than a unison cry for more funk—not for fake funk, not for "the placebo syndrome" (according to Clinton, dance music had to be rescued from the blahs), but for real funk, for the only funk able to provide existential pleasure, happiness, and hope. Or, as is claimed in an ad campaign for Parliament from the mid-1970s: "'Mothership Connection' is more than an album. It's a solution."[15] One should simply join the mothership brothership, tear the roof off the sucker, and cry out for another "chance to dance our way out of our constrictions":[16] one nation under a groove!

Analytical Afterthoughts

Perhaps a heavy funk groove ought to be seen as a struggle between two forces. One pulls down, while the other pushes forward. As the groove moves further from the One, it regains its push forward; its gestures are loosed from the grip of the One and given new momentum, only to be caught in the force field of the next One. The forward motion leads straight on to the next beginning, to the next black hole, absorbing the groove with a force that gathers strength exponential to the diminishing distance to the center of gravity. When the P-Funk grooves are at their best and deepest, they get the most out of this tension: the groove has weight, though it is always in motion. The musical gestures stretch the pulse and inner relationships of the groove to a maximum without cracking. The over-mature funk groove balances on the edge of its own dissolution.

This balance of forces is thus probably of utmost importance. In a P-Funk groove like "Up for the Downstroke," the weight down-low overwhelms the push forward: in spite of the title, one never gets sufficiently up from the extended downstroke. However, there is also a danger in moving forward too much. The necessary resistance can be completely lacking, so that layers slide into each other without friction: the weight is replaced by a sauntering lightness. This actually becomes more and more audible toward the end of the 1970s, in the music of both James Brown and P-Funk, when they become influenced by disco and the light funk of fusion.[17]

In light of history, it might seem as if funk's dueling forces went in different directions at the end of this golden decade of funk. Both the One, with its distinctive combination of heaviness and snappy attack, and a counter-rhythmic gesture of sixteenths based on the figure of four against three were characteristic of 1970s funk—in addition to shimmering flared pants, bare bellies, and huge golden jewelry. At some point, however, it seems as if the right *combination* of heaviness and forward push becomes a feature in short supply. The light version of the funk riff lived on in discofunk, and, after a while, in many other contexts as well. For some years it was almost a means of signifying "funk" in other musical contexts, even wandering all the way to the techno of the 1990s, where the same counter-rhythmic figure every now and again pops up, if in a more stiffly phrased, "schematic-synthetic" design.

As for the One, it becomes a distinguished, "funky" trait of many styles other than funk, from the late 1970s heavy funk of Mother's Finest through the music of Prince in the 1980s to the Red Hot Chili Peppers's "Funky Monks" (1991) or Me'Shells's "Shoot'n Up and Gettin' High" (1993). Finally, in rap music, it almost has arrived back home. In Public Enemy songs like "911 Is a Joke" (1990) and "Gotta Do What I Gotta Do" (1992), the One is irresistibly heavy and nevertheless fixed at the same time, probably because music technology has made it possible to stretch the heavy beat in a way that was unthinkable at the time of the classic funk grooves of James Brown. Today, the One can start extremely early without using a traditional syncopated note as an early kick-off. The One is continuously deep and heavy all the way, from its sharp attack far beyond any metrical limits; the One introduces, almost demonstratively, its own pulse. The whole idea of a syncopation, of anything deviating from the One, is all but abandoned.

However, neither the One nor the counter-rhythmic figure by itself is funk. A groove needs exactly the right combination of heaviness and forwardness, of the down-low and the up-tight, to move the body in a manner typical of funk. Both are necessary: the One—starting with the early attack and swelling out in suspension before being ended, or closed off, very sharply—as well as some syncopated small notes to push one's body forward, hitting just enough across the expected, keeping the body in (dis)interested, relaxed motion on the way to the next One.

The songs of James Brown show how this works in small doses, as when the entire rhythmic fabric, just before the one of "Sex Machine," unites in a unison downbeat in anticipation. They are both saying and doing it: they "Get up!" (for the downstroke). The whole intersection takes place at the margins; it is a slight impatience, as if one lets loose the attack of the One a little too early, thereby concentrating the energy for a moment before the release arrives and a new repetition commences. Parliament, alternatively, realizes the unique combinations of funk in the form of overdoses, by way of gestures that are unbearably heavy and excitingly snappy at the same time.

In other words, what was a modest little gesture in the grooves of James Brown, a little extension of the beat in time, becomes strikingly obvious. The small tension between slightly ahead of and straight on the beat in "Sex Machine" is now spread over several musical dimensions, gaining height, depth, and fullness. It has been devised on a new scale, making it both the same and something different. However, the way funk music hits the body probably endures, from James Brown to P-Funk and beyond. The body then contracts immediately, its energy concentrated for a moment before spreading out from the center in waves of release.[18] With James Brown the stroke is rather short and accurate. With P-Funk it is as if the surface meeting the body has become larger, and the body seems to be more relaxed or less composed in the first place. The effect is more saturated, deeper, longer lasting.

It is, however, not easy to define what this quality that inheres in a funk groove and is repeated every time really *is*. As for the grooves discussed in this study, it should be emphasized in closing that they are of course more than what has been presented through analysis. The "recipe" of the analysis can never create a groove. First, the recipe is highly insufficient. Second, a worthy funk groove is probably deeply dependent on the quality Adorno calls *die Kategorie des Einfalls*, the quality of hitting at something special, something unmistakable.[19] One has to find a particular matter and cultivate it to its optimal shape.

Perhaps, at least on the side of production, this is exactly what the funk groove is about. It cultivates some golden moments of creativity through musical dialogue, within the framework of the genre. An excellent groove is certainly not about putting it all together before its performance. The groove comes into being by working on a particular matter—time—in time itself.

IV

"Once Upon a Time Called Now!"

Temporalities and Experience

"The Payback"

The introduction of "The Payback" (1974) is a long, twisting maneuver, building up tension and supplying energy in order to prepare the listener for the events to come. The song has not started yet, and we know this. We are still allowed to keep our distance.

The pattern of the intro is quite similar to what will follow: it is open and clean, a dialogue of distinct elements with a clear outline that is slightly emphasized at the expense of the push forward. Guitar answers bass in a way that makes the guitar's chord hang in the air for a moment before it is picked up again by the bass. We have not yet been absorbed by the musical movement or fallen into its time. The figures are allowed to be drawn clearly, to step forward as complete entities, almost like spatial gestalts.

When the tension increases at the end of the intro, a change is forcing its way through. The patience of the listener is brought to a breaking point, as is the music itself. In the course of the intro's last bars, more and more voices pile on top of one other. In addition, the amplitude of the vibrato increases. Then, all of a sudden, this accelerating expansion closes in on the first downbeat in anticipation. In this critical moment, it is as if the rising trajectory of the extended introductory gesture intersects with the level of the main groove. The extension in time suspends us before we are whirled into a compelling push forward.

The main groove is characterized by an open and ordered sound at the limits of asceticism. The division of labor among instruments is clear and complied with in an almost pedantic way. Yet the groove has a momentum that the intro lacked: percussion keeps the push forward steady throughout, forcing us ahead without a moment for hesitation, reflection, or second thoughts.

The clearly drawn rhythmic pattern is repeated with minimal changes over almost seven minutes, forming a rhythmic basis for a constantly varied lead vocal line. The rough, raspy voice of James Brown appears to operate freely atop the strictly controlled groove. There is no musical movement outside of the duties required by the groove. The different elements step forward as distinct units in a musical dialogue—or, more precisely, in several dialogues located on different levels from high to low. The elements do not melt into a homogeneous sound, and there is almost no depth. Only one layer of musical texture is passing in time, like a strictly organized foreground whose background is empty.

At uneven intervals, the fabric of rhythm is torn by the vocal "lunges" of James Brown—by his unpredictable, urgent expressiveness. The pattern is forced to the background, but just for a while. When the voice leaves, the pattern returns. The gestalts come forward with their common shapes, swinging us back into the pleasure of repetition, as if the groove was always there and always will be.

The State of Being in Funk

In Brown's "The Payback," the basic unit of the song is repeated so many times that our inclination as listeners to organize the musical material into an overall form gradually fades away. Instead of waiting for events to come, we are submerged in what is before us. Our focus turns inward, as if our sensibility for details, for timing inflections and tiny timbral nuances, is inversely proportional to musical variation on a larger scale. When funk is experienced in this way, music ceases to be an object that exists apart from us. The relation of subject and object is almost suspended. We operate within a continuous field where the limit between music and listener is not yet established or has vanished. Dancing, playing, and listening in such a state of being are not characterized by consideration or reflection but rather by a presence in the here and now of the event. Charles Keil has referred to this way of being in music as the *participatory mode,* and it may engender an intense, almost euphoric feeling; in the words of Keil, "you are 'at one' with the entire universe or at least with very large chunks of it."[1]

In Europe in the 1970s the most important venue for this kind of experience was the dance floor, which was typically found in a discotheque or a club. The rise of a dance culture linked with clubs and discos was, needless to say, not a local phenomenon but part of an international trend that in many ways culminated with the formidable success of *Saturday Night Fever* in 1977. However, this trend, where soul-derived black dance music monopolized the dance rhythms of the Anglo-American influenced world of pop and rock—a field traditionally dominated by the culture and values of white, heterosexual, male fans—started long before that, perhaps with the commercial breakthrough of American soul in the mid-1960s. The development peaked with the explosion of disco in the late 1970s, and, as has been discussed previously, this process affected black dance music in various ways. According to Kai Fikentscher's book on underground dance culture in New York City in the 1980s and 1990s, it also entailed a process where disco, which was initially linked with the urban gay subculture, was "heterosexualized."[2]

My experiences with funk in the late 1970s, which provide the context for the discussion of the experiential aspects of funk in the following chapters, was no doubt part of this overall trend within the Anglo-American world of pop and rock. However, as Iain Chambers points out in his discussion of black music in Britain in the same period, the influence of soul on British pop music and culture may be summed up as twofold: on the one hand, soul influenced the mainstream; on the other, it formed the musical basis for typically "specialist tastes" like Northern Soul, a cluster of subcultures that focused on music released on obscure labels, as well as typical fan activities of various kinds.[3]

A similar division between mainstream and subcultural influences is also present in the reception of funk in the Anglo-American–influenced pop and rock audiences of the late 1970s. Funk both attracted a cultish following more concerned with collecting records and other fan activities than with dancing and at the same time made a significant mark on the mainstream pop and dance music of the time. In this respect, the fact that I have chosen to focus on funk as a means of transcendence on the dance floor is probably not accidental. It was mainly girls that filled the dance floors aimed at a heterosexual audience, at least in Scandinavia. The male connoisseurs in the rock audience, several of whom were into funk as well, were only occasionally part of the dance and disco culture. The crossover funk that was played in discos was probably too polished, too mainstream, and too overtly commercial to fulfill their need to cultivate the obscure. One may rather assume that the heterosexual male funk fans were attracted to the potency and the sexually loaded power traditionally linked with black musicianship and apparently present in an enhanced form in the heavy, "dirty" funk grooves. Also, the cool yet excessive style of bands such as Sly and the Family Stone and Parliament probably challenged the semiotic competence required by males to become fans.[4]

In this respect, the different forms of male and female engagement with funk might be said to follow the lines drawn up by Richard Dyer in his discussion of the difference between the erotic appeals of disco and of rock: "The difference between them lies in what each 'hears' in black music. Rock's eroticism is thrusting, grinding—it is not whole-body, but phallic." Dyer distinguishes between whole-body and phallic eroticism to explain the link between gay culture and disco: "Partly because many of us have traditionally not thought of ourselves as being 'real men' and partly because gay ghetto culture is also a space where alternative definitions, including those of sexuality, can be developed, it seems to me that the importance of disco in scene culture indicates an openness to a sexuality that is not defined in terms of cock."[5] Fikentscher also, in his interpretation of gay culture in New York City, stresses the opportunity offered by the dance venue to step outside the restrictions, conventions, and norms of the outside world.[6] In the same way, and probably due to the same feeling of marginality vis-à-vis the dominant rock culture, dance floor experiences in the late 1970s could be used by female fans to undermine prevailing cultural values and subvert the dominant order of things. In this respect the female response to the crossover of black dance music shared certain characteristics with the subcultures from which it emerged. Chambers also comments on the openness regarding alternative identity formation that marginalized white fans could find in black dance music: "Its [soul music's] bodily connotations are rarely exclusive—girls can usually appropriate them as well as boys. Enveloped in sensuality, sexuality does not disappear, but is for the moment diffused."[7] Moreover, the sophisticated, polished sound and commercial appeal of crossover funk no doubt alienated this music from the male connoisseurs. Thus, embracing these aspects worked as a basis for the dissident strategies of both gay culture and women aiming at queering the heterosexual masculinism of the dominant ideology of rock.

While the rock connoisseur's take on funk developed at a safe distance from both the dance floors and the likes and dislikes of the mainstream pop audience, the experience-oriented understanding of funk that is at the core of this study materialized right on the dance floors. While it has much in common with the gay interpretation of disco and other black dance music, there are also some differences that ought to be pointed out. First, contrary to the gay dance culture discussed by Fikentscher and Dyer, the dance culture that makes up the context for this book did not take place within a typically subcultural setting. It was mainstream culture. In line with this, the black dance music played on the dance floors was commercial pop and dance music aimed at the general pop market.

There are also differences regarding musical preferences that may be linked to differences in the function and interpretation of disco and other black dance music between gay male and straight, mostly female, audiences. Walter Hughes addresses one aspect of this in his article "In the Empire of the Beat" (1994), pointing to a possible link between the fascination for militant "four-to-the floor" disco and the presence of themes of dominance and submission in gay culture: "Disco . . . represents, for certain gay men, a form of violence done to a conventional self in order to refashion it, much in the manner of military, religious or sadomasochistic discipline."[8] In line with this, Hughes also comments on how the songs of the Village People, such as

"YMCA" and "In the Navy," tended to couch "the open secret of their homo-eroticism" in the very language of recruitment and evangelism. According to Hughes, a militant beat allows for a process whereby the self is refashioned not from within but due to a power above and beyond it, making the process of destruction (of a dominant heterosexualized masculinity) and re-creation of (a gay) identity a matter of having no choice. These themes of dominance and submission were not a conspicuous aspect of the dance culture dis-cussed in this study; the state of being in funk was not achieved by submis-sion to a militant beat.[9] Rather, it was achieved by an involvement in main-stream pop songs with obvious funky qualities such as Earth, Wind, and Fire's "Serpentine Fire" (1977), Chic's "Le Freak" (1978), or Michael Jackson's "Don't Stop Till You Get Enough" (1979). In my view, the importance of black dance music in this context should rather be sought in the transcendent, em-powering qualities of the dance floor experience. In line with this, as will be argued toward the end of this book, there is an alternative way of understand-ing the attractiveness of dancing to funky grooves that exceeds the body-mind dualism present in the common interpretation of funk as sex and as bodily pleasure.

The Groove Mode and the Song Mode of Listening

A striking aspect of the state of being in music, characterizing what should be called *the funk experience* (to separate it from funk as a musical-analytical object), is that it feels like it could go on forever. To reach this state, however, the interaction of listener/dancer and music does have to last, uninter-rupted, for a long time. As Fikentscher touches upon in his study of under-ground dance music, the requirements of a dance-floor setting influence the musical side of the music/dance interaction on several levels. The impor-tance of "the continuous dynamics of a dance floor atmosphere," as Fikents-cher puts it, applies, for example, to the overall dramaturgy—pauses between tracks or songs have to be eliminated, for one thing.[10] Moreover, it influences the repertoire selected. The situation clearly favors music with an emphasis on rhythm, and with what might be called a non-linear temporal-ity. This means that developmental musical structures have to be avoided.

Conversely, the interaction of music and audience may be encouraged or constrained by habitual expectations of the listeners/dancers. When dealing with the northern European reception of black dance music in the 1970s, the constraints are certainly of interest. Even though grooves were already rec-ognized as part of songs, this audience was not used to responding to music with groove as the overall principle of formal organization—that is, to music without the traditional formal structure of a song. In order to understand the "mainstream" funk experience of the 1970s, therefore, it is important to consider how the dominant listening *habitus* of this audience may affect the process of getting into a state of being in funk.

As has been discussed previously, the meeting of black dance music and the values of the Anglo-American axis of pop and rock changed funk forever. This may, of course, be explained on the level of market forces and commercial interests. However, an important aspect of this is also the clash between two rather different modes of creating and listening. While much African American funk of the pre-crossover era foregrounded rhythmic qualities, the main focus of Anglo-American pop and rock was still on melody and chords; while the primary formal entity in funk was the basic unit of the groove, the equivalent entity in pop and rock was the chorus.[11] Rhythm and groove were, of course, significant parts of the latter as well, but they were not the primary identifying aspects either in the shaping of a tune or in its reception. I have chosen to sum up these two different modes of creating and listening as the "groove mode" and the "song mode," respectively.

One might take exception to this, arguing against the implied contradiction between them. Certainly, a perfect rock tune ought to score high on both counts. However, within a cultural context dominated by the song mode of listening, a poorly performed groove will still work if the vocal parts or the riffs are catchy enough. Last but not least, and this is important in this context, when one is in the song mode, listening to a groove alone feels like waiting for something to happen—that is, for the song to begin.

In line with this, one may argue that the crossover of black dance music in the late 1970s was characterized by a discrepancy between production and reception, not only at the level of discourse and culture—that is, regarding the understanding and interpretation of music—but also at the prediscursive level of subjective experience—that is, at the level of being.[12] One might argue that this friction between groove-based funk and the more song-directed listening strategies of Anglo-American–influenced audiences was "solved" with the musical changes that occurred in funk during the crossover era. But it is not that simple. Even though crossover funk dealt with its audience's predisposition toward songs, that same audience also sought in black dance music precisely the transcendent experience linked with dancing, with participating in a groove. Thus, despite an unfamiliarity with groove-directed music, and the obstacles that this produced in the process of achieving a state of being in the groove, that groove was still the key to a deeply different musical experience for many new funk fans. The presence of a groove in musical terms was not enough; it was the groove *experience* that was sought after by this audience.

In this part I will focus on the experiential aspects of funk within the context of northern European pop and rock culture in the 1970s, with a special focus on the incongruity of groove-based funk and the prevalent song-directed listening strategies of the time. I will consider how funk encourages us to enter into the condition of being in a groove, and what the connection might be between the musical features of funk and "the state of being in funk." I will do this, however, not by dealing with typical hits from that era but rather through analyses of how some James Brown tunes may or may not comply with the demands of the dominant listening habitus among these new fans. I will concentrate on two tunes by James Brown that have been discussed earlier, namely "Sex Machine" and "The Payback," because they are particularly suited to a demonstration of how a listener who expects a song may experience a funk tune governed by the logic of the groove. This raises the question of how funk is organized in time, also on a larger scale, as well as how this musical form is experienced while it is taking place.

In chapter 8 I will present the backdrop for the inclination toward song-directed listening among the mainstream pop and rock audiences of the 1970s. I will also reflect on the important issues of time and repetition in music, focusing in particular on what these might be when in a participatory mode such as the state of being in funk. I will then relate these reflections to the findings of the analytical investigations of part II and III. In chapter 9 I will investigate the connections between large-scale musical form and the state of being in funk in "Sex Machine" and "The Payback." Both tunes are characterized by a form and temporality that seem to prepare for the state of being in funk, more so than the album-formatted *songs* of Parliament. At the same time, the groove-based form of these Brown tunes—their lack of a traditional song structure—raises issues regarding how an inclination toward song-directed listening might hinder the process of entering the state of being in funk. Then, in chapter 10, I will reflect upon the funk experience from the "inside," from within the state of being in funk. I will conclude with more general aesthetic and epistemological reflections and in the last chapter finally reconsider the relationship between the actual experience of funk and its dominant image in the West.

8

Time and Again

The Dominance of Linear Temporality

From the Baroque period to our own time, Western art music has often been experienced and described in terms of a teleological process. The music seems to form large-scale curves of tension, often building up to a climax before reaching a conclusion that is felt to be well prepared and quite natural. However, this is really only one way of shaping musical time, and it is in fact something of a historical parenthesis. Linear, teleological, or "closed" musical forms are in a larger historical and geographical context the exception rather than the rule. All the same, they hold a privileged position in the West, not only within musicology but in the general populace: the underlying values of this notion of music, such as unity, development, and complexity, have come to characterize the very notion of music itself.

Many contributions within the fields of music theory and music psychology rest on this notion of music as a teleological process. Among them are Leonard B. Meyer's classic "expectation theory."[1] According to Meyer, "intramusical" meaning can be explained as a temporary suspension or blocking of the resolution of musical expectations. The bodily correlate to this process is a state of undifferentiated physiological arousal. The experience of suspension is, according to Meyer, aesthetically valueless unless it is followed by a release that makes sense in the given context.[2] This also applies to the work as a whole and suggests that music is organized as a hierarchy: it has to be divisible into more or less closed parts and include certain points of more or less complete resolution. Tension has to be followed by release also with regard to the overall structure, and the natural ending of a work coincides with the point where *all* of the tension has been released.

In Meyer's *Style and Music* (1989), this aspect of the theory is expressed as an unavoidable demand for *closure*. Closure is regarded as a *prestylistic* feature: it is something music has regardless of its style, and the question is not whether or to what extent all music is characterized by closure but rather how its closure may be achieved more or less effectively in different musical parameters.[3]

Meyer concentrates exclusively on the tonal music of the Western canon. In *The Time of Music* (1988), Jonathan Kramer attempts to systematize and analyze *different* types of musical time. His point of departure is a theoretical division between linearity and nonlinearity. Musical linearity is defined as "the determination of some characteristic(s) of music in accordance with implications that arise from earlier events of the piece," while nonlinearity is "the determination of some characteristic(s) of music in accordance with implications that arise from principles or tendencies governing an entire piece or section."[4] Put another way, in a linear mode musical meaning is developed in a teleological process and is connected to the preceding and succeeding events, while musical meaning in a nonlinear mode is simply "uncovered." In practice, it is difficult, even impossible, to distinguish one from the other, and Kramer does admit that all music exhibits both linearity and nonlinearity.

In this vein, Kramer develops categories of musical time as variations and combinations of linearity and nonlinearity. The first is goal-directed linearity, which covers the repertoire that makes up the foundation of Meyer's theory of musical expectation. One interesting aspect of Kramer's description of Western tonal linear music is his emphasis on its nonlinear aspects:

> Consider pieces in which the texture, motivic material, and rhythmic figuration are virtually constant. Chopin's Prelude in C Major, opus 28, no. 1 (1839) and Bach's Prelude in C Major, from the first volume of *The Well-Tempered Clavier* (1722), are good examples, as is Schumann's *Stückchen* from the *Album for the Young* (1848) . . . In such music the context is not a consequence of the way the piece begins, but rather it is determined by the surface of the composition, which is in certain aspects unchanging. The music's texture exists throughout the piece but does not grow or transform itself as the work unfolds.[5]

According to Kramer, it may be argued that a constant context invites a linear mode of listening. After a few bars of unchanged texture and surface rhythm, the expectation arises that the next bar will be similar: "Eventually the expectation for consistency turns into virtual certainty, and (in information-theoretic terms) the texture and surface rhythm become redundant."[6] Attention, thus, is turned toward those musical aspects where the linearity unfolds, in particular melodic contour, harmony, the use of different registers, and in some cases the dynamics.

Kramer also deals with linearity in Western atonal music. However, this form of linearity lacks the clearly defined goal of the tonal system—that is, the inevitable return to the tonic: "In the absence of the tonal system's *a priori* goal definition, early atonal composers faced the challenge of creating cadences contextually."[7] Apart from Kramer's division of text and context, which does not seem to be properly thought out, the idea that linearity can be overtaken by musical aspects that are not dependent upon pitch, such as tempo, texture, figuration, instrumentation, rhythm, is a good one.

Meyer refers to these as "secondary parameters," because with the exception of rhythm, which may act as both a primary and a secondary parameter, they are characterized by their inability to specify exactly when something is going to end: "Lacking syntax . . . such processes cannot specify definite points of termination . . . they may cease, but they cannot close."[8] According to Meyer, it is only parameters like harmony, melody, and rhythm that may be described via class-like relationships—in other words, "digitized" and understood as discrete entities—that may be governed by syntactical constraints. When such a parameter has a syntactical function, he refers to it as "primary" and sees it as fundamental: "In general, the possibility of hierarchic organization depends on the existence of different kinds and strengths of closure created by syntax."[9]

The musical procedures of the tonal tradition, and especially absolute music, are commonly regarded as signifying on a musical level only. But as Susan McClary points out, even these procedures do cultural work too, and there can be striking resemblances, at least after the fact, among the musical forms and the dominant ideas and discoveries of a certain time and place. Tonality and functional harmony, for example, may be interpreted in light of the mechanistic worldview of eighteenth-century Europe. Moreover, the dramatic developmental forms of nineteenth-century music may be read as an unfolding of conflicting forces within the newly invented psychological subject. McClary notes further that music is both a possible expression of the common values of a society and a way of learning to cope with those claims:

> In any given tonal composition . . . various strategies serve to postpone that expected arrival [of closure]; these strategies, although they initially withhold certainty, eventually confirm the belief that rational effort results in the attaining of goals. The self-motivated delay of gratification, which was necessary for the social world coming into being in the eighteenth century, worked on the basis of such habits of thought, and tonality teaches listeners how to live within such a world: how to project forward in time, how to wait patiently but confidently for the pay-off.[10]

Until recently, the historicity of musical conventions and procedures such as tonality, functional harmony, developmental forms, unity within the work, and so on was to a great extent transparent both within musicology and to the general public. The features of music made within the world of Western tonal art music had almost taken on a metaphysical character: they came to represent, in some transhistorical sense, "the way music [was] supposed to go," as McClary puts it. The process of revealing the underlying ideology of this notion of music has lasted for several decades and is, by now, thoroughly debunked.[11] However, even though our reliance upon a classical-romantic aesthetics has been brought to the surface, central features of this music still affect our expectations of how music in general is supposed to go. Both Meyer's expectation theory and Kramer's account of the goal-directedness or teleology of tonal music, thus, express what might be called the dominant listening strategy in Western music culture. Not only the music but the listening to it can be called in a certain way teleological: one expects something to happen, certainly involving the aspects of music most often implicated in shaping such large-scale time spans, namely melody, harmony, and musical form. The notion of music as teleological motion is, then, not only (at least occasionally) a good description of music. It is also a description of a common music listening *habitus* within the European and Euro-American parts of the Western world.[12]

The fact that this notion of what music is (and should be) occupies a primary position within the Western music-cultural field affects how music is experienced within the field of popular music as well, and especially its Anglo-American strands. The notion surfaces in both production and reception as a relatively primary interest in songs, understood as melody and chords, rather than grooves. (Also, when it comes to copyrighting music, the melodic and harmonic aspects of a song are the ones that count.) In the next chapter I will discuss how this may have affected the interaction between funk and the new audiences that were recruited for black dance music during the crossover era. As we shall see, however, the influence from the dominant listening habitus described above did not cause these new audiences to reject groove-directed black dance music altogether. It only made it more difficult for them to meet the music in a way that allowed them to reach the state of being in funk.

Eternal Present vs. Eternal Presence—On Different Nonlinearities

The dominance of this notion of music has other effects as well. While texts dealing with other traditions have to delimit the scope of their validity by specifying their interest in "pop music" or "folk music" or "African music," Meyer, in his somewhat old-fashioned manner, may speak of his tradition as "music" without any further qualification. There is also a tendency to relate all other musics to this first music—that is, to unconsciously consider other music to be the opposite of this first music, as when Christopher Small describes African music this way: "The repetitions of African music have a function in time which is *the reverse of our own music*—to dissolve the past and present into one eternal present, in which the passing of time is no longer noticed."[13]

With Kramer's theory, this structural hegemony is embedded in the fundamental opposition of linearity to nonlinearity: the "One" side is defined in positive terms, while the "Other" is the negation of the One: the Other is the not-One. Thus everything except possible variants of linearity remains rather indistinct. All nonlinear music tends to appear the same, because the interesting thing about it is exactly its nonlinearity, and the fact that it may work as an antithesis of Western tonal art music. Kramer's category of "vertical time," which is nonlinear musical time at its purest, is to a considerable extent described in terms of negation: "A vertically conceived piece . . . does *not* exhibit large-scale closure. It does *not* begin but merely starts. It does *not* build to a climax, does *not* purposefully set up internal expectations, does *not* seek to fulfill any expectations that might arise accidentally, does *not* build or release tension, and does *not* end but simply ceases."[14]

Nonlinear musical time might include funk, but only if one leaves out all of the significant internal differences within nonlinearity. When considered simply as contrary to the linear, however, nonlinear music's internal differences disappear, as if its very difference stands in the way of discovering the various characters of different nonlinear musics. They all become "nonteleological," to use a term of Meyer's.[15] It is indeed striking that despite the fact that the actual musics sound rather different—repetitive rhythmic music differs from the contemporary art music that forms the basis for Kramer's category of "vertical time,"[16]— the counterpart of teleological linearity is described in much the same way by both Small and Kramer. Kramer links the "eternal present" with music that completely lacks phrases or is almost devoid of temporal articulation, as if one single present is being stretched out, covering the entire work:

> Just as the twentieth century has seen explorations of the subtleties of discontinuity, conversely it has seen experiments in extreme consistency. Some recent pieces seem to have adopted the requirements for moments (self-containment via stasis or process) as their entire essence. When the moment becomes the piece, discontinuity[17] disappears in favor of total, possibly unchanging, consistency. Compositions have been written that are temporally undifferentiated in their entirety. They lack phrases (just as they lack progression, goal direction, movement, and contrasting rates of motion) because phrase endings break the temporal continuum . . . The result is a single present stretched out into an enormous duration, a potentially infinite "now" that nonetheless feels like an instant.[18]

The work becomes like a sculpture that can be listened to from different angles. Meyer also describes "non-teleological art" as standing still; it is not kinetic but instead directed toward timbre or sound—the materiality of sound, not its relations: "One is not listening to the relationship among the sounds presented, but just to the sounds as sounds—as individual, discrete objective sensations."[19]

However, a groove does not stand still. Even though it is unchanging, consistent, and of a potentially infinite duration; even though the principles comprising it are supplied in advance, in the sense that the groove defines "its bounded sound-world early in its performance and stays within the limits it chooses";[20] and even though the groove is not proceeding toward a definite goal, it is—to the last second—in motion.

Both forms of musical time—the one potentially characterizing contemporary music's sculptures of sound and the other potentially present in repetitive rhythmic music—may be described as states of equilibrium.[21] However, we might find ourselves in a condition of stasis either because we are actually standing still or because we are moving at a steady speed in relation to something else moving equally fast and in the same direction. In each case the passing of time is no longer noticed. However, this last aspect is also to be differentiated according to the two states described above: either we do not notice the passing of time because no time passes—that is, because the work manages to convey the impression that no time passes—or we do not notice the passing of time because we move together with time. For what is time when one is being in time? It is only by stepping out of the stream of time that we might say "time passes": we notice the passing of time because we are no longer moving along with it.

Repetition vs. Repetition

One consequence of Kramer's model is that cyclical forms of musical time seem to disappear from view. Due to the fact that they are not able to either confirm or negate the primary position of linearity, they end up as external to the linear/nonlinear dichotomy and are therefore excluded from it. This means, for example, that the greater part of the folk music of the world and most of the field of popular music are not dealt with at all. In his classic book *Studying Popular Music* (1990), Richard Middleton accounts for at least some of this huge field, operating with *three* categories of time/form in his discussion of the significance of different forms of repetition for popular music. Linearity is one of them, along with the lyric and the epic. The lyric mode transcends the dichotomy of linear and nonlinear discussed so far and covers a regular pop song, a binary, symmetrical form with verse and chorus. The epic mode is thought to cover forms ruled by repetition or varied repetition. In Kramer's system they would probably have been labeled nonlinear.

Middleton's main concern is to work out a theoretical framework for understanding repetitive structures in music. Though it is useful on several points, however, his theory of musical repetition has a weakness, in that he makes rather too automatic a connection between variation and the linear mode, as well as between repetition and the epic or mythic mode. As an aid for analyzing syntactical structures in music, he presents a model of a so-called syntagmatic continuum. The two poles are absolute repetition ("monadic plenitude") and infinite or absolute variation ("infinite set"). When connecting these to a gestural level, Middleton seems to claim that repetitive structures always work as a way of stopping the musical motion, while any change is heard as movement toward a goal.[22]

Middleton is not the only one to link repetition to a musical standstill. Quite often, the repetitions of repetitive music are given full recognition for having transported us to a state of being outside time and space, or perhaps, quite to the contrary, *in* time and *in* space. The fact that there are repetitions in repetitive rhythmic music is, of course, of great importance. Endless repetition would likely contribute to bringing the listener into a state where the passing of time is not noticed. However, this would only happen in certain situations, because the effect of repetition is highly dependent on musical as well as social contexts. Repetition is, in other words, not automatically equal to nonhierarchical or nonlinear forms, or to different trancelike, meditative, or regressive conditions (depending upon your perspective).

Moreover, there is also repetition outside the groove. In "Structure and Function in Musical Repetition" (1979), David Lidov points out the ways in which repetition contributes to segmentation and hierarchy in Western art music. When repetition works in this way, he calls it *formative:* "Formative repetition (as repetition refers or directs attention to, and marks the material repeated) is the kind of repetition which fulfills the various grammatical functions outlined so far: it defines units of a musical work, and establishes their position in a hierarchy of longer and shorter segments."[23] Formative repetition is conventional and necessary, attracting little attention if the unit repeated corresponds to the constructional units of the hierarchy—or, in Lidov's words, "If the repetition is hierarchically conformal, its necessity and sufficiency neutralizes its interest. Interest passes to the material."[24] Formative repetition is, in other words, an almost transparent aspect of musical structure, and according to Lidov the absence of formative repetition is actually much more striking than its presence.

Formative repetition works, as a rule, in the form of two equal units following each other in immediate succession: "The two units will tend to form a larger group—according to the laws of Gestalt perception—because they are both similar and adjacent."[25] Whether this happens according to laws or not, this kind of repetition is fundamental to establishing, for example, the hierarchy of sequences in a standard pop tune, which is built up in accordance with such a principle. One measure plus another makes a unit of two, two plus another two makes a unit of four, four plus four makes eight, and so on. This repetition is not a topic in itself within this kind of musical form; it is simply formative and transparent.

Most often, the two equal units are not absolutely equal, but this does not change the effect very much. "Varied formative repetition" will, according to Lidov, merely tend to establish "equivalences and oppositions between different features of the material"[26]—as, for example, when a phrase is answered by a similar but different phrase in a symmetrically organized form. One's focus tends to stay on the aspect that changes, not on the aspect that repeats—for instance, a rhythmic pattern—even though the latter to a large extent must be said to form the basic framework for the phrase.

Contrary to Middleton, who tends to put too much stress on the length of the repeated unit, Lidov analyzes the varied effects of repetition using the number of repetitions as his starting point. When the number of units exceeds two, which is the typical number for formative repetition, the fact that something is repeated will attract attention in itself. This type of repetition he calls *focal:*

> The structures most frequently associated with the self-referential or focal type of repetition are a three- or four-fold immediate repetition of a musical unit, or a two-fold (i.e. single) repetition which crosses the boundary of a longer unit. The usual single repetition is neutralized by fulfilling a grammatical role; the extra repetition or, in the second case, the displacement is an immediate signal for a change of attention. Instead of focusing on the repeated material only, we focus on the repetition as an activity per se, and seek a symbolic interpretation of it.[27]

Lidov mentions the classical sequence as an example of a form of repetition that attracts attention as repetition while at the same time being strongly progressive: "Does a three-fold sequence comprise a focal repetition? Certainly, but it is also something else (e.g., a progression)."[28] Such repetitive structures might, in other words, give a feeling of an accumulation of time rather than the opposite. Middleton continues, "Sequence composes time (rather than marking time or obliterating it, as straight repetition, especially if musematic, seems to do)."[29] In general, one might say that sequence is both repetition and variation, and that it is probably just the interaction of the two that has an effect.

The interplay of repetition and variation is, however, no less important when the unit is less obviously varied than in the case of a classical sequence.

Repetition with a Difference

The question as to whether repetition in a groove is repetition of the same thing depends first upon the resolution of the "processing": if the resolution is good—if the listener is sufficiently attuned to details and other events on a micro-level—there is almost always something different in a given repetition. Conversely, a non-confident listener will probably tend to hear the same thing in spite of considerable differences from one repetition to the other. It also depends upon the extent to which listening is directed toward difference rather than similarity. When an important aesthetic orientation in African American culture is summed up as *to repeat with a difference*,[30] this means that every repetition is different, and that the focus is on difference—not difference in itself but difference stepping forward in relation to the same, to a figure, a formality or convention, perhaps even tradition itself. (In practice, tradition will also contain the expectation of difference.) In other words, repetition in a groove is a sort of micro-level signifyin(g): it is repetition and revision in one and the same maneuver. The aim is twofold. On the one hand, it is important that the same is repeated every time and recognized or categorized as such. On the other hand, it is equally important that this same is different. However, this difference must not exhaust the category but instead occur in the form of what could be named *intracategorical variation*: the difference is a difference within the repeated same.

Even a strictly repetitive tune like "The Payback" is, on the level of structure (meaning the content that can be pinned down some way or another, by notation or another form of representation) an example of a changing same. The change is rather discreet and happens over a long time, but it is there. First of all, it is the response guitar that "develops" in this way. The funky wah-wah riff is extended so that the gestures gradually get bigger and looser, occupying more space and more time. However, we never think of this change as a change, probably due to the fact that it is contained in the act of producing the same. For this reason, it is probably also a mistake to speak of variation in this case. It is perhaps more accurate to speak about optimization, about subtle perfection, about shaping the riff so that it can make itself even more comfortable within the whole.

This continuous work on getting at the optimal solution is often described as "locking the rhythm" or "nailing the rhythm." It is not a thought process, and it is never finished; it goes on automatically and continuously, manifested in the form of better or worse periods. In the better periods the technical skills of musicians and dancers are completely absent (such things as precision and timing tend to be audible or visible only when they are lacking; ideally, they attract no attention to themselves).[31]

In most of the tunes by James Brown and his bands, this is exactly the case. All of the parts are completely reliable, and in a normal or "absorbed" mode, one need not consider the manner in which the groove is played; an alternative is never introduced. However, we might also miss how "right" this is. For us, the groove simply has a good feel to it, and as long as this remains so, it is never apparent just how difficult it is to let things alone, to avoid disturbing the state of being in a groove. Almost anything can bring the audience, dancers, and musicians out of the stream of time, out of the moving music, and it is actually very hard to avoid doing so.

In other words, when the groove proves successful, we tend not to consider or analyze it. However, this does not mean that the state of being in a groove is thoughtless—"thinking" is not the same as "thinking about." We are thinking all the time, but when we think about the groove, it is perhaps because the groove has failed: our first thought is usually that something is wrong.

Repetition in Time

The trustworthiness of a groove, one in which the technical skills or competence-related aspects of the performance are transparent, is very important so that the groove's partakers can get into the groove and remain there, in the participatory mode, for a long time. However, when this happens, not only the groove's "craftsmanship" disappears but also the sense that the same basic musical unit is being repeated throughout. In a song like "The Payback," this repetition leads us deeper down into the groove. However, repetition is in a sense absolutely without interest for those of us who are being moved. It is almost transparent.

In other words, the fact that there is repetition is not the focus of the experience. On the contrary, a presupposition of the "condition of funk" is that repetition is not heard, that it is out of focus. In Lidov's analysis of "textural repetition," he points out that it "cancels out its own claim on our attention and, thereby, refers our focus elsewhere (to another voice or to a changing aspect)."[32] Lidov suggests that this might happen already by the fourth or fifth repetition. For Lidov, this kind of repetition—if it is successful—leads one's attention to "another voice or . . . changing aspect" without losing its repetitive effect: "The figure maintains, nevertheless, a transcendental influence on our musical consciousness."[33] Perhaps this is how repetition works in, for example, the minimalism of Steve Reich. The repetitive texture "cancels out its own claim on our attention" and becomes a curtain of sound while our attention wanders in other directions. The listener waits for something else to happen—another event, a new element, a little change—but all the while without the repetition disappearing or losing its effect. We hear things differently from when there is no repetition.

Even though Lidov's musical universe is far from funk, his description is interesting because it focuses upon how, as time passes, repetition is absent, though it is still there. His description is probably even to some extent relevant for how a Western pop- and rock-confident audience approaches a song: its repetitive strata largely remain unfocused. However, this does not mean that they lose their effect, and contrary to the minimalism of Steve Reich, they will probably be directed toward motion. Nevertheless, one's attention will—due to the dominant mode of listening—settle instead on the musical aspects that are varied.

The thought that repetition is not experienced as repetition must, however, be further clarified on two counts. First, the fact that a song contains a lot of repetition is no guarantee that the repetition will disappear or be ignored by the listener. Repetition may equally well remain the listener's focus; to use an expression by Lidov, the claim on the attention of the listener is never canceled out, as the listener is bound by the repetitive structure and has not moved from focal to textural repetition. If, for different reasons, one is not able to give oneself up to the groove, repetition will probably become a repetition of the same. This may be when and why repetition sometimes becomes unbearable. To experience the "joy in repetition," as Prince calls it, one has to move, or one has to be moved. If one is not, repetition may soon become a repetition without difference: the same is no longer transparent but rather too pronounced, almost obtrusive, nerve-racking, perhaps even, as for

Adorno, a sort of torture.[34] Viewed this way, intracategorical variation is as fundamental to the aesthetic phenomenon of repetition as the repetition itself; the intracategorical variation is the strictly necessary supplement of repetition. This is a crucial point regarding the mainstream pop and rock audiences' meeting with funk grooves, because the inclination toward song-directed listening may inhibit them from moving together with the groove. Instead of giving in to the moment, they continue searching for the syntactical structures of overarching forms, such as the periodicity created by melodic phrases, chord progressions, and the like.

Second, when the repeated actually is exactly the same, repetition may still be experienced as repetition with a difference: the question remains as to whether repetition is repetition. Even in music where every basic unit is exactly like the preceding one and where the basic units, if taken out of time and placed on top of one other, are identical—for example, because the music is performed by machines and not human beings—every repetition is still different, because the time in which it occurs is new.[35]

Repetition as Production

As stated earlier, the groove is, in one sense, only a groove to the extent that we are moving together with it and are absorbed in the participatory mode. A groove works when it is allowed to and/or manages to conquer us for the state of being in the groove. If one takes such a participatory mode as a point of departure, repetition does not exist apart from its supplementary difference; as an experiential aspect of the groove, repetition is probably absent. In other words, when we are in the music, we hear only difference, but not in the sense of a deviation from what has come before. Rather, the synthesis in time that has to take place to make repetition into repetition never takes place, at least not on a level that brings it into focus. The fact that "what is" is the same as "what was" is pleasurable but never considered.

In *Difference and Repetition* (1994), Deleuze states that the constitution of repetition already implies three instances of repetition. The first one he calls "repetition in itself," but as he points out, this leaves repetition as unthinkable. Repetition has no "in itself": it cannot be attributed to the object repeated but rather, in the words of Hume, "change[s] something in the mind which contemplates it."[36] The second instance of repetition relates to this effect of repetition and implies a "passive synthesis in time," as Deleuze says, which is not carried out by the mind but occurs in the mind as it contemplates, prior to all memory and all reflection. On this level, repetition takes place but is not recognized as such; it is still repetition for itself, or rather, repetition before the act of understanding repetition. The third instance of repetition is repetition constituted as such, as "repetition for us," but this act of understanding is, as Deleuze points out, superimposed upon and supported by the two underlying levels.[37]

In line with Deleuze, one might say that in a participatory mode, repetition remains repetition for itself. It never becomes repetition for us. Moreover, Deleuze also points to the fact that repetition is production in the first place. It has no "in itself." Due to this, when one is in the process of *creating* a repetition, repetition cannot be explained by its identity in concepts or representations. He gives the following example:

> Consider . . . the repetition of a decorative motif: a figure is reproduced, while the concept remains absolutely identical . . . However, this is not how artists proceed in reality. They do not juxtapose instances of the figure, but rather each time combine an element of one instance with *another* element of a following instance. They introduce a disequilibrium into the dynamic process of construction, an instability, dissymmetry or gap of some kind which appears only in the overall effect.[38]

The process is fueled by a productive dissymmetry. This productive force is in the process, in the sense that the whole process is considered to be a sign of this force at work. At the same time, however, it is not in the process, because the very goal of the process is to cancel it.

Along these lines, Deleuze finds it necessary to distinguish between two types of repetition, dynamic and static, which correspond to repetition as experienced from positions inside and outside the process, respectively. The latter concerns only the overall static effect—it *results from* the work and refers back to a single concept, which leaves only an external difference between the ordinary instances of a figure. The former concerns the acting cause and is the repetition of an internal difference that it incorporates into each of its moments. According to this interior perspective, the figure is not shaped at once but rather comes into being like the "evolution" of a bodily movement—or, in other words, like a gesture. Deleuze writes, "In the dynamic order there is no representative concept, nor any figure represented in a pre-existing space. There is an Idea, and a pure dynamism which creates a corresponding space."[39]

Also within a groove, repetition is production in the sense that one is continuously producing, or co-producing, rhythmic gestures in an ongoing process. In the groove mode, the entire rhythmic pattern is neither played nor experienced at once; it is instead experienced over time. Every gesture has to be effected, and in one sense, repetition is like a kind of continual re-*petition*, a re-appeal or request that requires a follow-up. The request takes place every single time, and it happens over and over again in the form of the same, yet new (re)petition. It has to be done, and it has to done in time, sequentially.

In other words, rather than repeating a prefabricated figure, one repeats an internal difference. One makes up one part and answers with another in an eternal rhythmic dialogue. Every time the answer is the same, but this may only be because it is the right answer. The groove requires exactly that answer at that point; a different answer would take the whole process off course, and the entire fabric of rhythm might fall apart.

Repetitive Production in Grooves

Many of the features of the James Brown and P-Funk grooves presented in parts II and III contribute to this sort of productive dissymmetry. Both the structural tension of rhythm and counter-rhythm and the figure of on-and-off, as heard, for example, in the pattern of pick-up gestures in "Sex Machine," seem to have a certain driving, dynamic effect that leads the process onward. If we take the figure of on-and-off as an example, we seem to have to choose between getting lost and following the pattern's movement from on to off and back again. Beginning with our first confusion surrounding the critical point where the figure is inverted and we have to sort out the change, through the part of the pattern where the figure actually *is* inverted, to the point where everything is back in place again, we are probably busy with our perceptional processes as we sort out the interplay of rhythm and counter-rhythm. The groove does not allow for other, more time-consuming activities to take place before the part of the pattern where the basic pulse is confirmed by the main rhythm, without being threatened by a counter-rhythm. Not until the figure installing the offbeats as main beats is corrected by the complementary gesture reasserting the regular onbeats is there room for a shift in our concentration, for a looking back or a looking ahead.

However, because this phase of relative stability normally arrives at a point in the process when the introduction of change is almost unthinkable, namely right in the middle of the pattern, or rather at the end of the first part of the basic unit, the pattern might be said to contain a certain built-in circularity. The metrical structure of the main rhythm leads the pattern toward a mini-"closure" at the end of every basic unit, but this potential stage of greater symmetry is neutralized by the counter-rhythm. As is often also the case with the cross-rhythmic figure, the off-beat rhythm usually fills up the second part of the basic unit, hence increasing the dissymmetry or instability in this part of the groove. In other words, the counter-rhythm is either directly or indirectly at work when the natural point of closure arrives, and perhaps also slightly after it—usually, it takes some time to get things back in order.

James Brown's "Get It Together" (1967) is not a funk tune, but it is an excellent example of how dissymmetry may work as a productive force within the basic unit of a groove. The tune is a somewhat strange combination of a traditional verse/chorus structure and a groove-based, strongly circular form that lacks any division above the level of the basic unit. The rather unstable but at the same time highly energetic groove leads nowhere other than back to its own beginning. The combination of the circular bass line and the rather exceptionally obscured conditions surrounding the One make the act of rhythmic grouping difficult on a micro-level, even regarding the identification of the beginning and ending of the basic unit. This is primarily due to the polyrhythmic disturbances caused by the horn section that, by means of an enduring figure of four against three, make a serious attempt at introducing an alternative pulse (see fig. 32). This figure is so long that the fourth of the five indications of the alternative pulse is displaced, with considerable effect. Due to the sustained presence of this cross-rhythm, the instability increases toward the end of the pattern, and this is largely responsible for the circular character of the groove. It makes it difficult to delimit the basic unit and obscures the potential point of closure, the point where it would have been possible to break out of the circle, namely the One.

"I Got the Feelin'" (1968) is also characterized by conflicting forces. In this song the horns mark out the transition from one pattern to the next by projecting a real desire for the One, but they never follow up this movement by introducing a serious heavy One. The One ends rather abruptly: we are still waiting for the gesture to continue, to be accomplished, when we realize that it has actually passed and the horns

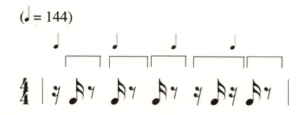

Figure 32. Cross-rhythmic figure in "Get It Together," played by the horn section.

are once more spreading out their small quick notes on the verges of the beats. All in all, the time signature is forced to the background in favor of isoperiodicity. The borderline between the basic units is almost erased, and this somewhat seasick feeling of being pulled toward the One only to be jettisoned on the other side is explored to the bitter end, when the fourth level of the blues sequence finally arrives. It begins on an unambiguously marked one, catching the listener, by this time lagging considerably behind, unawares.

In both of these songs, the isoperiodic character of the pattern on the first and primary tonal level contributes to an effective "closing" of the groove, not in Meyer's sense but rather the opposite: the pattern becomes circular.[40] Both grooves display a One that is considerably destabilized and rather weak, and this makes breaking out of the pattern difficult. The grooves do not settle down at any point or contain points of closure in the sense of Meyer. There is no time for introducing fundamental changes or for moving to another section or level. To the extent that closure occurs, it never coincides in the different voices.

As we discussed earlier, as funk becomes funk its texture becomes more open and easier to grasp. Viewed this way, there are several songs from the main funk years of James Brown that are too dense, complex, or unstable to be viewed as typical funk tunes. They are situated, instead, at the edge of the style. "I Got the Feelin'" is one of these songs. Even though it shows up with many of the typical features of a funk song—the phrasing is extremely snappy, and there is a strong tendency toward cross-rhythm—the groove is too unclear.

A song like "Soul Power" generates a similar doubt, particularly in groove 2. Here the pattern never becomes stable. In this section of the song, one feels vaguely that the groove has been inverted in the middle of the bar. However, the stable phase of the figure of on-and-off—that is, the first part—is extremely short, almost nonexistent. This is particularly due to the intricate figure of the bass. Bootsy Collins's playing is designed to make the whole fabric of rhythm drift by generating musical hypotheses in the bass for how to understand the sounding events—and how to reject them—almost nonstop.

In the beginning of the bar, the question is open as to what constitutes the basic motif in the figure. The doubled sixteenth, followed by a pause and a single sixteenth, may be continued as a 4:3 pattern or, in other words, with a single note on one-and (see fig. 33). However, when the note arrives, it is a double, suggesting a basic motif that is slightly different from what was probably expected in the first place. One has the immediate impression of a cell that is about to be repeated, lasting for six sixteenths, as follows: two played, single rest, one played, double rest (see fig. 34). In the middle of the repetition, after the first rest, the single played sixteenth never materializes. Instead, one sixteenth later, on three-and, the figure starts from the top and is then completed in its entirety (see fig. 35).

Understood this way, the second accomplishment of the basic motif is displaced one eighth with regard to the basic pulse, and this is probably what contributes to the vague feeling of the rhythm being turned around in the middle of the bar. However, it is impossible to say exactly when this occurs, due to the moment of confusion arising when the last part of the motif does not appear after beat three, and neither does anything else. When the doubled sixteenth shows up on three-and, the situation is still unclear. The figure does not become clear until after the fact, until the single syncopated sixteenth occurs on the sixteenth after the fourth beat. However, the position of this tone is so unstable, and

Figure 33. The opening of the bass line of groove 2 of "Soul Power"; possible continuation in brackets.

Figure 34. The first half of the bass line of groove 2 of "Soul Power"; possible continuation in brackets.

the sixteenth is so hesitantly played, the motif never settles fully into place. Even when the rhythm turns back by way of its normal beginning at beat one, we remain unsure.

The pattern of this groove seems to be designed to achieve a certain feeling of losing firm ground: the potential regularities of the pattern are subdued almost at the moment they emerge. Certainly the performance of the pattern also contributes to this. In fact, such a groove is quite telling regarding the speed at which a pattern may be established, and the minimal effort it takes to break it down, as well as the aesthetic satisfactions of rules violated. However, it may also say something about the limits of perception when it comes to one's ability to understand the pattern as a pattern. This is, however, deeply dependent upon how familiar the style is to the listener.

Circularity and the One

It is not typical for a funk tune to be as unstable as the grooves discussed above. In funk, the big questions are quite uncomplicated. At least one knows what the questions are, as well as most of the answers: there is no doubt as to when the pattern starts and ends, or which pulse represents the basic regular beat. Nor is it difficult to identify the outline of the main gestures, even though it might be difficult to tell exactly when they happen. In line with this, one might anticipate that the less structurally complex funk grooves would lack the kind of productive dissymmetry characterizing the unstable grooves discussed above.

As shown in parts II and III, however, many of these "simpler" grooves present a similar productive force as a certain ambiguity at a micro-level. Even though it might be easier to understand *what* happens

Figure 35. The bass line of groove 2 of "Soul Power."

here, the question of *when* is perhaps even more thrilling, and this contributes to keeping the listener within the movement of the groove. On one level, the answers to the "big questions" of the groove are pretty obvious: we have no problems getting familiar with the beginning and the ending of the pattern, as well as with the dominance of the main rhythm. The relatively few independent gestures give clear instructions as to the main outline of their patterns. On another level, however, the answers are less obvious. The ambiguity is fairly constant and often more developed than in a groove with a more traditional, structural complexity. It never becomes entirely clear when the dominating rhythm takes place or the transition from one pattern to the next happens. The figures that are there are, simultaneously, not there. So, even though the answers are given, the questions are still posed. And every answer becomes a new question, because while making one relation stable, it makes another unstable.

In a funk groove the force field surrounding the One is very important to this process. In the songs described above, the groove would seem to turn on itself due to a *weak* One. In the P-Funk grooves the opposite occurs. The first beat is no longer implicit and unstable. It is overwhelmingly explicit and unavoidable: we are being pulled toward an extended One with a force that makes it impossible to think of anything else before the metrical beat one has in fact passed. Parliament's "P-Funk (Wants to Get Funked Up)" is one example: the One has grown so big, so heavy, that we may almost speak of a slow layer of pulses consisting of just one heavy beat, carrying enough power to influence the whole groove. This means that we are barely free from the impact of the previous One when the next absorbs all of the musical energy like a black hole, locking us in the groove at the very point where a new pattern or change could have been prepared. The One is so powerful that nothing can possibly happen until it is restated; the acceleration toward the heavy beat is so strong that any force pulling in another direction is neutralized. The situation may not be surveyed until after the One, but by then it is again too late.[41]

In a song like "P-Funk (Wants to Get Funked Up)," as well as the rather unstable grooves of James Brown discussed above, the groove is characterized by constantly tugging at its own lack of symmetry as it strives for a more stable phase that never arrives. On the side of the listener or partaker, this tugging demands an almost constant presence in the (re)productive process of the groove. There is no room, or time, according to one's approach, for distanciation. We are constantly moving along together with the groove. In other P-funk songs, there is a little breather between the heavy Ones, as for example in Parliament's "We Want the Funk." Not only the structure but the experience of the groove may be described as circular (even though the circles are rather small). This feeling of circularity depends upon a stable phase during the basic pattern, where the partaker for a moment is able to maintain some distance to the actual events, observing her own movement. But this stable phase never coincides with the end of the pattern as indicated by the meter. When the level of "gestural disturbance" is at its lowest, the meter, as a virtual structure of reference, leads the groove further on, and vice versa.

"Make It Funky" (1971) is a circular groove from James Brown's hand, yet one with a marked tendency to stress every beat. Yet this is the rare James Brown song where the One is entitled to swell out, almost as in the later P-funk songs. Similar to those heavy grooves, this groove is in many ways less complex than "I Got the Feelin'" or groove 2 of "Soul Power." We are not busy with syntactical problems all the way through. Actually, not much happens between the few gestures that exist. The effect of those gestures, however, is so strong as to hardly allow time for recovery. Similar to P-Funk grooves such as "Up for the Downstroke" and "P-Funk (Wants to Get Funked Up)," the force field surrounding the One almost overwhelms the whole pattern. It seems impossible to act until the extended One has passed.

In the example of the spatial figure given by Deleuze, the process continues until the pattern has gained a certain stability. In a groove, the productive dissymmetry never brings the process to an end in the same way; it never ends up in a stage of further symmetry. Rather, the instability seems to be particularly striking in the important phase where one pattern is accomplished at the exact time another starts. In other words, exactly at the time when a distanciation is likely to occur—when a synthesis in time transforming "repetition for itself" into "repetition for us" is most likely to happen—the productive lack of symmetry seems to be particularly high. In such a groove there is no closure; rather, the circle itself is closed. There is always a "last" answer being answered by the beginning, a last question that needs to be answered by the One.

According to Deleuze, "Repetition is a condition of action before it is a concept of reflection."[42] When moving along in this closed circle, when being somehow forced as a listener to follow the groove all the way through, repetition *remains* a condition of action. The groove moves, and we move along. We are present in the groove, in a moving present, or, simply, in time experienced as presence. In such a mode every repetition is lived: it is produced and co-produced. Repetition is never allowed to be a vehicle of reflection: it remains an unfocused aspect of an ongoing movement, repeated time and again.

In order to fully understand and enjoy a funk groove, we must be able to move together with the groove in this way. Put differently, the state of being in funk is equal to the groove being experienced as a process of repetitive production. As was pointed out previously, however, the listening habitus among the Anglo-American pop and rock audiences may constrain such a process, because their inclination toward song-directed listening may inhibit them from reaching for a deep involvement in the events of the groove. Instead of giving in to the moment and concentrating on the musical events as they fold out inside the basic unit, they continue to wait for the first *actual* traces—a melody, a riff, a sequence of chords—of the common *virtual* schemes or forms within the song mode of listening. This meeting of a musical habitus influenced by the temporalities and forms of Western musical traditions and a music that ultimately requires a different approach is the subject matter of the next chapter.

9

Between Song and Groove

Groove Becoming Song

Normally, a standard pop/rock tune consists of a repetitive layer where the groove runs nonstop as well as a hierarchy of sequences that order the basic units into larger groups of four, eight, sixteen, and so on. The drums and bass usually form a basic two-bar pattern, while the guitar often plays a riff across four bars, or two basic units. The vocal may in turn be ordered across eight bars; when repeated, this comprises a verse of sixteen bars. In other words, even though the pop tune's rhythmic basis may be totally leveled out, in the sense that it is organized as a continuous repetition of a pattern of one or two bars, it nevertheless has an easily recognizable form due to the phrase-based symmetrical organization of these basic units.

When one expects that musical events will be ordered in this manner, pure grooves can be aesthetically dissatisfying. Music that is almost nothing but a groove may in fact cause a form of restlessness, because nothing happens with regard to melody and chord progressions, the musical aspects that most commonly contribute to forming this hierarchy of sequences.[1]

The P-Funk songs exemplify how this need in crossover music for a mix of song and groove can be addressed. At least in the album versions, their songs to some extent fulfill the expectations regarding form of song-oriented pop and rock audiences: they are both pop songs and riff-based grooves. Even though songs like "P-Funk (Wants to Get Funked Up)" and "We Want the Funk" appear inclined toward a participatory mode of listening through the circular effect of the heavy One as well as the structural ambivalence of their gestures (as discussed in chapter 7), they do present a hierarchy of sequences, more or less. These songs even have a verse and a chorus, although the two are very closely related.

Moreover, the central role of the four-bar melodic riffs contributes to the construction of a symmetrical phrase-based hierarchy, grouping the basic units in four, eight, sixteen, and so on. The riff of "P-Funk (Wants to Get Funked Up)," for example, lasts for four bars and may be schematized as in figure 36. As mentioned, the riffs are grouped in alternating sections of sixteen or thirty-two bars. In this regard, some P-Funk songs adapt a standard song structure, even though the shift from one section to another is marked by a change of *texture* rather than of chords. In "We Want the Funk," for example, the movement from verse to chorus is carried out by the vocals, which exchange one riff for another, as well as by the bass, which plays the riff in unison with the rest of the band instead of acting independently. Despite such subtleties, this song lends itself to the framework of a traditional pop-song structure; its phrase-based symmetrical grouping of basic units may at least to some extent fulfill the desire for a song in the traditional sense.

When a funk groove is experienced as a song, its song aspect is likely to overshadow its groove aspect—one's attention will not be on the groove *as a groove.* Due to their listening habitus, the pop and rock audiences will immediately start searching for hints of a hierarchical grouping of the song's basic units. And if they can confirm the virtual scheme of a traditional song structure, a funk song will become, first and foremost, a *song:* the "processing" of the musical events will take place at the cost of a presence in, and hence a sensibility for, the groove. Although the pleasures of the groove might still move the audience subconsciously, their primary attention will be elsewhere.

Of course, it does not need to be this way: a structure like the one found in "We Want the Funk" is not necessarily an obstacle to the groove mode. The time spans formed by the riff are not that long, and the changes from one section to another are not very dramatic; if the partaker is comfortable with the aesthetics of groove, she may, of course, still sink into the subtleties of the changing same. However, when the cultural predisposition—the virtual constraints—are pointed not toward the subtleties of the fabric of rhythm but toward the formation of patterns on levels above the basic unit, then a hierarchy of sequences may block one's process of harmonizing with the movement of the groove, because in order to achieve a presence in the groove—in order to enter its participatory mode—we must temper our fixation

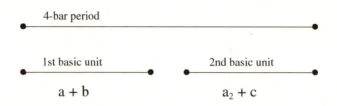

Figure 36. Schematic outline of the riff of "P-Funk (Wants to Get Funked Up)."

with linear aspects such as traditional melody, chord sequences, and hierarchical organization.

Sometimes, it is as though James Brown intervenes in the pop and rock audiences' complex, ambivalent reception of funk in order to recruit for the groove mode by way of the traditional form of a pop song—or, rather, by way of something that appears to be such a form.

The Dissolution of the Hierarchy of Sequences

Most of the funk and funk-related grooves of James Brown are simply "turned on," for example by a small shout from Brown himself. Then the groove continues until it is "turned off" again. Still, there are often clear tendencies toward groupings on the level above the basic two-bar unit. In contrast to, for example, "The Payback," many of Brown's songs are more melodically developed as well. In some of these groove-directed tunes, James Brown's lead vocal builds up an expectation of symmetry in phrase structure, then tears it down in the next breath.

"Sex Machine," for example, is marked by extraordinary manipulation with regard to its periodic structure. We are almost spun into the song's rhythmic motion by a melody pretending to be the start of a regular verse. We are tangled in an emerging linearity that then vanishes before reaching closure.

The basic unit of the song is one bar long, and the song's beginning prepares for a grouping of four plus four measures. However, instead of concluding this format in the sixteenth measure, James Brown starts from the top once more. After seven bars of what appears to be another attempt at a sixteen-bar unit, the groove's characteristic piano riff arrives. It is played twice (by Brown himself), forming a clearly ordered period of eight bars that represents a moment on firm structural ground before the song again shifts back to ambiguity. When building up to the bridge,

grouping of bars suggested by the vocal
grouping of bars suggested by the vocal "after the fact"

Figure 37. Schematic outline of form in "Sex Machine" (/ = 1 basic unit)

however, Brown's vocal suspends all inclinations toward periodic structuring. New vocal onsets break up the patterns by continuously introducing "first bars" at unexpected moments. And finally, the bridge arrives as a pure release: one is lifted to another musical level, where the stored energy floats freely on top of an open, less controlled groove.

The lack of regularity in the overall structure of the song obscures its formal identity, yet we are engaged by a form of linearity, albeit one leading nowhere. The bridge does not occur according to intramusical logic, but it is not a surprise. Due to the increased intensity, we certainly know that something is going to happen, but we do not know exactly when.

From the same time period, "Give It Up or Turnit A Loose" and "Mother Popcorn" are also characterized by this way of using the lead vocal. In the latter, James Brown even hints at a kind of verse, but as he moves into it from the introduction he disturbs any regular scheme by starting to sing in the beginning of the sixth basic unit, in measure 11. (The "standard" timing would have been represented by measure 17, or perhaps measure 13, in the case of a blues.) The pattern that was about to be established is broken down by, or rather on, one beat through this indication of a new first bar. And this turns out to be the strategy throughout Brown's series of unusual vocal onsets. The song's basic unit becomes the only safe clue for understanding its musical process; there is nothing to be gained by grouping four plus four bars because, exactly when we are about to get things in order, Brown breaks through, tearing down the structure, forcing us to start again from scratch.

This process goes on for so long that the hope for a B-section, a chorus or a bridge, ultimately fades away. We have to surrender to an almost infinite series of repetitions and accept that nothing else happens. Our attention starts wandering into the puzzle of the groove. Then the bridge arrives: we are brought out of the condition and restored to "consciousness."

After the bridge, the groove lasts three times as long, almost to ensure that the expectation for anything else really has let go. But then, when it is completely out of sight, the bridge arrives again, perhaps even more surprising this time.

Eventually, after the groove has returned from the second B section, the song starts building up to a climax with the "reintroduction" of the soloing saxophone (in keeping with the structure of a standard song, the main solo is likely to appear before the second B section.) In many other musical contexts, this would indicate the traditional conclusive culmination, where the dynamic curve is expected to move in

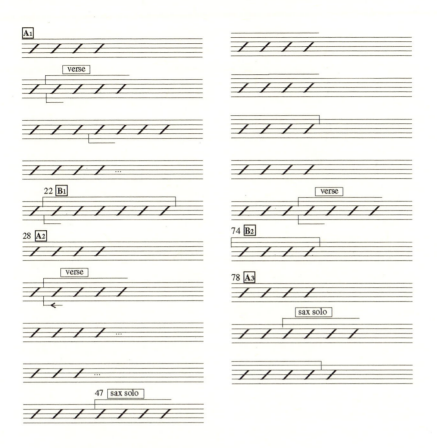

Figure 38. Schematic outline of form in "Mother Popcorn" (/ = one basic unit)

one direction: up and out! Just as we come to expect this final blowout after minutes bursting with sameness, the song ends, as if Brown decides to cancel the whole operation with a snap of his fingers.

Song Becoming Groove

As we discussed previously, African American culture seems to be double-voiced at heart.[2] African American popular music, thus, often speaks with tongue in cheek. Perhaps the funk grooves of James Brown also had to communicate on several levels, passing both as pop songs and as grooves. On the one hand, a tune had to stand up for inspection in a groove-directed mode of listening: it ought to survive the confrontation with a sensitive, groove-confident perceiver in a mode of absorbed participation. On the other hand, it had to answer to the demands of the more song-directed, pop mode of listening (and the demands of the Western music industry). This required a striking melody, a catchy chorus, and a well-adjusted, effective form.

Many of Brown's songs negotiate this span between a song mode (of listening) and a groove mode (of participating). In line with this, funk can be simplistically defined as a hybrid of black and white. This does not mean that funk has a black part belonging solely to a black musical culture and vice versa. The point is rather that funk is nourished by two different traditions and relates to two different groups of listeners.

However, in reality this reception situation is much more complicated. Funk's ambiguity is not only present on the side of reception, in the sense that one group of listeners connects with the groove and another with the catchy riff (or, for that matter, the extraordinarily hip attitude). The span between the two approaches to the music—the mode of listening directed toward melody, chords, and a hierarchy of sequences on the one hand, and the desire for presence in the "eternal" motion of the groove on the other—can also be present in one and the same person, who might, for example, experience the song when listening and the groove when dancing. In fact, these two approaches can be present in the same *act* of listening-participating. On the one hand, the *lack* of form in the traditional Western sense, as in a pure repetitive groove, prevents participation. The listener gets bored; repetition comes to the fore as repetition. On the other hand, if there is form in this sense, the preference for so-called "linear" listening will be triggered. The listener becomes engaged in the groove, but not primarily as a groove. In other words, when a certain form is the virtual norm, a lack of sensibility for the groove seems to be the final result either way.

It is exactly in this regard that "Sex Machine" has some extraordinary capacities. It plays on a possible inclination to linear listening, which, when triggered, might be explored for quite different agendas. It engages the "body" by way of processual deviations and ambiguous phrasing. It engages the "head" in the sense that the restless pop and rock audiences who might perceive the easily graspable pattern with a poor resolution is swirled into the song's motion by the many suggestions of a phrase-based form.

In a song like "Sex Machine" this quasi-form is used to engage the potential partaker who might not be able to engage in the groove by herself. The syntactical constraints of the melody, those that commonly serve a grouping function, now prevent us from considering the fact that the song's motion leads nowhere. The funk song is not experienced as having the traditional form of a song; however, it is not experienced as *not* having such a form either, even though this is nearer to the truth. By playing up the traditional syntactic function of melody while subordinating it to the actual primary syntactic aspect of this song— rhythm—the issue of form never arises. Even partakers expecting a "song" as such fail to ask the question. We just never start wondering why this song never becomes a "song."

In this way, James Brown not only manages to entice pop and rock audiences into the groove but also realizes the groove as a groove, in the sense that a hierarchical-symmetrical grouping is never allowed to overrule the experience of the groove. Brown intervenes in the potential formal scheme to deny his own tentative division of the musical course. As a consequence, there are no points of closure in this song; we are continuously on the move. It is thus able to engage with an audience whose cultural preferences require both groove and song, in a way that is likely to transform the song into a groove experience, thereby dissolving its "lack" of form in time.

To repeat myself (with a difference), a funk song will not offer a funk experience until its groove is experienced as a groove. The song is in this respect secondary, and the fact that many funk songs are not songs in the traditional sense may simply be because groove rules the form. Some songs seem to prepare for this in a particular way, using form to overrule the expectations inherent in the dominating mode of listening within the Western pop and rock audiences, making the song into the desired negation of form. However, what about when there are actually no song traits whatsoever? It is now time for "The Payback."

The Pure Groove

In James Brown's "The Payback" (1974), there are no hints of a song structure in the traditional sense. We do not even find a play with form, either from a blues sequence or a hierarchy of sequences; the musical aspects that create large-scale time spans in music are completely diminished. The harmonic course of the tune is hardly a course at all: the key note never changes, and overlaying it is a riff based on a B-flat minor seventh scale. It is the same chord all the way through, although it is somewhat differently colored. Moreover, the tune has no melody in a traditional sense. Indeed, it is quite impossible to reproduce the tune by singing it, and James Brown's lead vocal consists of various shouted short exclamatory phrases such as "I'm a man!" "Gotta deal with you!" "The brother get ready!" and so on. All in all, the vocals seem to lack any regular periodic structure and provide nothing that might be used in order to identify periods on levels above the basic unit.

After a few bars within the world of "redundant" harmony and a vocal part that never seems to make any attempt to establish a larger phrase structure, one either gets bored or changes one's expectations from progression to stasis. The lack of chord progressions and melody soon becomes a virtual fact, a normal condition, and we can focus instead on the level where details step forward and become significant, processing the music with high resolution in real time. There is no need to store information about what has been performed in order to understand what might follow, in order to grasp a larger formal structure. The song's entire formal capacity might be explored within a short period of time. In this way, the acts of listening, dancing, or even producing the groove are directed toward the core of the song—that is, toward the levels of the groove where things are supposed to be taking place.

Even though "The Payback" is close to a pure groove, it is not without form. The tune takes some time to build up energy to a suitable level for the main groove to start, but as soon as this interplay between the support drums, the unvaried rhythmic foundation, and "master drummer" James Brown is established, we get the feeling of a groove that could go on forever.

However, before arriving there, we must be recruited for the groove. In a song like "The Payback," the process of whirling the listener into the musical course, building up energy, putting the potential partakers in motion, has to be taken seriously. When the main groove starts, we must be prepared to enter it. If we do not, the whole event may collapse.

Consecration, Cut, and a New Beginning

The musical form of "The Payback" resembles the most common form of live funk groove, including among more traditional funk songs. In a live setting, the groove aspect is likely to be strongly emphasized at the expense of any traditional song structure, precisely in order to achieve the presence in the groove that is sought after at such an occasion. However, the appearance of this form on the A side of a 1970s single is, to say the least, more surprising. When a pure groove is realized within this frame-work, there has to be some negotiation between the format—which typi-cally required an immediate appeal and a limited duration—and the spe-cific rules of the groove. There is no time for building up energy or for the groove to appear infinite: the "consecration" has to be quickly effected. Furthermore, the groove, as discussed in the previous chapter, has to be integrated with a formal scheme that is ideally both asserted and tran-scended at the same time, and in a surprising and enticing way. Last but not least, the end has to arrive before the energy has actually dissipated.

The latter is most commonly solved by a fade, while the beginning often has the form of a hook, as with the characteristic powerful shout James Brown makes in "I Got You (I Feel Good)," the sustained chord of "Papa's Got a Brand New Bag," the little "Hit it!" in "Doing It to Death," or the forceful strokes performed in unison by the horns and the band in "Sex Machine" (following the well-known, energetic shout-ing of James Brown). The songs may also start with a few waves of the groove as a short intro, as in "Cold Sweat" and "Soul Power," or by Brown simply counting up the band, as in "Funky Drummer." Such be-ginnings grab our attention and prepare the ground for the "real" song. In other words, "The Payback" is in more than one respect a rather spe-cial case in the impressive series of successful Brown singles, and it is also a quite uncommon solution for its time. It lasts for more than seven minutes, its intro is extremely long, and the end is not a fade.

As mentioned, "The Payback" may be said to explore the dramaturgy of a live setting in miniature, and as such it displays several typical fea-tures.[3] The consecration is carried out by a long introductory gesture, in-troducing the participant to the "community" of musicking: we are lifted up to the level of the groove and readied to enter its motion. The eight-unit intro (each unit equals two measures of 4/4) expands heavily at the end—more and more voices are piled on top of one other, while the am-plitude of the vibrato increases. The whole gesture suddenly closes in on the first beat of the main groove as the first downbeat in anticipation.

This transition from the introductory gesture to the main groove is one opportunity for the groove to end something without achieving the effect of closure; it is called *the cut*. Traditionally, the cut refers to the point in the musical course where one or more tracks or layers are taken out of the groove so that the remaining voices receive more attention.

Figure 39. The drum pattern of "Funky Drummer."

However, in line with the dialogical logic described by Chernoff,[4] our attention goes in the opposite direction as well. Not only does a certain voice achieve renewed attention when other voices are cut around it, but a voice may also acquire attention as it is itself cut.

This happens, for instance, in James Brown's "Funky Drummer"; the drums go on their own for eight measures (at approximately 5:50) while Brown appreciates them through repeating the outburst "Ain't it funky!" The immediate effect of the cut is clearly that one becomes aware of the layers of bass, Hammond organ, guitar, and horns that had previously accompanied the "funky drummer"; we hear the dimensions that are gone; gaps are exposed. At the same time, our attention shifts to the extraordinarily tickling drumming by Clyde Stubblefield, and a groove that, when running alone, seems to be both less and more complicated than when it was played together with the rest of the band (see fig. 39). On the level of figure, it is more straightforward and open than we might expect. On the level of gesture, however, the drum playing is more intricate than may be perceived when it is only part of the sound of a full band. Both the strokes belonging to the basic pattern and the more ornamental strokes are extremely well placed and most often marginally ahead of themselves.[5]

The beginning of the classic break beat in rap is also an instance of the cut: it is a *break* where several voices—especially those that have previously attracted the most attention—are cut in order to let the *beat*, comprised of some of the distinct rhythmic layers of the repeated basic unit, continue on its own for a while. In a rap context, the break beat brings the underlying layers of rhythm into focus, because the rap itself attracts the attention otherwise. Besides, there are also often elements in the sound of a more traditional musical-thematic character. Due to this, in her book on African American rap music Tricia Rose describes the break beat as follows: "The thematic elements of a musical piece are suspended and the underlying rhythms brought center stage."[6]

In a rap production, a break beat is usually a particularly striking or challenging rhythmic passage from another record. It can be based on a "historical" break of longer or shorter duration: it may be a manual or an electronic extension of "the best part of a great record."[7] One may sample the whole basic unit of a groove, for example from a song like "Funky Drummer," or a shorter break, such as the ones that are interjected into the main groove of "The Payback," which is then made into a loop. In case of the latter, the break will almost be realized "to the second power": the break is made into a subject for repetition, and not only in the sense that it has occurred earlier in another musical time. What was a break in a former musical continuity is looped into a duration that then acts as a break in the new context; or, in the words of Rose, "Rap music relies on the loop, on the circularity of rhythm and on the 'cut' or the break beat that systematically ruptures equilibrium. Yet, in rap, the 'break beat' itself is looped—repositioned as repetition, as equilibrium inside the rupture. Rap music highlights points of rupture as it equalizes them."[8]

The cut is not really similar to the break or to the break beats of rap; it simply refers to the kind of break where something is cut, momentarily, while something else is continued. It works as a new beginning, and it implies an abrupt drop in dynamic level and often a more open texture as well. The transition from the intro to the main groove in "The Payback" is typical. Here the new groove is cut into the rising introductory gesture. The beat starting with the cut is, however, not an interlude but the main groove, and the dynamic effect is *forte piano*. Instead of moving right into the cut, the song prepares for the cut by building up energy, then dispelling it, as in the break beat. In "The Payback" this transfer takes place after a previous increase in energy, while in a break beat the cut indicates a lowering of energy from a previously stable level.

In James Snead's discussion of the cut, both of these variations are mentioned, as well as several others. However, first of all he places the cut within a repetitive, circular setting: "In black culture, the thing (the ritual, the dance, the beat) is 'there for you to pick up when you come back to get it.' If there is a goal (Zweck) in such a culture, it is always deferred; it continually 'cuts' back to the start, in the musical meaning of 'cut' as an abrupt, seemingly unmotivated break (an accidental da capo) with a series already in progress and a willed return to a prior series."[9] Snead gives many examples from music and literature. In James Brown's funk, the cut is the return to the groove after a bridge. In John Coltrane's jazz improvisation, the cut is "the unexpectedness with which the soloist will depart from the 'head' or theme and from its normal harmonic sequence or the drummer from the tune's accepted and familiar primary beat."[10] In the field of literature, Snead points to Ishmael Reed's *Mumbo Jumbo:* "Reed, in the manner of the jazz soloist, cuts frequently between the various subtexts in his novel (headlines, photographs, handwritten letters, italicized writing, advertisements) and the text of his main narrative."[11] At first glance, Snead's account seems to include so many different gestures that "the cut" comes to mean almost anything. Through closer inspection, however, a pattern emerges. Common to all his examples is a fractural transfer from one level to another, from one thing to something else (and, one may add, the latter is never equal to nothing).

The fractural character of the end of the intro and the fractural transfer to the new beginning at a lower level of intensity are the most striking features of the first break in "The Payback," where the intro culminates and the main groove begins. By means of the cut, our focus is redirected toward the main groove, and this is done *without* triggering the expectations of a sequential hierarchical form, because the intro is never ended but is instead cut midstream and replaced by a new beginning.

Continuity and Breaks

As mentioned already, as soon as the main groove of "The Payback" is running, we have the feeling that it might go on forever. Even though James Brown's vocal interference sometimes may be misinterpreted as the beginning or ending of a four-bar period—misinterpreted because it almost never matches the actual circumstances—the musical course gives no clues to an overall form of sequences.

This "eternal" continuity is, from time to time, interrupted by breaks. But while the first break in the musical course of "The Payback" is a typical cut, the many later breaks have a different character. They do not advance the ongoing events or direct focus from one level to another. They merely halt the ongoing movement for a little while, in the form of a short trembling, before moving on again at the same level. And even though they are critical points in the course of the tune, they are not "dramatic"—there is no preceding increase in tension or subsequent change in the fabric of rhythm. They are, in short, neither changes nor transitions. After every little "shock" we return to the same, to the continuous stream of musical gestures. The breaks are suddenly just there, as a contrast to continuity.

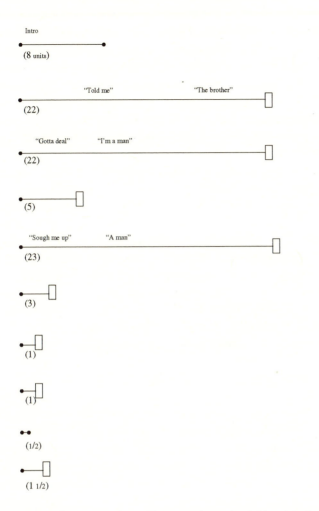

Intro

(8 units)

"Told me"   "The brother"

(22)

"Gotta deal"   "I'm a man"

(22)

(5)

"Sough me up"   "A man"

(23)

(3)

(1)

(1)

(1/2)

(1 1/2)

Figure 40. Schematic outline of form in "The Payback," break indicated by ☐

However, *when* these breaks occur is probably not accidental. In order to avoid an experiencing of the breaks as something more than pure breaks, they are positioned at places other than the expected ones. They are almost anti-prepared. After the intro, which lasts for eight basic units, it takes twenty-two (not twenty-four!) units before the first break arrives.

On two occasions during this period, James Brown might give us the impression that he starts on a new sequence—namely on the beginning of the eighth (not the ninth) unit after the main groove has started, and three units before the first break. However, these tendencies in the direction of an emerging periodicization are soon denied by other vocal events.

The break itself is designed in such a way that under normal circumstances it would have been placed at the beginning of a sequence of two units or of multiples of two. However, the break does not happen when we expect it to; instead, it shows up at the beginning of the fourth unit after Brown's last quasi-beginning. To the extent that we can anticipate what is going to happen due to this clue, the break then occurs either one unit too early or one too late.

The timing of the breaks in the tune as a whole is of utmost importance to the maintenance of the groove mode: the breaks must be placed in such a way that they do not imply a grouping of the basic units. This is especially important in the context of an Anglo-American pop/rock reception; in order to encourage a groove mode of listening, the conventional pop formats, with their traditional hierarchy of sequences, have to be out of focus. In "The Payback" there are no allusions to such standard schemes: the breaks—which certainly are points where a traditional song could begin to take form—are placed across a natural division into larger sections of four or eight basic units, making the possible groupings impossible.

This is also the case with the second break, which occurs after another period of twenty-two units. However, by this time one has no feeling of these two first periods being of the same length. First of all, this is because there have been so many repetitions of the basic unit without a grouping of the units. Also, at some points during this second series there are singular utterances from Brown that might be heard as the beginnings of something. However, these do not equal any pattern. Moreover, they are in positions other than the quasi-beginnings during the stretch before the first break. Also, this time the most pronounced instance is some units before the break, but now it is not three but four units after James Brown shouts "I'm a man!" before the break occurs. Seen this way, the arrival of the break is both right and wrong: it is wrong according to the previous break but perhaps more right according to the design of the break itself.

This time the break takes up only half of a unit, although this might in fact be a quite misleading statement, since the break is an entire entity in itself, a completely completed figure. The length of the break is, however, one half of the length of the basic unit, and not a whole unit as last time, and this is probably the "correct" version—at least this is how the breaks are later on in the tune. Moreover, the first break sounds rather weak. Interestingly, the break is never "completed," either by a pause or a supplement in the form of the second half of the basic unit. Due to this, among other things, the break does not work as part of a potential symmetrical form. Rather than forming the first half of the first unit of another section or sequence, the break is interjected into a series of basic units as a rupture.

As important as the breaks themselves is what happens *between* the breaks. In his interpretation of African Takai music, which is also based on the repetition of short, relatively simple units, Chernoff directs our attention to this aspect:

> It is the duration of time that a drummer plays a particular rhythm, *the amount of repetition and the way rhythms change*, to which the drummers pay attention, and not so much any particular rhythmic invention. The aesthetic decision which constitutes excellence will be the *timing* of the change and the choice of a new pattern . . . The way a drummer changes, above all, is to be prized for a kind of *smoothness and fluidity*, for the music must both move forward and be steady in order to be interesting and danceable.[12]

As Chernoff points out, rhythmic innovations in themselves are not the main concern within this form; what matters is the continual flow between the breaks, as well as when the breaks occur. One can still change the music, if the change is done smoothly—that is to say, if the music is changed without changing the music. Or, alternatively, one could change everything at once.

In the case of the former, the change has to be so discreetly conducted as to be hardly perceptible; as Chernoff notes, "Those drummers considered to be the best . . . take their time."[13] In "The Payback," the response guitar is changed in this way; the funky wah-wah riff is allowed to get bigger and looser, occupying both more space and more time. This "optimizing of the same" links one basic unit more tightly to the next, and the groove becomes more of a closed circle. Its gestures gradually become less distinctly outlined, and the response riff starts to spread out on the first beats of the next unit. The ambivalence of the response riff is, in other words, allowed to work longer, influencing as well the first part of the basic unit, which had been dominated by the slightly too straightforward figure of four against three (at least when considered in isolation). All in all, it brings to the whole some unarticulated depth, a little extra "stickiness."

According to Chernoff, the arrangements of James Brown are especially pleasing to an African ear due to their stability and the way they are open to new voices. The tunes of James Brown employing a more traditional song structure and different sections are also appreciated, since the changes from A to B are of the second kind discussed above; they do not happen gradually, but rather "all the instruments change together and then return to their former relationship."[14] In Chernoff's African context, James Brown is praised due to his ability to time these changes extremely well. At the core of this challenge is the relation between continuity and breaks, where the play with relative duration is of great importance. In "The Payback" it is obvious that the long gets longer in relation to the short, and vice versa.[15] After the second break, which arrives after the second long series of twenty-two units, there follows a somewhat surprising short series of five (not four!) units. When the next and third long series is played, which is almost as long as the previous ones (twenty-three as opposed to twenty-two units, but still not twenty-four!), *it feels much longer*. And then, when the really short arrives after this third (prolonged) long series, it feels even shorter. After another three units comes the fourth break, which thereby breaks down a potential pattern consisting of two long series, one short series, and then two long series. Immediately after—that is, one unit later—there is another break, and then, after one more single unit, yet another one. The end is near, the energy is about to ebb away, and the whole thing is probably going to be quieted down.

However, after the last break and the following half unit, where bass and guitar leave the sound box and the drums alone accompany Brown, the rest of the band suddenly gets back into the song. It might seem that the frequent breaks were only an interlude and that this cluster of breaks indicates a form on a higher, as yet unacknowledged level. However, halfway through the second unit, after the band has been playing together for some time, the tune is suddenly turned off by a short, scant stroke on the snare drum, straight on the first beat of the basic unit's second bar.[16]

Groove vs. Nonsong

As in "Sex Machine," rhythm is the primary formative aspect of "The Payback" on a larger scale. However, while "Sex Machine" may be more adapted to serve the conflicting demands present in the ambivalent pop/rock attitude toward funk, "The Payback" is more unequivocally situated within a repetitive, groove-based aesthetic framework. While the groove of "Sex Machine" is played out between the formal requirements of groove and song, the groove of "The Payback" seems to govern the tune's form right away. In short, this tune displays many of the formal characteristics typical of groove based music, such as open-ended repetitive form, the cut, and breaks that work to increase intensity but not to mark hierarchical sequential form. Put differently, "The Payback" relies completely on a groove heard as groove, on the listener being transformed into a partaker in a groove experience. There are no points of closure and no formal divisions above the level of the basic unit. The groove does not even attempt to appear as form in this sense: there is no "quasi-song," nor are there any longer melodic phrases. Rather, the groove is cultivated as its own form.

As such, "The Payback" clearly displays the connection between repetition and depth.[17] Given the premise that the groove works well, and that we are ready to give ourselves up to it, repetition is likely to contribute to the process of focusing on performance in real time by directing our attention toward the unfolding of the unit that is repeated. The focus becomes the shaping of this basic rhythmic cell, because when the repetitive structure is allowed to work as a groove in this way, the participant's attention seems to stay within the time span of the groove's basic unit.[18] A potential tendency toward organizing the musical progression into an overall form gradually fades away. The focus turns inward, as if a sensibility for details, for timing inflections and tiny timbral nuances, is inversely proportional to variation on a larger scale. The senses process information with an even better resolution in time.

And even though this absorbed condition of getting deeper and deeper into the groove is interrupted by breaks, they do not create a form in a traditional sense: the breaks do not have the effect of (re)directing attention toward larger time spans in the musical course of events. They do not work as closures.

Contrary to the repetition caused by mechanical reproduction— which, as mentioned earlier, has probably been the model for cultural-critical discussions of the repetitive aspect of repetitive music (see also chapter 8)—the interesting aspect of repetition from this perspective is that it allows for perfection, or variation, or just absorption in "the same." As Chernoff says with regard to African drumming, "A drummer uses repetition to reveal the depth of the musical structure."[19]

Repetition indeed gives depth; the rhythmic pattern may be sharpened through the "subtle perfection of a strictly respected form."[20]

In other words, the relation between the pure form of a groove, with its repetitive structure and cuts and breaks, and funk's main musical "challenge," namely the subtle perfection of the basic two-bar pattern, is not accidental. However, this also means that, as a musical form, the pure groove hides no weaknesses. When all attention is on the groove and almost nothing else is happening, even small mistakes become distinct. The pattern has to be kept steady and relaxed all the way through, and this requires quite extraordinary musical skills.

Just how important this is for the final outcome is only obvious when the musicians do *not* manage to maintain steady time all the way through, or when the gestures run cold. In "The Payback," for instance, there are tiny variations as to the overall feel of the groove. In some periods, the musicians seem to struggle a little to arrive at a perfectly right and relaxed agreement among the different rhythmic layers. In the introductory phase, for example, everything feels a little uptight; the gestures proceed—almost in a literal sense—according to scheme. Then the different parts begin to find their place within the whole, and the groove really starts to settle after the first break (at 2:40). After four minutes things are absolutely right, but rather soon (approximately 4:20) the groove gets a little stiff again, as if somebody started to think things over too much. Following this, there is a period where the energy and presence are slightly diminished before the band once again becomes focused. From approximately 5:30 onward, the groove sounds better than ever. The gestures interlock in a flexible, dynamic, and relaxed manner, and the groove settles, running almost by itself.

A groove may, in other words, reflect a continuous reworking of an optimal solution. Moreover, as a musical form the groove seems to arrange its events in such a way as to *expose* this process, and in case of the pure groove, the neutralization of the other musical dimensions makes it almost impossible to escape it. As a consequence, the quality of the rhythmic "mattress" of those strata that most pop and rock songs use as an unattended but nevertheless important foundation for other musical aspects—melody, chords, and so on—becomes precarious.[21] There is nothing to hide behind. Even the ambivalent, restless pop/rock listener is forced to focus on the groove. "The Payback" is not a groove in disguise, like "Sex Machine," which may be able to get the pop/rock listener to swallow the bait by way of a phraselike quasi-song. It does not "mimic" the structure of verse and chorus, as in the studio versions of the P-Funk grooves. Nor is it a more or less plain combination of song and groove, as in much crossover funk.[22] Even the voice is mainly serving the groove, due to its fragmentary, fill-like character. So, while "Sex Machine" might be able to keep questions regarding form at a distance, "The Payback" is rather outspoken in defying them: it is a pure groove that does not relate to the conventional universe of song-directed listening.[23] After the lengthy introductory gesture, all that remains is whether one is ready to enter time, taking interest in the small movements of the groove, or not.

This is, however, not necessarily likely to happen. As was pointed out previously, the focus on goal-directedness and developmental forms within white Western musical traditions also expresses its dominant listening strategy. Not only can the music be said to be of a teleological kind, but even the listening to it is in a certain way teleological: one expects that something will happen, certainly regarding the aspects most often involved in shaping such large-scale time spans, namely melody, harmony, and musical form. In the field of Anglo-American pop and rock in the 1970s the traces of this notion of what music is and should be, which have occupied primary positions within the Western music-cultural field, existed as an interest in songs understood as melody, chords, and form rather than grooves. When a funk tune like "The Payback" encounters such a listening habitus, the incongruity between the mode of production and the mode of reception may hinder the engagement in the groove, because there is simply nothing else to the tune. Instead of becoming a groove experience, "The Payback" may end up as a nonsong, as a denial of the expectations inherent in the dominant habitus of listening of the mainstream pop and rock audiences.

In light of my previous discussions of the relations among different musical temporalities and the funk experience, therefore, it is not especially surprising that the funk of the crossover era adapted to the traditional pop/rock format. Together with the changes in sound and content of its lyrics and so on, this structural change most clearly points up the subsequent changes in cultural orientation and economic influence that characterize this period in black musicking. The new cultural situation encouraged musical forms that met with the requirements of the song mode of listening but also offered a groove experience to the wealthy white mainstream pop and rock audiences in the middle of discovering the thrills of black dance music. In what follows, I will approach the funk experience from within, and in the last chapter I will to turn to the question of why this experience was so important.

10

Feeling, Intensity, and the Sublimity of the Event

When one is in a funk groove, the experience of time is—somewhat paradoxically—not really an experience of time. There is no distancing from the musical events: one is continuously engaged in the co-production of gestures; there is a total presence in the groove. Time dissolves. Repetition never becomes repetitive. The distancing required for time and repetition to become time and repetition for us does not take place.

Strictly speaking, it is impossible to explain such a state of being in funk, to explain what being in time is like before one becomes aware of the fact that one is in time. In the very moment one starts considering funk in this way, one's state of being is changed. In other words, to place oneself in time, distancing is required; one's experience must be placed in relation to something else, to *other* events or *other* places. We may also view this in reverse: there is no state of being in funk before it is understood and labeled as such. Viewed this way, the potential, as well as unavoidable, distancing from the state of being in funk is constitutive of the state itself.

In this chapter, I will subject the funk groove experience to more general aesthetic and epistemological reflection. I take the funk experience for granted and presume that the enduring groove causes no frustration in the listener, positing for convenience that the state of being in funk is a totally stable condition.[1] My primary concern is not to discuss how we arrived there, or what aspects—in the music or in a culture—may support or threaten this state of being in funk. The whole discussion of contextual factors is hereby suspended.

My discussion will be informed by theoretical contributions from different sources. First, I will situate the state of being in funk within a more general hermeneutic discourse, applying Paul Ricœur's account of discourse as a dialectic of event and meaning on the case of being in funk. Second, I will explore this state of being in a groove for a long time with regard to the Deleuzian notion of intensity, as well as from the point of view of Jean Francois Lyotard's reinterpretation of the aesthetics of the sublime.

Before delving further into this musical event as such, however, I will give a brief account of the dramaturgy of the occasion that is most likely to encourage full participation, that is most likely to transform funk into a groove experience, or, as will be a main focus in this chapter, into pure event: the live concert. Within such a context, the problems of reaching a point of full participation discussed in the preceding chapters may be absent or, at least, less present. Within such a context, even a pop/rock-confident audience will probably work together with the groove in order to reach a point where the motion is carried on almost by itself, without thought for any other option.

Funk (A)live

There are situations where the restless Western pop/rock-confident listener—who normally expects a certain musical form and tends to hear a lack of song when there is nothing but a groove—seems to be especially open to a groove experience. On a modern dance floor or in a live music setting, even a rather reluctant song-directed participant is probably "set" to enter the state of being in funk. When taking part in what is probably better described as an assembly or a party, the situation demands that one surrender to the event: the conditions are right, in other words, for experiencing the literally drawn-out consequences of a pure groove and its predisposition toward infinite duration.

In these cases, extended versions of tunes are the norm, and the musical event as a whole is expected to take its time. The "consecration phase" may last for a long time, and the groove does not end before reaching its own end—that is, before reaching a point where the energy is on the decline, inducing a self-regulating winding down. The situation may actually act to suspend the whole question of form; in the words of Christopher Small, "A performance may go on for several hours or all night, and will have no formal beginning or end; rather it will take some time to gather momentum and probably just fizzle out at the end when the musicians run out of energy or enthusiasm. There is no limit time set."[2] A typical P-Funk event starts, gains a certain momentum, and then carries on until the occasion is exhausted. For example, in the previously discussed live recording of P-Funk All-Stars from the Beverly Hills Theater in Hollywood, the introduction of the band lasts for more than thirteen minutes. When the groove is moving, the experience of time is extraordinary, in that there is no experience of time; it dissolves, and, as I discussed in chapter 8, although this condition is often described as being *outside* of time and space, the opposite is rather the case. One is totally present *in* time and *in* space. Master drummer George Clinton does not disturb this situation, often allowing the groove to run nonstop for several hours. Even when there is a change of "song," the groove as a whole is not interrupted. The passing of time is not noticed until the end, until we are taken down, or out of time, slowly but steadily returning to another time.

In contrast, James Brown tends to manipulate the audience through his intervention. The opening of his concerts is characteristic: the band and MC Danny Ray warm up the audience well in advance of the principal character appearing on the stage. In the live version of "It's a New Day" from the third *Live at the Apollo* recording (1971),[3] we are connected to the musical course a little after the show has started, but before this, the MC, by means of horn bleats and drum rolls, has brought the audience up to and beyond the level of the main groove.

Brown enters the stage at the moment when this introductory gesture culminates with two turns of a rather energetic, up-tempo, showy r&b groove, à la the Blues Brothers, with a heavy backbeat. "Mr. Dynamite" is not only surfing atop a shouting audience but fronting a very concentrated musical energy. With such a starting point, one can carry straight on: for an audience now paced physically faster than the groove itself, the main groove is experienced as a slowing down. The groove opens up, inviting the audience to participate. From here onward, the whole event is more a question of bringing us up and down, back and forth, according to the different moods and levels of energy required by the material. (Of course, this is also about sustaining the fundamental premises of the whole event: time has to be steady; the transparency of the technical skills must remain undisturbed; the figures of the groove must be right and rightly performed, and so on.)

Within such a context, once the audience is overwhelmed by the groove it guides itself toward the condition of moving together with the groove, toward the pleasure of experiencing the groove as a presence in time.

The Imploding Event

When one is in the ideal state of being in funk, there is no distance to the event at all—there is instead total presence in the groove.[4] However, within the Western philosophical tradition, this presence is not understood as presence, because when one is in the mode of being, understanding is absent.

In his lecture "The Hermeneutical Function of Distanciation," Ricœur works out this topic with regard to discourse, proposing to understand discourse as a *dialectic* between performing and understanding, or, in his words, event and meaning. According to Ricœur, to say that discourse is an event is to say several things at the same time. Discourse is realized temporally and in the present: it "has time," as Ricœur says. Furthermore, it is characterized by the fact that someone is speaking: it has subjectivity. Finally, the speaking takes place and refers to a world: it includes others.[5]

The other pole of the dialectic is equally important to the constitution of discourse: namely, meaning. And in line with the hermeneutic tradition that began with Heidegger, Ricœur situates distanciation *within* being-in-the world:

> In *Being and Time*, the theory of understanding is not tied to the understanding of others, but becomes a structure of being-in-the-world. More precisely, it is a structure that is examined after the structure of *Befindlichkeit*, state-of-mind. The moment of understanding responds dialectically to being-in-a-situation, as the projection of our own-most possibilities in those situations where we find ourselves.[6]

Ricœur 's notion of meaning is tied to the unavoidable distanciation that is a part of discourse itself, and the very first distanciation is, as Ricœur writes, "The distanciation of the saying in the said."[7] But what is said? Ricœur opens up the notion of meaning way beyond the more common use of meaning as *Bedeutung*. The notion of meaning is left very available in a positive sense, here implying all of the aspects and levels of exteriorization that make the inscription of an event possible. Inscription is unavoidable, but it may take place on different levels.

With the speech act theory of Austin and Searle as a starting point, Ricœur analyzes discourse as potentially activating three levels of meaning. The first level is the *locutionary* act, or the propositional meaning, in the sense of "what is said." The locutionary act exteriorizes itself in the sentence, which can be identified and re-identified as having the same meaning, as being the same utterance (*Aus-sage*)—for example, "Close the door!" The second level is the *illocutionary* act or force, "that which we do in saying," or rather, *how* something is said (is it an order or a wish?). The third level, the *perlocutionary* act, is located in and with the very act of uttering; it is the fact *that* something is being said. Perlocutionary action is discourse as stimulus, and it produces certain effects—for example, fear (in the case of a command): "It acts, not by my interlocutor's recognition of my intention, but sort of energetically, by direct influence upon the emotions and the affective dispositions."[8]

Even in those cases where meaning is present solely on the level of perlocutionary action, even though the meaning is no more than a "that something was," the event does not escape distanciation. The event will always be turned into some form of inscription.

Following Ricœur, one might say that the state of being in funk is also actualized as event and understood as meaning. There is always a dialectical response to the being-in-the-situation. What this immediate meaning amounts to in the case of funk will be further explored toward the end of this chapter. So far, I shall only argue that even though funk requires a total presence in the event, a shift to meaning is unavoidable. Sooner or later the event will go beyond itself into meaning. Actually, the very naming of the event is by itself a shift to meaning; it is always-already after the fact or after the event.

The paradoxical relationship of the floating temporal experience and its identifiable meaning, referred to by Ricœur as the dialectic of event and meaning, is a fundamental condition of being in general. What Ricœur points out regarding discourse might also be pointed out about music: all music is actualized as event and understood as meaning. The relationship among the three levels of meaning may, however, differ considerably from the meaning of discourse. The hierarchy should probably be turned upside down: due to the lack of ability to produce a traditional referential meaning, the locutionary act is relatively unimportant. The illocutionary level, "that which we do in saying," is, however, very important. Ultimately, though, the perlocutionary action, "that which we say by saying,"—the way music "can stir up certain effects," to paraphrase Ricœur, and have a "direct influence upon the emotions and the affective dispositions"—is probably the bottom line in many cases.

Regarding the dialectic of event and meaning in the case of funk, one might say that the state of being in funk is characterized by an intensification of the event as event: the state of meaning is never allowed to arrive; it is instead postponed or set aside. It is put out of play by the play, so to speak, of the music. Instead of responding dialectically to being-in-a-situation with a moment of understanding, we find ourselves absorbed in a delay of meaning. The presence in the event defers the presence of meaning. In this way, the intensifying of the event may be explained as a reversal of the delay caused by the circulation of signs. The intensifying is a delay in the opposite direction: what is deferred is the very entrance into the circulation of signs.[9]

This "implosion" in the event defers the transition to the very moment of understanding, where meaning is allowed to sum up the happenings, for example, by naming the event an event. The shift to meaning is completely out of sight. One is in the event as if there were never anything else, perhaps to such an extent that one even after the fact is likely to deny that a shift to meaning ever took place.

I Feel Good!—The Feeling of Feeling

It is time to move from hermeneutic to aesthetic considerations: what, or rather *how*, is this particular imploding event in terms of aesthetic experience? What is funk about when we are there, in the groove, in the state of being in funk?

It is probably no coincidence that the few words in James Brown's funk that have a meaning—"I Feel Good," "Cold Sweat," "I Got the Feeling," "I Am Superbad," "Get Up," "(I Feel Like Being a) Sex Machine," "Get on the Good Foot," and so on—deal with feeling. This has been interpreted as some kind of self-centered hedonism, and perhaps rightfully so. However, these utterances may also be understood as being about funk's own aesthetic standard: the feel.

Feeling is no doubt a key aesthetic notion in this kind of music, because funk without feel is not funk. In this musical context, feeling has nothing to do with an extrovert style of performance or with expressing actual innermost feelings. It is about cultivating the right swaying motion; about accurate timing; about being in place, in time; about precision and relaxation at once. Playing all the correct figures means nothing unless it is carried through in the right way. If this is not achieved, the whole "body and soul" of funk immediately collapses. The only indication as to when it is right—whether one is dancing or playing—is a feeling, and not just any feeling: funk is about the "right" feeling.

In some respects, this right feeling recalls Kant's analysis of aesthetic judgment, or what he calls "the satisfaction in the beautiful." The notion of the beautiful might be somewhat misleading in this context, but Kant's description of the act of judging as dwelling in a condition of "purposiveness without purpose" is nevertheless relevant. The right feeling is also characterized by an indeterminacy according to *what*, but at the same time a certain determinacy according to *how*.

Kant's aesthetic judgment relies on sensation, because the pleasure at stake can only make itself known this way. In Lyotard's interpretation of Kant's analytic of the sublime, he points out how sensation is fundamentally self-referential—it is at once a state of being and the sign of this state of being. Lyotard works this out with regard to the role sensation plays in informing thought of its state: "Thought only judges according to its state, judging what it finds pleasurable. Thus this state, which is the 'object' of its judgment, is the very same pleasure that is the 'law' of this judgment. These two aspects of judgment, referentiality and legitimacy, are but one in the aesthetic . . . [this] remarkable disposition of reflection I call *tautegorical*."[10] When it comes to reflection in the theoretical and practical realms, the tautegorical aspect of sensation is combined with a heuristic aspect; thought feeling its own state is always combined with thought turning toward the knowledge of, for example, objects. However, when dealing with reflection within the territory of the aesthetic, this tautegorical function is all that is left, because it does not and should not lead to anything but itself. According to Lyotard, aesthetic judgment is only a series of sensations considered to be judgments and must be analyzed as such, or, as he asks toward the end of the lesson on aesthetic reflection, "Should one not conclude that reflection, when left to itself [as in aesthetic judgment], can only say 'I feel, I feel' and 'I feel that I feel' tautegorically?"[11] Pure aesthetic feeling is no more than a feeling: a feeling of feeling.[12]

When, with euphoric authority, James Brown cries out "I feel good!" he may, in other words, be passing on an *aesthetic* judgment. The message is, to use yet another title of his, "Ain't That a Groove!" Again and again he is compelled to express that he feels that he feels the right way.

However, the feeling of the right feeling is not necessarily expressed in this way. Even though the right feeling is present in the event, it may remain more or less concealed on the level of meaning. And one may ask: Why do I know that this feeling of feeling took place? How, or perhaps rather *when*, is it that I feel that I feel? If the state of being in the groove is that of a total absorption, and there is never any distance, one feels, pure and simple. There is no aesthetic reflection: one does not feel that one feels. The presence in the event, in the groove, takes place as if nothing else ever existed.

This may be exactly the time for an intervention to take place. James Brown enters the "unawareness," giving the absorbed participant a little shake. He makes us aware of the state of affairs—"I got you, I feel good!"

Give Me a Break!—Intervention and Intensity

As discussed earlier, the many breaks in the musical course of "The Payback" do not make up a form. Even though aesthetically the breaks are critical points in the course of the tune, they are not dramatic in any sense of the word. There is no preceding increase in tension, and they are not followed up by any change in the fabric of rhythm; they are neither changes nor transitions. The breaks are suddenly just there, as a contrast to continuity. After every little "shock" of this sort, we return to the same continuous stream of musical gestures.

Nothing really happens, nothing is actually changed. Yet, for a little while, something *is* changed. When the musical movement is interrupted, one's attention transfers to what is actually going on, and when the groove continues with more of the same, it is nevertheless different. The return to the groove after this small disturbance is extremely satisfying. The minor alteration gives an instant of intensified feeling, as if we suddenly sense the state of being that we have moved away from, and now return to, in a new way. This "new" beginning underlines the qualities of that which was and now is: suddenly, there is a difference;

for a moment, I feel that I feel. However, this difference does not imply that the right feeling is being transformed to something else. It is rather being experienced as heightened sensation, as intensified feeling, as intensity itself.

According to Deleuze's discussions of intensity in *Difference and Repetition*, intensity is difference. However, it is not the form of difference that occurs when one quantity is subtracted from another. Such a difference is actually a canceling out of difference, because one is left with a synthesis of difference in the form of a certain remainder. This is not the case with the intensity of the experience above; one state of being is not compared to another. The intensity at stake is rather an intensifying of one state of being as such.[13]

Intensity is, moreover, not a difference between different intensities. This is also highly relevant with regard to the intensity of the breaks in a song like "The Payback": the intensity caused by the break is not a heightening of the level of intensity, in the sense that we move from one level of intensity before the break to a higher level after the break. Actually, there is no intensity prior to the intensifying moment. It is the break as such that installs the difference as a difference in intensity, by inducing virtual intensities on each side of itself. As Deleuze states, "Every intensity is differential, by itself a difference. Every intensity is E–E', where E itself refers to an e–e', and e to ε–ε', etc. Each intensity is already a coupling."[14] In other words, while experiencing intensity, intensity also seems to be projected onto the rest of the experience, even though, strictly speaking, there is no intensity outside the moment of intensity. Prior to the break, there is no intensity, and when the break is history, the intensity is gone. The right feeling is not intense. It is just a feeling of things having to be like this and not any different. Outside of the moment of intensified feeling, it is instead the transparency of reliability that rules. The situation does not step forward before some kind of distanciation takes place.

Distanciation may also happen due to a breakdown of reliability, such as when the groove lacks a steady beat, or when the strokes are too late or inaccurately performed, or when the voices of the rhythmic dialogue seem to speak for the parts of others, or when somebody is making too much out of a part. However, such a break does not induce intensity in the sense above. It does not elucidate the right feeling but represents instead a breakdown of feeling. We cease to feel the right feeling. In order to arrive at a situation where the right feeling is likely to occur, it is, on the contrary, crucial that the matter of course is allowed to rule undisturbed. The effect of intervention relies on a previous implosion in the event. Intensifying in the aesthetic sense is not possible until presence in the groove is total. In order to initiate the aesthetic break, the little distanciation that makes us feel that we feel, the reliability of the groove has to be intact, and the right feeling must already be there.

Intensity does not come forward in the form of a certain quality. In "The Payback," the intensification of the right feeling does not mean that the right feeling is being explicated or transformed into something outside itself: the fact that James Brown intervenes in the state of being in funk does not cause a feeling *of* something. However, the premise for such an alteration to take place, for the difference to remain implicated, so to speak, is that it is sudden. The alteration has to be unprepared and also remain "unqualified": there is no summing up of the musical events so far. The break implies no act of reflection upon the musical form, or upon repetition as such. There is no closure, no synthesis in time. Rather, the music has to ensure that the absorbed condition lasts right up to the break, that the non-noticing of time continues all the way up to the "aesthetic now" and continues on the other side of it in a way that makes the now once again disappear, without proceeding to quality.

The break is not supposed to activate anything but "the reason of the sensible," as Deleuze calls it. Nothing is being "explicated in extensity"; intensity is not "drawn outside itself, in extensity and in the quality which fills that extensity."[15] Still, there is just feeling, and feeling of feeling in the sense of feeling judging itself. There is no heuristic activity, no category involved, no shift to meaning. The distanciation induced by the break is pure "tautegorical activity," pure aesthetic reflection in the sense of Lyotard. The event is summed up neither as form nor as meaning. It is only an emerging "it happens."

"Once Upon a Time Called Now!"

Eventually, a serious "change" has to occur: the tune's ending. Sooner or later this total distanciation has to take place. The deferral of meaning—whether in the form of a "what has happened" or a "how did it happen" or just an "it has happened"—has to come to an end. We are distanced from the situation: the event "goes beyond itself in the meaning."[16] What happens at this point, in the moment after the event, which in the case of funk may have lasted for quite a while?

The traces of the event are still there, located within the body in the form of sensations, as traces of a rush of a certain vitalizing energy. We are tumbling out in one or another sense: we regain consciousness. We become aware of the event, or simply come to terms with it. The event is becoming an event of understanding.

By this time, we are also regaining a consciousness of time, because when we stepped out of the time of the groove, temporality became situated. The temporal event is now objectified as an event. Now meaning happens; now the *temporality of meaning* is transparent, while the temporality of the event may be summed up as "time." The event as such is distanciated, while the event as meaning is installed in time. In other words, from a state of being characterized by an absence of meaning, it is now the event that is absent; the presence in the event is replaced by a presence in meaning.[17]

In this very moment that the event has come to an end, the process of understanding the event begins, and the "quoting" of the event may start. However, in the case of funk, there is a considerable immediate resistance to inscription. Any of the attempts to account for the meaning of the event, embedded in the process of distanciation, become meaningless, as if the traces of the event refuse to be led out of the body. They struggle against the transition to meaning. Funk may be an event whose meaning is to *never be* meaning, an event where meaning dissolves in the very moment of distanciation, where the point is to avoid the dialectic of event and meaning so as to remain within the event, within the state of being in funk. Its point may be to avoid stepping out of its musical course in order to delimit and understand it.

Somewhat paradoxically, this understanding may not be reached before the unavoidable shift to meaning actually has taken place. We acknowledge, and we acknowledge the act of acknowledging being irrelevant. We acknowledge in the very moment that we declare that the whole experience was not about acknowledging. The uncovering of meaning happens as an uncovering of the fact that meaning, in this case, was invalid: the appearance of meaning is an appearance of nonmeaning.

The distanciation from the state of being in the groove activates the problem of representation, which is also on the agenda with regard to the analytic of the sublime of the third critique of Kant, the *Critique of Judgment*.[18] This has been realigned by Lyotard's reinterpretation of the sublime as the "it happens" that is impossible to represent, and it becomes crucial when facing an experience that takes place in an almost completely absorbed mode of being. It is exactly those aspects of the event that belong to the very being-in-the-situation—for example, the right feeling and the feeling of feeling as such—that tend to disappear in the shift to meaning. We are rather qualifying the event as an experience *of* intensity. Intensity in this explicated form becomes the meaning of the event, while intensity as such is hidden under the quality "intensity," which may, in fact, block the light upon the state of being in funk where intensity took place.

While being there, however, when the "it happens" actually happens, we are completely uninterested in the fact that the main aspect of this condition may disappear in the moment that it is being ended. When playing or dancing or listening in a participatory mode, time is not forgotten. On the other hand, nor is it remembered: we are in time, we *are*, or rather we *act*. We are committed to the production and co-production of gestures, marking time with movement whether we are moving or not. Funk may be a music for the dance in a wider and more basic understanding of *to dance:* whether the dance takes place in space, or the "dance" involved is entirely a mental one,[19] we are in motion. The movement is not yet frozen. Time is not yet measured time.

Nevertheless, by way of its claim on taking place in time, on being lived as productive repetition—every gesture being a new answer at the same time as being the same—the groove is actually an extraordinary occasion within which to experience time. A funk groove creates nothing beyond: it is not too early, or too late; it happens now, a now that is not to be grasped in posterity. The state of being in funk takes place exactly in that now that remains unknown to consciousness, the now that consciousness is unable to think, the now that it even forgets in order to constitute itself, that it may only account for in another time, after the fact: "Once upon a time called now."

11

Presence and Pleasure

Trying to put that thang called funk into words is like
trying to write down your orgasm. Both thrive in that
gap of time when words fall away, leaving nothing
but sensation.

—Barry Walters, *Village Voice*

Funk is whatever it needs to be, at the time that it is.

—George Clinton

Being in a groove, feeling the right feeling, letting presence happen, from the inside, from a position within time, within the experiential now, this is probably what funk is all about, and we should perhaps leave it at that, in all its meaningful non-sense.

However, the funk groove already has a meaning in a traditional sense; or rather, funk has different meanings according to the cultural setting. Within the field of black American popular music, within what we may call funk's primary social context in both a historical and a musical sense, funk has to a great extent been regarded as an expression, as well as a means, of spiritual upheaval, of achieving strength and pride. This focus on the spiritual aspects of funk should, however, be understood within a non-dualistic conception of the relation of body and mind: in this setting spiritual upheaval does not exclude bodily pleasure. The opposite is rather the case, or, quoting Dr. Funkenstein, move your mind, and your ass will follow.

Within the larger field of Western popular music, dominated by the ideology of Anglo-American pop and rock, funk has, on the other hand, been understood according to a highly *dualistic* framework of body and mind as a form of bodily pleasure linked with sex and desire. As I discussed in part I, we can start to explain this via the common opposition of nature and culture in the West, and its historical linking of black culture to nature, as well as via a general "othering" of rhythm in relation to musical aspects like harmony, melody, and form within the musicological tradition. This understanding of rhythm as a more spontaneous and natural aspect of music than, say, harmony, as well as the notion of "hot rhythm" as it emerged in the jazz era in the early twentieth century (see also my discussion in chapter 2), has no doubt had a significant impact on the way the mainstream pop and rock audiences for black dance music in the 1970s have approached the musical qualities of funk, in many cases reducing them to a consequence of certain animated bodily conditions.

In light of the discussions in the previous chapters, however, we may now identify some additional aspects of this primitivistic reading of funk. As part of this, I will re-play some of the issues discussed in part I, now with a focus on how the dominant tradition of Western thought may have constrained our understanding of the state of being in funk. Thus I will ask once more: What is the meaning of funk within the Anglo-American influenced field of popular music, or rather, how did it become what it is? And how does this intersect with racial ideology?

The Veiling of Musical Means

The first aspect to be discussed in response to these questions links up to the fact that in the Anglo-American–influenced field of popular music the state of being in funk, and the interlinked lack of traditional meaning discussed above, takes place within a culture in which presence in music in this sense is accounted for primarily as absence (of mind). As French philosopher Jacques Derrida points out, the Western metaphysical notion of presence works as a privileging of consciousness, understood as that instance that has been granted the power of synthesizing what might be called "traces of Being." However, a category such as this—that is, the subject—has never been imaginable without reference to presence understood as self-presence. According to Derrida, the precedence given to consciousness therefore implies the precedence that is given to the present in this particular sense.[1] When interpreted within this "ether of metaphysics," as Derrida calls it, the state of being-in-funk turns out to be nonmeaning or absence (of self-presence). Viewed this way—and given that this meaning is a negation—funk *does* have meaning in a traditional sense. A translation has already taken place: the claim of the funk groove on absorbed (and concerned) participation is interpreted as absence, and this interpretation, absence of self-presence, is almost present beforehand.

Another aspect of the primitivistic reading of funk that may now be brought into light is linked to the fact that the technical-rhetorical, *musical* qualities of funk largely remained transparent to the crossover audiences. As has been revealed through this study, the shaping of a funk groove is a musical process that requires both specialized technical skills on the side of the performers and a highly developed sensibility for grooves on the side of the listeners. In line with this, one might ask how dedicated funk fans, familiar with the style and capable of identifying a successful groove on the dance floor, have been able to overlook this fact. This may now be understood in light of the fact that the musical means of a funk groove aim to cultivate a temporary possibility of presence in the musical motion; the means of art are explored to bring about immediacy.

In order to understand how this immediacy plays a role for the primitivistic understanding of funk, the general distrust of exteriority and the resistance to acknowledging the technical-rhetorical aspects of the production of meaning—both of which characterize the dominant tradition of Western thought—is important. The suspicion regarding exteriority can be traced in Western culture's twofold relationship to writing; as Derrida says, there is a good writing and a bad writing. The good writing is writing in a metaphorical sense: "Natural, divine and living writing is venerated; it is equal in dignity to the origin of value, to the voice of conscience as divine law, to the heart, to the sentiment, and so forth."[2] Such writing is prescriptive, it is immediately united to voice and to breath, and it is the voice one hears upon retreating into oneself "in the intimacy of self-presence"[3] Bad writing links up with the process of mediation—for example, the fact that writing is written. Writing in the common sense is condemned: "The representative, fallen secondary instituted writing" is exactly what infects the good writing, making it impure.[4]

Good writing has always been "comprehended as that which had to be comprehended."[5] Put differently, good writing is meaning; it provides the answer to the question of what happened. Bad writing is technique and materiality; it is the answer to the question of how. In "the

ether of Western metaphysics" bad writing is artificial and almost per-
verse; ideally, it should be exterior to the meaning. However, in line
with Derrida, we might conclude that the reason bad writing is perceived as so bad is exactly that it does *not* leave meaning alone. In fact,
bad writing is a presupposition for the production of meaning. That it
remains unfocused in the process, its materiality and means dissolving
in the very act of mediation, does not mean that bad writing is absent.

A main issue in this study of funk has been that when one is in the
state of being in funk, technique and materiality ideally do not make
themselves known as anything other than the right feeling. In other
words, when taking part in a funk groove, when in the temporality of
the event, the means of art disappear as an effect of the means of art.[6]
Even though the lack of distance characterizing the state of being in
funk is not at all the same as the music being unmediated—even
though manner is absolutely fundamental to whether the groove actually happens in accordance with the sublimity of the "it happens," and
even though the tendency to keep the listener continuously in motion is
an effect of *how* the groove is enacted—when a groove actually takes
place, its manner is transparent. Put differently, we might say that the
aim of achieving a state of being in funk rules both form and the realization of form. In order to arrive at a state of being characterized by total
absorption in the groove, the technical aspect of the musical means has
to be covered.

In funk, this interplay of musical rhetoric and experience encounters
a culture where concerning oneself with form or rhetoric—in short,
with the "surface"—is inherently suspicious. As a consequence, the formal or technical aspects of the groove remain unfocused *outside of the
event* as well: we do not talk about *how* the meaning or nonmeaning was
produced when the event has come to an end, but rather about *what* the
meaning was. As was pointed out in the beginning of this book, the
process of understanding an experience like the state of being in funk
implies that the latter is unavoidably objectified in a process of distanciation, as is inherent, for example, in social discourse. This process unavoidably implies transforming what is to be understood into something other than what it was. The funk experience as a state of being
seems to be especially difficult to grasp, primarily because the very process of grasping it tends to conceal the distinctive qualities of its initial
events. Also, due to the highly processual character of its meaning,
funk is about how things are in "real time"—how the groove unfolds in
performance, right then and there.

In the context of the reception of crossover black dance music in the 1970s these difficulties regarding the process of grasping the experience of being in funk—together with the suspicion of exteriority inherent in the dominant Western culture and the interlinked downplay of the importance of "bad writing"—may have encouraged a situation where the musical means remained veiled also in the understanding of funk following (as well as preceding) the event—that is, in discourse, in "the speech about music," as Steven Feld once put it.[7]

This repression of formal aspects, of the *technical-rhetorical* qualities of funk, becomes almost completely unavoidable when, in addition, the bad writing is black, because in this case the Western tendency to overlook things that cannot be accounted for as meaning in the traditional sense coexists with a traditional primitivistic reading of blackness as nature. In other words, as regards the primitivistic understanding of funk this ignorance of "bad writing" or mediation has probably coincided with the notion of hot rhythm bound up in "the dialectics of modern racial ideology" discussed previously.[8] As a consequence funk has largely turned into a twofold question of descent and desire. Following Radano, we might say that along the historical axis of this crossroads unfolds an extension to a natural, pre-civilized past, while at the horizontal axis we find the threat of the excessive power of black rhythm, of "private desires [getting] public display."[9]

As should be clear by now, such an account of funk does not accord with the findings of this study regarding the musical features of a funk groove or the experiential aspects of the state of being in funk. The aesthetic leading star of funk is *not* lack of control or "hot," unmediated desire but rather personal coolness, or a focused, relaxed presence in the rhythmic events.[10] In line with this, the discourse of the Black Arts Movement in the 1960s was focused on the uplifting forces of black music. Even though the focus on descent within this discourse, understood as a possible unbroken line to an African past, may be influenced by a common nineteenth-century notion of rhythm as a more natural musical expression than, for example, harmony—and thus, as Radano claims, may be said to originate in the same racial ideology as the dominant Western primitivistic reading of black music (see my discussion in chapter 2)—music was nevertheless regarded as a primary tool in the search for a new spirituality. It was not regarded as a barbaric leftover from a pre-civilized world but lauded as a black expression demonstrating a high level of artistic sophistication. As pointed out previously, most 1960s and early 1970s funk, for example James Brown's, was deeply spiritual for the African American audience. And as we have seen, the cool element is indeed striking with Brown, and not only because of his musical focus on moderation, asceticism, and discipline. Several texts and titles within his diverse and voluminous catalogue reveal a clear focus on anti-regression and the promotion of spiritual strength, pride, independence, and involvement, including "Say It Loud, I'm Black and I'm Proud," "Get Up, Get Into It, Get Involved," or "Soul Power."

Nor is the effect of funk grooves regressive in the world of Clinton and his alter egos. Rather, it comprises a central means for achieving the kind of collective spiritual state of being necessary for the process of unifying the black nation and fighting the setbacks within black communities. In this way the "philosophy of funk" projected by George Clinton is thus linked to black struggle and black consciousness, even though he combined black pride with psychedelic dimensions. One might also say that the coolness projected by Clinton and the rest of the P-Funk party, especially when it came to style and visual appearance, is a highly calculated and cultivated artistic practice that is neither primitive nor natural.

In the northern European 1970s context, this horizon of black musicking was not visible. In one sense, however, it was audible, because even though it was not recognized as such, it was nonetheless the well-formed quality of the groove that paved the way for the experience, the state of being in a groove, that was sought after by this audience. However, as pointed out previously, when the groove is a success in this respect, this experience is characterized by its musical means being veiled. The transparency of the musical rhetoric is a presupposition for the absorbed and, according to Western metaphysics, "mindless" experience. As a consequence, the fact that the shaping, the very *production*, of a good funk groove is *not* a matter of desire in a raw, unmediated sense but quite the reverse—it relies instead on holding back, on an imperative of the form, on tedious articulation—was not acknowledged.

In other words, the transparency of musical means at the level of experience, the "ether of Western metaphysics" that condemns the rhetorical level as superficial, and the long tradition of primitivistic readings of black rhythm in the West all contributed to the ignorance of the musical qualities of funk characterizing the Anglo-American field of popular music's understanding of it. It has probably also led to what might be called a general confusion of "hot" and "cool" regarding black music: The hot reception has lead to an assumption that the production is also hot.[11] A lack of focus on the musical-rhetorical level goes together with an unthematized primitivistic reading of black culture as more natural, making the funk groove work almost as a mimetic utterance: the means of mediation disappear into that which is mediated. And the latter, the meaning that is left after the event, is immediacy. The fact that funk is artifice has been totally discounted in favor of a meaning (rhythm as nature and body) that leaves no room for artifice. That the funk groove cultivates the immediacy and sensibility of a state of being-in music (a being-in that, accordingly, is made possible by "trickery" and artificial means) is confused with the music itself being immediate. And when the question of meaning is activated after the event and there is no meaning in a traditional sense (except for an absence of self-presence, which in line with the privileging of this form of presence is interpreted as an absence of mind), the ability of the groove to bring the listener into the state of being in funk is exchanged for a meaning that is immediately filled up with "body" and "nature," in keeping with the genre's black origins. The sounding events are regarded as unmediated body, and this bodily character is interpreted under the influence of a primitivistic reading of black rhythm as hot, as a direct expression of the threatening presence of primary needs: as, for example, raw, unmediated desire.

Externalizing the Internal Other

The racist dimensions of this interpretation of funk, as well as the reduction of the musical qualities of funk that it implies, have never been fully disclosed. In fact, however, the mainstream pop and rock audiences' deficient comprehension of funk and other black dance music in the 1970s has much in common with the mainstream American reception of jazz in the 1920s. Like ragtime, funk is perceived as a pre-artistic "it grooves," as if the quality of making a groove groove is something that resides in the (black) body as such. The highly artificial character, the musical sophistication, and the micro-rhythmic complexities so crucial to the state of being in funk are ignored as regards understanding, exchanged for interpretations stressing the supposed natural origins of musical rhythm. In line with this, the impact of the music is explained by comparing it to corporeal activities like heartbeats or sexual intercourse.

As has been touched upon previously, one might ask how it was possible to overlook the implicit barbarization of black culture inherent in this reading of funk, in the reduction of the musical qualities of funk to questions of body and nature. Part of the answer lies in the fact that there was a focus on rhythm instead of blackness: black dance music was perceived as rhythm music, and although we know better now, the link between rhythm, nature, and body appeared as a form of "universal truth" that transcended racial inclinations. Another aspect important for the sustainability of the primitivistic understanding of funk among these audiences was the absence of blackness. This may be approached at several levels. First, there was a physical absence: Scandinavian urban areas in the 1970s were, contrary to the situation today, still characterized by a rather homogenous population regarding color. Perhaps even more important, however, was the absence of a mediated cultural manifold. In Norway in the late 1970s, for example, there was almost no visible blackness in the mass media.[12] Last but not least, there was an absence of blackness in that the sociopolitical circumstances of the production of much black dance music, for example as regards the music of James Brown, were "removed" from the new sounds. As a consequence, the struggle of black America was not at all in the minds of the mainstream audiences for black dance music when they were listening or dancing to it. Iain Chambers describes the parallel impact of African American popular music on British youth culture in the late 1960s and early 1970s as an instance of blackness being both present and absent at the same time: "In Britain, soul music obviously had a different, far more mediated presence . . . The deep black American undertow that frequently shaped these sounds was widely removed from white British experience."[13]

All these forms of absence of blackness—physical, mediated, and what might be called sociohistorical—are important aspects of the cultural backdrop for the reception of funk among the mainstream pop and rock audiences of the 1970s. Put differently, one might say that there was no "blackness on the loose" at these dance floors, nor was there an indirect confrontation with black culture in the form of today's widely mediated images of popular black culture: black dance music implied, in other words, no threat for these audiences. Black dance music was also not a place for ethical considerations regarding racial discrimination or inequality, because there was no link from it to the history of African America. Most important for the resistance among these audiences to acknowledging the high artistic level of black musicking and laying bare the barbarization of black culture inherent in the primitivistic reading of funk, however, was probably the fact that black dance music, like minstrelsy in the United States in the late nineteenth century, met "a need in white culture"[14] In a way similar to the re-interpretation of the life and work of Robert Johnson that took place in British blues in the 1960s, black dance music could be made "to fit another story already in place."[15]

Contrary to black minstrelsy, however, black dance music was not used as a means of approaching a manifest color line, as with the black mask in nineteenth-century American society, but of negotiating the relation to the *internal* Other of dominant white Western culture. Through the musical and cultural codes of black dance music, there was still an *audible* difference in play, as well as a different experience on offer, and it was no accident that the need to get in touch with this internal other, the other of the self-presence described by Derrida, was lived out by way of black dance music. First, as has been demonstrated in this study, the musical organization of a funk groove, both on a micro- and a macro-level, encourages an experience that actualizes this internal other of dominant Western culture—the unavoidable supplement that within a dualistic conception of body and mind may be named body but which is also the experience of giving in to the moment (I will return to this shortly). Second, there was the need for *externalizing* the internal other, for living out this other side by way of a culture that was still in some way or another "foreign." For, as Chambers points out in his discussion of black music's impact on British youth culture in the same period, there was only an *apparent* absence of blackness: "Returning to the centrality of dance in this unforeseen cultural exchange, there were also—rarely perceived, but subconsciously received—a deeper series of connections activated."[16] Lipsitz also observes that the very existence of racism adds to the mystery, distance, and inversions of prestige enacted in the reception of black music, or, as he writes in his discussions of the prevalent romantic understanding of Robert Johnson's life and art within Anglo-American blues audiences: "With African-Americans relegated to primitive, natural, and mystical domains the consumption of black culture salves the alienations and identity problems of European Americans."[17]

So even though the differences of the sounds of funk and the interlinked experience were not used as a way of demarcating and negotiating the boundaries between a primary position of whiteness and a *present* black other, the grounding of this difference in such an interracial relation was still crucial for how these sounds were used to negotiate with the internal other of dominant Western culture. In other words, there was, and probably to some extent still is, a strong *interest* in holding on to an understanding of black dance music as closely linked with the body and desire. In fact, the dynamic associated with these audiences' embracing of black dance music in the 1970s turns out to be quite similar to the one described by Lott with regard to black minstrelsy. To paraphrase Lott, one might say that the interpretation and engagement with funk and black dance music was also a manifestation of the desire to get in touch with the other of the dominant culture. And furthermore, this domain of otherness, for the time being labeled body, was at the same time so attractive and so threatening as "to require a cultural marker," as Lott puts it.[18] In this sense funk and black dance music were used as a mask: they made it possible to engage with this "othered" domain in a way that at the same time kept it at some distance.[19]

Body vs. Time—Renaming the Internal Other?

There is a long tradition in white Western culture for living out the internal other of the dominant culture by way of an external other. According to Lott, black minstrelsy was probably the first culture industry of the United States that met this need in white culture, and also the first example of what might be called a commodification of blackness that seems to have accompanied the black musical tradition all the way from minstrelsy to rap. In the case of funk, this borrowing of what was perceived as a primarily musical otherness was used for subversive means in relation to the dominant culture. It worked as an unavoidable supplement to dominant values and culture, to the complex described by Pattison as the "the official super-ego of the West."[20]

As long as the dominant white Western culture seems to constantly produce a need for subverting this dominant order, we may assume that there will remain a substantial resistance to giving up our understanding of black culture as a bearer of nonconformity or a means of distanciation from the mainstream—in short, as a bearer of a potential experience of otherness. African American rhythms probably still constitute a field of otherness; the involvement with much African American music has remained a means of catharsis, of dealing with the "prohibited" pleasures of the body. Or, put differently, for many funk fans within the mainstream pop and rock audiences of the 1970s it might still to some extent be raw, unmediated nature that is drawn upon when James Brown howls or his band starts to groove.

The difference of the experience of a well-formed funk groove may, however, not be fully explained by such a perspective; it is not constituted solely by this link to racial ideology but also by the potential temporality of such a groove. In my view, mainstream pop and rock audiences in the 1970s also felt in funk an experience of time that was external to the self-presence privileged by "the ether of metaphysics" of Western thought. Even though it is impossible to separate the music's disposition for such an experience from the cultural aspects and the racial ideology discussed above, it is also important not to *reduce* the impact of funk to the latter. The state of being offered by a funk groove is different from that of, for example, country and western, and in this process musical features and cultural aspects work together.

In other words, it might still be that the *musical* qualities of funk, or rather, the interlinked experience, also make it important for this audience as a possible place for living out the "internal other" of the dominant Western culture: the dance floor is still there for those of us who are looking for a refuge from the presence of self-presence, for those of us seeking the presence given by the groove but forgotten by Western metaphysics. If one calls such a relation to funk a presence in the body, which may be likely within the framework of a Western, mind-centered, dualistic approach to the relation of body and mind, almost everything is the same. The meaning of funk is still to be found in the interaction of music and body, in how the music hits the body. However, it may no longer be that easy to reduce the funk groove to its supposedly barbaric nature. The state of being in funk may rather be interpreted as an experience not of being out of place, out of time but *in place, in time.* When connected to the groove, it is not its barbaric nature but rather its deliberate form that causes the particular sensational state of the body that is the right feeling.

It is not possible to reflect upon music while it happens. If we try to consider music while it is being performed, we unavoidably affect the current state of being, changing the situation that was to be reflected upon. At its root, this is a problem that affects all interpretation, which is given over to the process of translating the immediate aesthetic experience into an experience of conscious reflection. However, when it comes to funk, the question of meaning becomes particularly precarious. That the musical means can be thematized in an analytical discourse—the fact that a groove grooves is not only due to some presupposed elusive dimensions of performance but to some systematically occurring musical features—does not make the problem of translation less immediate. The problem with regard to funk may be that the effect of the musical means is an extraordinary occasion of being-in. The groove requires an almost total presence in the music; it requires absolute simultaneity in the "processing"; it has to be enjoyed in real time. It does not work without full participation in the actual events. The processing of large-scale time spans has to be subordinated to presence in the perceptual now.

However, while placing this happening *in* time in the deepest sense, an abyss is also exposed between the experience that offers itself to Being as immediate presence, as a letting-presence, and the experience bearing the character of reflection after the fact. Funk is experienced as highly meaningful, but the meaning is a very different one to hold on to. At the very moment we try to articulate the meaning, it disappears.

Thus, in addition to being understood as the music of others—that is, black music—funk is a form of music activating the dominant Western culture's internal other, that which falls outside of the presence of Western metaphysics, of meaning, that which is only indirectly present in the understandable spaces of discourse. The fact that funk after the event is almost meaningless in a traditional sense is exactly the thing that makes funk able to bear witness to the event, almost in the way Adorno, probably with a quite different soundscape in mind, prescribed as the main task of the "new music."[21] The shift to meaning, or rather to no meaning, is of such a character as to point toward the event as the radical other. In fact, the shift to meaning is characterized by the breakdown of meaning typical of much modernist art. In the Adornian version of modernist aesthetics, the technical or formal aspects of the work play a particularly important role in this experience: the work as form, drained of content, of meaning, may point to the event reminding us of the absence of absence implied by the objectification of the process. Discovering the artificial character of art becomes a testimony to that which no longer is, thus bearing witness to the "non-identical." The process emerges through the shift from event to meaning, or, in Adorno's words, from process to object. This is not due to the object character carrying the truth but to the fact that the object character of music, its formal aspects, refers to something that is not an object. According to Adorno this is the paradoxical nature of art: "The movement of artworks must be at a standstill and thereby become visible. Their immanent processual character—the legal process that they undertake against the merely existing world that is external to them—is objective prior to their alliance with any party."[22]

In other words, the character of process, or the fact that the groove needs to take place in time, is a constant reminder of the "it happens" that consciousness, according to Lyotard, is not capable of thinking and even forgets in order to constitute itself. However, the consummation of a funk groove is not to bear witness to the event. Its goal is not that "Truth establishes itself in the work."[23] The end is not the leap out of the state of being in funk. It is the state itself. Furthermore, because what matters is the being in the event, there is actually no point in realizing the process as work. When the groove is a success, when the music hits the body in exactly the right way, the state of being in funk is a totally focused experience. To refer to the cliché that most commonly accounts for it, it is a forgetting of time and place—that is, of a certain understanding of time and place.

Probably it is only within the framework of a truth-seeking Western philosophical discourse that the leap out of the event becomes a major focal point. Funk's potential meaning as non-meaning is probably produced in and with the meeting of a musical form praising presence in the absent now, the "not-yet uncovered," as Heidegger says, with a philosophical context where the ability of the music to testify to the radical other takes on an almost existential subversive power. In the moment when one moves beyond the immediate situatedness within the body and tries to introduce funk in the universe of thought—that is, of reflection—the experience of funk activates the limits of representation. Then the groove advances as a threshold experience, as the only memory of a state of being that never announced itself as having a past tense.

However, the funk groove and the state of being in funk do not primarily belong to such a discourse. Funk is not made with regard to such an avantgardist task: it is not made in order to call dominant Western modes of thinking to account. It is rather a form of music deeply linked with a musical tradition where "the presumption of the mind with respect to time"[24] seems to have been less present than within Western philosophy, and where one has been less afraid of the "bad writing"— one might actually like it or even encourage it. *The Signifying Monkey* is actually a hero, because he is a master of a rhetorical strategy where "styling . . . is foregrounded by the devices of making a point by indirection and wit."[25]

To reduce the importance of the funk groove to the critical shift from event to meaning would be to lead the groove back to a place where it does not belong. Just as funk is not the body in a narrow sense, funk has not come to earth in order to bear witness to the event. Even though a funk piece of music might lean in that direction, to claim that it actually fulfills such a task would be to overlook the very central role of funk as a place for being and letting presence happen, as an occasion for uplifting, empowering forces to enter the body and the soul, as a refuge offering the opportunity to be without distance in a world where the room for absorbed participation, for being-in, is limited and the threshold for giving oneself up is rather high.

In this context, the whole point of funk may be to take some time off from reason, both the pure and the practical, from the very imperative of meaning, including the nonmeaning required by the critical discourse of Adorno and his followers. It is not the absence of the absence of the metaphysical presence that is the point of funk, but rather the absence of absence in the actual Presence in the groove.

In a Western mind-centered universe, this radical other—also labeled the event—is probably compelled to reside in the body. In light of this and held together by its close link to black culture, it is not very surprising that the radical otherness of the state of being in funk is accounted for in terms of the body. Perhaps "the body" is only one attempt by the Western mind to straighten out this now that is never to be straightened out, and that we as Westerners therefore attempt to control in a double movement of repression: first by capturing it, taking control of it, and giving it a name, and then by rejecting it as something subordinate, secondary, and "primitive."

However, strictly speaking, funk is as much a condition of mind as of body, and actually in a way that makes it rather meaningless to distinguish between mind and body: funk is body *and* soul, a body-soul. Its radical otherness may equally well be accounted for as a matter of time. It is the fact that funk happens before the (after)thought that causes trouble: it is the presence in the "not-yet uncovered," in the absent now, that makes funk intangible for Western reason. Similar to the dominant dualistic Western notion of the body, this now is also "on the other side," and there they may actually meet exactly in the place escaping thought; or, as Lyotard points out, the time of feeling is *now*.[26]

Setting this Western complex aside, however, the shift to meaning is probably rather undramatic. The meaning turns up as an "it happened," or a "that which happened is no longer happening," yet without ever implying that it was not happening! It was a happening, and it was great, when the groove took control, when the groove was able to bring us into a state of being in the rhythmic dialogue without distance, of giving oneself up to movement, to the unique opportunity a funky funk groove is for more or less reluctant, restless listeners to take part in a more radical sense: to be present in a presence that can never be present as such, to be present in something that may be called . . . pleasure.

Notes

Chapter 1. Whose Funk? (pp. 3–19)

1. Smitherman 1994: 118. This tendency to name the most important things by the dirtiest words may seem peculiar to an outsider. According to Smitherman, a linguist, however, the many inverted meanings in black talk, as well as the existence of a huge specifically African American vocabulary, goes back to enslavement and the need for a system of communication that only those in the enslaved community could understand (Smitherman 1994: 5).

2. Eileen Southern's book on the history of black American music and Dave Marsh's article on Sly and the Family Stone in *The Rolling Stone Illustrated History of Rock 'n' Roll* may serve as examples of these tendencies. See Southern 1997 and Marsh 1992.

3. In 1970 "Thank you (Falettinme Be Mice Elf Again)" reached the top position on *Billboard Magazine*'s pop chart and r&b chart.

4. Ricky Vincent's book *Funk: The Music, the People, and the Rhythm of the One* (Vincent 1996) is, as far as I know, the only book that deals with funk history; it is written from a journalist and fan's point of view. Even though the book gives an impressive overview of the activity of funk and funk-related bands and artists from the 1960s to the early 1990s, one might say that the history of funk as a *musical* style is yet to be written.

5. Palmer 1992: 164.

6. Brown 1997: 5.

7. Mills, Alexander, et al. 1998: 66.

8. Ibid.: 11.

9. Ibid.: 29.

10. Ibid.: 72.

11. Ibid.: 87.

12. Ibid.: 97.

13. Corbett 1994: 287.

14. See chapter 7.

15. Frith 2004: 21.

16. It may also seem that when "African American" is subsumed into the broader category of "black" (sometimes this category is simply named "African" after what is commonly regarded as the *Ursprung* of black culture),

this broader category tends to be used in opposition to "white" or European in a way that comes close to implying "non-Western" for the former.

17. Radano and Bohlman 2000: 33.

18. Radano 2003: 3.

19. Husserl's *The Phenomenology of Internal Time-Consciousness* and Heidegger's *Being and Time*, as well as his later works "Time and Being" and "The Origin of the Work of Art," are classic texts within these traditions. See Husserl 1991 and Heidegger 1962, 1971, and 1972.

20. Mikhail Bakhtin is one theorist outside of the continental philosophical tradition who has thematized this fundamental point in all hermeneutics and made the connection between individual experience and cultural formations evident (see Bakhtin 1986; see also Heidegger 1962, 1971, and 1972).

21. Although he argues from a different point of view, Radano advocates a similar critique of the essentialism of black music studies in his recent book *Lying Up a Nation: Race and Black Music* (2003): "Theories of retention, which underlie Afrocentric thought, commonly reduce the complexity of lived experience to a static and oversimplified phenomenology of blackness. These theories are oversimplified because they give weight to the assumption that black music grows, like a living, organic form, from fixed, predetermined origins, an assumption that, after all, betrays the legacy of the color line" (Radano 2003: 10). I will return to a discussion of Radano's critique in chapter 2.

22. Richard Waterman, A. M. Jones, and John Miller Chernoff are all examples of white ethnomusicologists who have studied African music.

23. The terms "self-knowledge" and "other-knowledge" were presented in a lecture by Gary Tomlinson at the research seminar "Musical Hermeneutics/ Musical Anthropology: New Models of Understanding in Contemporary Musicological Research" at the University of Oslo, October 16–20, 2002.

24. Mayfield 1972: 26.

25. Ibid.: 27.

26. Ibid.: 29.

27. Jones 1972: 117.

28. Ibid.

29. As they were decades ago, in the title of R. Waterman's classic essay "Hot Rhythm in Negro Music" (Waterman 1948).

30. Unless stated otherwise, all songs are picked from the *Star Time* anthology (1991).

Chapter 2. Two Discourses on Blackness (pp. 20–36)

1. Radano and Bohlman 2000: 32.

2. Hegel 1980 (1830): 177.

3. Ibid.: 176–77.

4. See Snead 1984: 63.
5. White 1972: 5.
6. Gran 2000: 47.
7. See Marshall Berman's *All That Is Solid Melts into Air* for an interesting discussion of how modernity's own discourse on modern life has always been both affirmative and critical, often at the same time: "Our nineteenth-century thinkers [Marx and Nietzsche] were simultaneously enthusiast and enemies of modern life, wrestling inexhaustibly with its ambiguities and contradictions" (Berman 1982: 24).
8. Small 1987: 154.
9. The ridicule of blacks also served as a protection against having to deal with the terrible conditions under which many people actually lived. Hoyt W. Fuller puts it this way: "The facts of Negro life accuse white people . . . the white viewer must either relegate it to the realm of the subhuman, thereby justifying an attitude of indifference, or else the white viewer must confront the imputation of guilt against him. And no man who considers himself human wishes to admit complicity on crimes against the human spirit" (Fuller 1972: 6).
10. Lott 1993: 6.
11. Said 1978: 42.
12. Small 1987: 152.
13. West 1994: 128.
14. West points out that the situation is different for black women because the dominant ideal of female beauty is different: "The ideal of female beauty in this country [the United States] puts a premium on lightness and softness mythically associated with white women and downplays the rich stylistic manners associated with black women . . . This means that black women are subject to more multilayered bombardments of racist assaults than black men, in addition to the sexist assaults they receive from black men. Needless to say, most black men . . . simply recycle this vulgar operation along the axis of lighter hues that results in darker black women bearing more of the brunt than their already devalued lighter sisters" (West 1994: 130).
15. Agawu 1995: 384–85.
16. Ibid.: 385.
17. Ibid.: 386.
18. Ibid.: 383.
19. Radano 2003: 247–55.
20. Ibid.: 255.
21. Ibid.: 258.
22. Alan M. Kraut in the *New York Times*, February 12, 1922, quoted in Radano 2003: 237.
23. Frith 1983: 19.

24. In a more recent book, *Performing Rites* (1996), Frith takes exception to the primitivism of the rock discourse on blackness and relates it to the mind-body split of Western thought: "There is, indeed, a long history in Romanticism of defining black culture, specifically African culture, as the body, the other of bourgeois mind" (127). In the chapter "Rhythm: Race, Sex, and the Body," his overall agenda is to loosen the close tie between rhythm and sex, which he sees as an ideological construction: "The equation of rhythm and sex is a product of high cultural ideology rather than of African popular musical practice" (141). Here, Frith reveals the traditional essentialism regarding the nature of blackness to be racist and focuses on blackness as socially and historically constructed.

25. Jazz was also perceived as subversive to the dominant values of establishment culture. In the words of Lawrence Levine, "Jazz was seen by many contemporaries as a cultural form independent of a number of the basic central beliefs of bourgeois society, free of its repressions, in rebellion against many of its grosser stereotypes" (Levine 1978: 293).

26. See Pattison 1987.

27. Radano and Bohlman 2000: 33.

28. Gates 1987: xxv–xxvi.

29. Gayle 1972: xxii.

30. Richard Gilman, quoted in Gayle 1972: xv.

31. Gayle 1972: xvii.

32. Ibid.: xxii.

33. See Marcuse 1969.

34. Gayle 1972: xix.

35. Fuller 1972: 7.

36. Gayle 1972: xxi. The female black subject seems to be almost as absent in the Black Aesthetic Movement as the black subject is within American society as a whole (judging by Gayle and his male co-writers).

37. Stewart 1972: 77.

38. Ibid.: 80, emphasis added.

39. Fuller 1972: 9.

40. In the so-called Herskovits-Frazier debate, E. F. Frazier responded to Melville Herskovits's pioneering study of Africanisms in African American culture, *The Myth of the Negro Past* (first published in 1941), by arguing that slavery was so devastating in America that it destroyed all African elements among black Americans. Herskovits, for his part, had emphasized the continuity of West African carryovers in African American culture. For a short presentation of the Herskovits-Frazier debate and the study of African cultural survival in North America, see Holloway's introduction to the anthology *Africanisms in American Culture* (Holloway 1990: ix–xxi).

41. Stewart 1972: 81.

42. Gates 1987: xxv.
43. See, for example, P. K. Maultsby, "Africanisms in African-American Music" (Maultsby 1990), and O. Wilson, "The Significance of the Relationship between Afro-American Music and West African Music" (Wilson 1974).
44. Wilson 1974: 20.
45. Wilson 1983: 3.
46. Wilson, for example, turns to James Brown's "Super Bad" to demonstrate reminiscences of African cross-rhythms in African American music (Wilson 1974: 12–13).
47. Ramsey 2003: 27–28.
48. Ibid.: 149.
49. Ibid.: 153.
50. Born and Hesmondhalgh 2000: 32.
51. Ramsey 2003: 38.
52. Ibid.: 19.
53. Radano 2003: 35.
54. To me it remains a bit unclear whether Radano himself believes in the power of black music as such, or whether he ascribes to the view that the power of black music may be fully accounted for at the level of discourse. If the latter, he may be accused of a form of reductionism that sometimes goes together with a certain misconception of the poststructuralist insistence on the constitutive character of discourse, as expressed, for example, in the slogan *Il n'y a pas dehors le texte*. With this utterance, French philosopher Jacques Derrida reminds us of the fact that all experiences are "always already" inscribed in discourse, in the sense that there is no inter-subjective or social experience as such. This is sometimes misconstrued as a denial—at the level of the individual—of all experiential modes other than the textual. In this study, even though I also ascribe to a nonessentialist view on the issue of cultural identity, I remain open to the importance and power of nondiscursive modes of experience.
55. Radano 2003: 276.
56. Ibid.: 272.
57. Ibid.: 271.

Part II. A Brand New Bag (pp. 39–42)

1. Palmer 1992: 167–68.
2. In the liner notes to *Star Time*, producer Jerry Wexler, who was then working with Aretha Franklin and other soul stars for Atlantic Records, says, "'Cold Sweat' deeply affected the musicians I knew . . . It just freaked them out. For a time, no one could get a handle on what to do next" (White and Weinger 1991: 31).

3. Schematically the standard form of pop/rock may be summed up as an ABABC(A)B form, where A is the verse, B the chorus, and C the bridge or interlude. The chorus at the end is often repeated and/or faded out.
4. Social theorist Max Weber's description of the nature of ideal-type concepts and their significance for the social sciences was worked out in his writings on the methodology of the social sciences. See Weber 1949.
5. The most correct label, at least in terms of the literature in question, would probably be "West African rhythm," but because all of these texts use African rhythm or even African music (often in opposition to another ideal type, namely European music), I will also use these labels when I discuss these works.
6. Weber 1949: 90.

Chapter 3. A Fabric of Rhythm (pp. 43–60)

1. Nketia 1974: 126.
2. It is perhaps misleading to refer to the basic pulse as an isochronic pulse. The distance between pulses will vary with regard to physical time. Instead, one might rather speak of an *experienced* isochronicity.
3. Arom 1991: 212.
4. I refer to these different levels as quarter notes, eighth notes, and so on, for practical purposes. However, the use of the names of metrical units should not be confused with a mathematically correct subdivision or with the units as they sound in other musical contexts—for example, in classical music. The subdivision in funk, especially when it comes to the smallest units of sixteenth and thirty-second notes, is almost always swung to a greater or lesser extent.
5. Nketia 1974: 127.
6. Ibid.: 134.
7. Waterman 1948: 25.
8. Nketia 1974: 133.
9. Deleuze 1994: 208. "Du virtuel, il faut dire exactement ce que Proust disait des états de résonance: 'Réels sans être actuels, idéaux sans être abstraits'" (Deleuze 1968: 269). The reality of the virtual can be called *structure*. However, according to Deleuze, one must avoid giving the elements and relations that form a structure an actuality that they do not have, or taking from them the reality that they do have. This is because, in Deleuze's words, "*The virtual is fully real in so far as it is virtual*" (Deleuze 1994: 208). "*Le virtuel possède une pleine réalité, en tant que virtuel*" (Deleuze 1968: 269, his italics).
10. This understanding of rhythm as an interaction of sounding events and a preunderstanding in the listener corresponds to a view of the perception of rhythm as a dynamic process where external sound events are syn-

chronized, or rather interact with, the listener's internal rhythmic processes. For an interesting attempt at working out a mathematical model of this interaction, see Large and Kolen 1994. That rhythm is a phenomenon indivisible from the listening act also underlies the empirical psychological research on rhythm carried out in Uppsala, Sweden, by I. Bengtsson, A. Gabrielsson, and others (1969: 57–58.)

11. In literary theory on rhythm, rhythm is also viewed as an interplay of actual events and virtual structures, the latter commonly referred to as meter. According to *The New Princeton Encyclopedia of Poetry and Poetics*, this distinction dates to the late fourth century B.C.E., to a pupil of Aristotle named Aristoxenus. The relationship of rhythm and meter is described as follows: "The established view is that ultimately meter is simply a subset of rhythm . . . but this is not exactly true: strictly speaking meter has no rhythm. Meters provide structure; rhythms provide movement . . . Without a structure no movement would be possible, but within structure a number of movements may be permissible" (Brogan 1993: 1068).

12. A similar distinction between virtual schema and actual musical event is found in T. Kvifte's work on playing technique. He distinguishes between digital and analog categories in the experience of music: "If we encounter a pitch somewhere between C-sharp and D, we divide the experience of pitch in two aspects, one digital (the note 'D') and one analog ('out of tune')" (Kvifte 1989: 94). One challenge for the research on so-called systematic variations and their importance for rhythm, however, is to determine the norm from which the musical events may deviate. According to the rhythm research group in Uppsala, the question as to what constitutes the norm, or rather the reference at play in the understanding of a rhythm, is quite open and may in fact be impossible to pin down. They maintain, however, that this is in principle not an argument against the investigation of systematic variations in music or, one might add, against the importance of such a musical dimension (see Bengtsson, Gabrielsson, et al. 1969: 96).

13. Bakhtin 1986: 71.

14. Ibid.: 71.

15. Ricœur 1973: 130.

16. Ibid.: 131.

17. Bakhtin 1986: 72.

18. It may also be assumed that a difference in phrasing between two musicians involved in the shaping of the same gesture, for example a downbeat, creates a more interesting gesture. In his article "Motion and Feeling through Music," Charles Keil notes that "In general, chunky bassists and on-top drummers combine effectively, while stringy bassists and lay-back drummers work well together" (Keil 1994a: 64). Keil has named such differences in phrasing or feel "participatory discrepancies" (PDs; see Keil

1994b: 96–98). He claims that PDs are responsible for much of the vital drive of a groove, a view that is thoroughly supported by the analytical work of this study.

19. Robert F. Thompson, quoted in Chernoff 1979: 47.
20. Wilson 1992: 329.
21. Ibid.
22. Ibid.
23. Nketia 1974: 137–38.
24. The sound box was first described in my work on the Prince album *Diamonds and Pearls* as an analytical tool for describing music produced in a recording studio; see Danielsen 1998. A rather parallel conception to the sound box is found in Allan F. Moore's book *Rock: The Primary Text*; see Moore 1993: 106.
25. Wilson 1983: 3.
26. Ibid.
27. Chernoff's account of African drumming (1979) is extracted from several years of studies in the Ewe and Dagomba provinces of West Africa.
28. Chernoff 1979: 51.
29. Ibid.: 55.
30. Ibid.: 54.
31. Ibid.: 55.
32. Nketia 1974: 134.
33. When complementary rhythms of contrasting sound are heard together, the result often sounds similar to the melody of language. Especially in African music, such sentence-like rhythmic melodies may be a duplication of language carrying a semantic dimension. This similarity of African language and drumming is commented upon by Chernoff, Nketia, and Jones, to mention a few; see Jones 1959: 230–51; Nketia 1974: 177–88; and Chernoff 1979: 75–87.
34. Chernoff 1979: 60
35. Ibid.: 59–60.
36. Ibid.: 113–14 (his emphasis).
37. Ibid.: 58.
38. Ibid.: 48–49.
39. This goes for more than just African music. In some Norwegian folk music, it is not easy for an inexperienced dancer or listener to identify the basic pulse. It may not be an explicit part of the music; also, many dances in triple rhythm are characterized by a considerable variation as to the length of each beat.
40. See Waterman 1967.
41. Chernoff 1979: 50.
42. Waterman 1967: 211.
43. Chernoff 1979: 114.

44. Ibid.: 159.
45. Gates has been accused of essentializing black culture. Radano writes, for example, that "what Gates has referred to as the musical basis of an oral 'superconsciousness' are little more than ahistorical, and, ultimately, idealist devotions to a 'vernacular' grounding that has been reformulated in the postmodern lexicon of elusiveness: signifyin', the blues matrix, deformation of mastery, and so on" (Radano 2003: 39). Radano's problem lies, however, not so much in these theories gesturing toward the vernacular, or in the underlying belief in creative resistance, but "in their perpetuation of anachronistic beliefs in music's ability to rise above the circumstances of political, cultural, and social change" (ibid.). In my view, however, there is absolutely nothing, at least as regards Gates's contribution, that may lead to such a conclusion. Quite on the contrary, the Bakhtinian "dialogic imagination" underlying Gates's work situates every act of signifying safely in time and space. See also my discussion of the relation of text and context in chapter 1.
46. The stories of the Signifying Monkey are versions of the following plot: the Monkey is intent on demystifying the Lion's self-imposed status as King of the Jungle. The Monkey's task is to trick the Lion into tangling with the Elephant by invariably repeating to the Lion some insult purportedly generated by their mutual friend. The Monkey, however, speaks figuratively. The Lion, indignant and outraged, demands an apology of the Elephant, who refuses and then trounces the Lion. The Lion, realizing that his mistake was to take the Monkey literally, returns to trounce the Monkey. According to Gates, "It is this relationship between the literal and the figurative, and the dire consequences of their confusion, which is the most striking repeated elements of these tales. The Monkey's trick depends on the Lion's inability to mediate between these two poles of signification, of meaning" (Gates 1988: 55). Gates claims that the research on this oral tradition has been too busy with the insulting aspect of "signifyin(g)," thereby overlooking it as "a pervasive mode of language use." According to Gates, signifyin(g) is synonymous with figuration: "Signifyin(g) [is] the black trope for all other tropes, the trope of tropes, the figure of figures. Signifyin(g) is troping" (Gates 1988: 80–81).
47. Gates 1988: xxii–xxiii.
48. Ibid.: 61.
49. Roger D. Abrahams, quoted in Gates 1988: 74. In *Talking Black*, Abrahams defines signifying as "a wide variety of verbal techniques united by the single strategy of verbal manipulation through indirection" (Abrahams 1976: 50–51).
50. Gates 1988: 123. Gates's theory of signifying has inspired several music scholars. In his analysis of Miles Davis's 1964 recording of "My Funny Valentine," Robert Walser, for example, demonstrates how Davis plays on

the history of the melody, signifyin(g) on all of the versions of the song he had ever heard (including his own), and therefore on many of the versions a listener would have heard as well. According to Walser, the melody of "My Funny Valentine" was so familiar to his audience that Davis did not even need to state it before signifyin(g) on it. After two brief phrases the song is already established. Moreover, later in the solo, Davis sets up "a tremendous silence, a charged gap of almost three full measures" (Walser 1995a: 176). Such a gesture relies completely on the history of the song resonating clearly for the audience. Moreover, it relies on the history and reputation of Davis himself. As Walser points out, "To create a pause of such length, during the most tense harmonic moments of the song, is, among other things, Davis's confident assertion of his stature as a soloist. Would an audience wait eagerly through such a gap for a lesser musician? Would a lesser musician dare to find out?" (Ibid.: 177).

David Brackett also relies on Gates's work in his analyses of James Brown's "Super Bad," applying it to a number of aspects of the song, the lyrics, the relation of lyrics and previous music history, the relation of polyrhythm and the pulse, and so on (Brackett 1995). For more music scholars using Gates's work and/or Houston A. Baker's notion of "the blues matrix," see Monson 1996, Tomlinson 1991, Floyd 1995, Ramsey 2003, and Zak 2005.

51. This is a paraphrase of Barthes's French text; see Barthes 1973: 1015.
52. Gates 1988: 61.
53. Ibid.: 124.
54. Small 1987: 234.
55. Bakhtin 1986: 79.
56. Ricoeur 1973: 137–38.
57. Gates 1988: 61.

Chapter 4. Rhythm and Counter-Rhythm (pp. 61–72)

1. *Dancing in the Street,* episode 9, "Make It Funky" (BBC/WBGH, 1996).
2. Don Knowlton, quoted in Wilson 1974: 7.
3. Wilson 1974: 9.
4. When I refer to rhythmic layers and figures as "cross-rhythmic" in the following discussion, I use the term in this weaker sense. Describing a layer in the rhythmic fabric of a funk groove as cross-rhythmic does not mean that it sounds cross-rhythmic in an African music sense.
5. See van der Merwe 1989: 158–60 and Chernoff and Johnson 1991: 69.
6. The swung or 12/8 version of the rumba pattern () is related to what A. M. Jones, in his classic study of African music, refers to as the "African signature tune": (Jones 1959: 210–13). The latter is also referred to as the standard pattern of African music (see Kauffman 1980: 397 and Chernoff and Johnson 1991: 67). Schematically it may be described as a pattern of 12/8 subdivided

into either [2+2+3]+[2+3] or, conversely, as [2+3]+[2+2+3], while the swung version of the rumba pattern implies a grouping of the 12/8 into 5+4+3.

7. Chernoff 1979: 98.

8. In his analysis of "Fight the Power" by Public Enemy (1989), Robert Walser finds that both the standard pattern of 3+3+2 and the figure of four against three are present in the polyrhythmic mix, but, in a way similar to a funk groove, these tendencies toward cross-rhythms are at work *within* the framework of a main rhythm of 4/4: "We begin to see that a variety of musical lines operates at different rhythmic levels, remaining within the overall organization of the meter and the two-measure unit, but filling the groove with complex tensions" (Walser 1995b: 202).

9. An articulation of a subdivision of sixteenths that is too clear cut may actually be experienced as a conflict with the groove as a whole. To some extent this happens in James Brown's "Funky President," where the sixteenths of the guitar are too evenly and accurately played to take up a position in the front of the sound box. The timbral clarity of the single-string playing is obviously an aspect of this. Although forming a 4:3 figure by way of its grouping, a straight subdivision like this does not fit in with the rest of the groove, and if the act of listening is focused on this layer, the groove is straightened out in a negative way. The straight subdivision does not give room for the ambivalence cultivated by the rest of the groove.

Chapter 5. "The Downbeat, in Anticipation" (pp. 73–91)

1. Brown 1991: 3.

2. *Dancing in the Street*, episode 9, "Make It Funky" (BBC/WBGH, 1996).

3. Here I distinguish between the one as a metrical unit—more precisely, the first beat of the measure—and the One as a sounding gesture (with a capital "O"). The latter is a characteristic rhythmic gesture in funk. It is centered around the first beat of the basic unit but may extend far beyond the metrical limits of the first beat (see also the discussion in chapters 7 and 9.)

4. Ghost strokes are soft taps played on the snare drum between the normal beats. They may be almost imperceptible, but they aid in keeping time and they color rhythm patterns.

5. A similar effect is present in "I Got the Feelin'" (1968), which also features Clyde Stubblefield on drums.

6. From Leeds's liner notes to *Star Time*; see Leeds 1991: 12.

7. In Bootsy Collins's own words: "Well, that space was always there, so I tried to play lead on bass to make things a little more entertaining" (Mills, Alexander, et al. 1998: 69).

8. In his analysis of James Brown's "Super Bad," David Brackett names this relation of downbeat and preceding upbeat the "downbeat/upbeat ellipsis" after Gates's description of how a musician "signifies" a beat: "He is

playing the upbeat into the downbeat of the chorus, implying their formal relationship by merging the two structures together to create an ellipsis of the downbeat" (Gates 1988: 123). With reference to Wilson and Gates, Brackett argues that in "Super Bad" these anticipations of the downbeat create an emphasis upon it and, moreover, that the upbeat to the beginning of another repetition is a musical space of utmost importance (Brackett 1995: 134; see also Wilson 1974: 12).

9. This gesture is particularly funky and is also one of the stylistic traits that is often imported by other styles to supply a touch of funk. Prince's "Purple Rain" is an example of this borrowing: this rather straightforward FM rock ballad has a distinct funky feel due to Prince's phrasing, both as a singer and a guitarist.

10. Waterman 1948: 25.

11. The vocals in "Sex Machine" may also be an example of the inclination toward percussive sounds in African American music. Even when the instrument is not necessarily percussive in character, like the human voice, sharp sounds, clear attacks, and a distinct articulation are preferred.

12. For further analysis of this, see chapter 9.

13. Fortepiano is a direction for performance indicating that a note should be played loud, then suddenly soft.

14. The B section of "Soul Power" (groove 2) seems to be less spread out in both space and time, and it is far less funky than the A section. The upper and lower parts of the sound fit together, and the basic unit is reduced to one bar. The question regarding density referent is also far more clarified. All parts of the groove supply the prevailing subdivision on the level of eighth notes, with the exception of the bass line, which unfolds in the open spaces. Due to its intricate counter-rhythmic pattern, the bass is also very destabilizing here (for further discussion, see chapter 8.) Though the congas play sixteenths, they are placed far back in the sound box and are no threat to any subdivision into eighths.

15. "Ain't It Funky Now" is from a live concert in Paris, one of the last with the Collins brothers. It should have been released on King as a triple live album called *Love, Power, Peace* but was withdrawn when Brown signed to Polydor in July 1971 (see White and Weinger 1991: 41).

16. See also my earlier discussions of the familiarity of the two versions of cross-rhythm.

17. From the entry "Funk" in *The New Rolling Stone Encyclopedia of Rock and Roll* (Romanowski and George-Warren 1995: 362).

Chapter 6. A Brand(ed) New Fad (pp. 95–112)

1. Vincent 1996: 86.

2. George 1988: 147.

3. Garofalo 1993: 231.
4. Brackett 2002: 68.
5. Ibid.
6. Ibid.: 69.
7. Garofalo 1994: 282.
8. Toynbee suggests that three "currents" have kept the popular music mainstream "flowing along its rocky course": hegemony, economy—involving how the music industry always tries to map a market onto hegemonic mainstream taste—and what he calls a popular urge to find an aesthetic of the center, some sort of "stylistic middle ground" (Toynbee 2002: 150). Along these lines, he identifies three different overlapping mainstreams in the history of popular music. The first he labels TiPAH (Tin Pan Alley–Hollywood). It runs from the early 1920s to the turn of the 1950s. Rock then constitutes the second mainstream, beginning in the 1950s and reaching its height in the 1970s. Since the 1980s, we have, according to Toynbee, been living in a moment characterized by plural, international networks and "glocal" phenomena like rap. In this period, he writes, successive singular mainstreams have been replaced by parallel multiple networks. He identifies three such networks: world music, glocal scenes, and regional blocs (Toynbee 2002: 159).
9. Garofalo 1994: 283.
10. Brackett 2002: 70. Even though funk as a style came to influence the mainstream, it may, in other words, seem as though traditional funk artists and funk bands did not attract their share of this new interest in black dance music. However, it is beyond the scope of this book to fully account for the range and complexities of the crossover processes going on in this period.
11. In an essay called "Ain't No Mountain High Enough: The Politics of Crossover," Steve Perry, for example, celebrated the integration taking place in the pop market in the 1980s; see Perry 1988. For a discussion of the debate between Perry and Nelson George on these issues, see Garofalo 1993.
12. George 1988: 129.
13. Ibid.: 150.
14. Brown 1997: 23–24.
15. In 1985 the single "Living in America" reached number four on the pop list and number ten on the r&b list.
16. McEwen 1992: 521.
17. Mayfield 1972: 27.
18. West 1994: 23.
19. Ibid.: 24.
20. West 1988: 181.
21. There are, of course, exceptions to this rule. The most striking examples from this period of spiritual funk with an appeal to a mainstream audience are probably Earth, Wind and Fire and Stevie Wonder. Both had several

Top Ten hits on the Billboard pop chart during the late 1970s. Whether the spiritual "content" of their songs was actually heard as spiritual by their new listeners is, however, still an open question. In his article on black crossover in the early 1980s, Brackett remarks upon the fact that crossover songs were party and dance numbers, arguing that this "inaccessibility" for black artists of the romantic ballad, "the widest public forum in popular music for the expression of serious emotions . . . might tend to project an image of African-Americans as frivolous, happy-go-lucky, and hedonistic, and therefore unready for the mature, romantic commitments available to white, pop artists" (Brackett 2002: 78).

22. West 1988: 182.

23. See, for example, White and Weinger 1991: 43, Palmer 1992: 169, and Vincent 1996: 84–86.

24. White and Weinger 1991: 43.

25. According to Garofalo, disco instituted a process of "reverse crossover," because in the late 1970s black radio stations were in the position of having to add white disco artists to their playlists in order to hold on to their listeners. The new, rock-influenced format of black-oriented radio (called urban contemporary) that followed the death of disco was multiracial, and "Urban Contemporary may have simply institutionalized the process of 'reverse crossover' which had begun during the height of the disco craze. UC outlets provided greater access for white musicians on what had been black-oriented stations, but African-American performers did not gain any reciprocal access to rock radio" (Garofalo 1993: 242–43).

26. Philadelphia soul was smooth—some would say slick—soul music characterized by sweeping strings, lush horns, and smooth vocal arrangements. The producer team of Kenny Gamble and Leon Huff created many of the instrumental textures that came to distinguish the genre. Its popularity peaked in the mid-1970s.

27. George 1988: 160.

Chapter 7. "Some Say It's Funk after Death" (pp. 113–40)

1. There are, of course, exceptions to this picture, like Stevie Wonder.

2. The title of this chapter is from the lyrics of "P-Funk (Wants to Get Funked Up)."

3. This inequality could be experienced in the consummate "Chocolate City," Washington, D.C., where the symbols of white power were situated only a few blocks from one of the poorest, worst-off inner cities in the United States.

4. Quoted in Corbett 1994: 7.

5. West 1988: 182.

6. Ibid.

7. Mills, Alexander, et al. 1998: 97.
8. West 1988: 182–83.
9. Brown 1997: 218–19 (emphasis added in the fourth sentence).
10. The main groove does not start until after two sections that almost work as intros. First, several voices sing the vocal riff "Tear the roof off the sucker" four times. After this section one expects the song to begin. However, the groove lacks grounding: "the ifs, the ands, and the buts" instead float freely. Actually, the groove does not settle until the first heavy One arrives after four bars (intro 2).
11. In general, gesture a2 is very similar to gesture a: it is also polyphonically realized by way of bass and vocals. However, this time the bass has taken over the cross-rhythmic function, while the vocals are allowed to weaken the effect of the cross-rhythmic pattern by placing the last syllable right on the fourth beat.
12. In a George Clinton interview by Greg Tate and Bob Wisdom, the interviewers characterize the live recordings from Beverly Hills as "awesome . . . funk on the Ellingtonian or symphonic level." Clinton answers: "Oh, did you hear that? Ain't that baaad? That is our baaadest shit, man" (Tate 1992: 37–38).
13. At one point Worrell actually plays the offbeat gesture as a 4:3 pattern.
14. See Chernoff 1979: 55.
15. Poster for the Parliament album *Mothership Connection*, released in 1975.
16. From the lyrics of the title track of Funkadelic's album *One Nation under a Groove* (1978).
17. As I mentioned, this is audible in P-Funk's "Bop Gun" (1977) and "Flash Light" (1977).
18. "Contract-release" describes a similar movement in jazz dance that focuses on the center of the body and begins with an attack generated by a locking of the midriff.
19. In the essay "Leichte Musik," Adorno writes that "light" music has become a refuge for a quality that was important for art music but has been lost, namely the relatively independent, distinct singular moment within totality. "In der leichten findet eine Qualität ihr Refugium, die in der oberen verlorening, aber ihr einmal wesentlich war, und für deren verlust sie vielleicht sehr zu zahlen hat: die des relativ selbständigen, qualitativ verschiedenen Einzelmoments in der Totalität" (Adorno 1973: 216).

Part IV. "Once Upon a Time Called Now!" (pp. 143–49)

1. Keil 1994b: 98.
2. Fikentscher 2000: 27–29.
3. Chambers 1985: 146.
4. For a discussion of male connoisseurship in rock, see Straw 1997.

5. Dyer 1990: 414, 415.
6. Fikentscher 2000: 75.
7. Chambers 1985: 149.
8. Hughes 1994: 150.
9. According to Richard Dyer, the importance of this form of disco may also be somewhat exaggerated in the interpretation of gay disco culture: "It depresses me that such phallic forms of disco as Village People should be so gay identified" (Dyer 1990: 415).
10. Fikentscher 2000: 44. The need for achieving this dynamic was the original reason for two turntables in a standard disco rig, so that pauses between songs could be avoided.
11. Interestingly, this is completely in accordance with David Brackett's work on the stylistic differences involved in the crossover processes. In a comparative analysis of George Clinton's "Atomic Dog" and Michael Jackson's "Billie Jean," Brackett finds that the latter has less syncopation or polyrhythm and a melodic design "closer to the norms of European art music. In experiential terms, listeners may feel a sense of periodic tension and relaxation, produced by the coordination of many musical elements, and aided by the way in which melody and harmony work together" (Brackett 2002: 76).
12. For a more thorough discussion of the hermeneutic concepts of understanding and being, as well as the relation between them, see the introduction.

Chapter 8. Time and Again (pp. 150–71)

1. Meyer's theoretical account has influenced the contemporary field of the cognitive psychology of music. Dowling and Harwood have developed a theory of musical affect that relies heavily on Meyer, and Narmour's "implication-realization" model also is close to Meyer's account (see Dowling and Harwood 1986: 202–224; Narmour 1989; Narmour 1991).
2. Meyer 1956: 28.
3. Meyer 1989: 3–37.
4. Kramer 1988: 20.
5. Ibid.: 40–42.
6. Ibid.: 42.
7. Ibid.: 33.
8. Meyer 1989: 15.
9. Ibid. In line with this theory, one might think of atonal linearity as parasitic to the linear gestures of tonal music, miming its processes of tension and release, as well as cadences, by means other than tonality.
10. McClary 2000: 67; see also Weber's classic study of Calvinist ethics and their significance for the emergence of a capitalist economy in early protestant Europe (Weber 2001 [1958]).

11. See, for example, Dahlhaus 1983, Kerman 1980, Kerman 1985, and Solie 1980. For a discussion of their influence in the field of popular music, see Danielsen 1998.

12. *Habitus* is a key concept in Pierre Bourdieu's sociology (cf., for example, Bourdieu 1990: 52–65). It signifies a set of culturally determined bodily dispositions to act, think, and feel in certain ways. Habitus is internalized and does not manifest in the form of beliefs or desires. It has no representative content and at no stage passes through consciousness.

13. Small 1996: 55 (emphasis added).

14. Kramer 1988: 55 (emphasis added).

15. Meyer 1967: 160.

16. According to Kramer, "Vertical music reached a pinnacle in the third quarter of this [the twentieth] century" (Kramer 1988: 386). He mentions Stockhausen's *Stimmung* (1968) as a consummate vertical piece, together with music by—among others—Steve Reich, Philip Glass, John Cage, and, not least, Morton Feldman.

17. Kramer here refers to the discontinuity separating the different moments of Stockhausen's "moment form."

18. Kramer 1988: 54–55.

19. Meyer 1967: 73.

20. Kramer 1988: 55.

21. In the typology of Kramer, "vertical time" is split up into two subcategories, "stasis" and "process." The latter may be designed to include repetitive rhythmic music. However, the repetitive minimalism that is linked with the subcategory "process" is also different from a groove, simply because it does not groove. Even though the figures of a minimalist rhythmic work such as Steve Reich's may be similar to the figures of, for example, Chernoff's West African drumming, the sounding or gestural difference is absolutely irreconcilable. With Reich the repetitive pattern becomes a backdrop of sound, working as a ground in order to make minimal changes come forward. The repetitive pattern does not move but rather draws attention to change on the micro-level.

22. Among other things, this leads Middleton to a description of the blues progression as a "mildly developmental" musical form. This progression is, however, an example of a cyclic form, where neither changes nor repetitions are accumulated and every sequence "erases" the previous one. The circle always returns to its own beginning, as if to wipe itself away, with difference only stepping forward in relation to the pattern, almost as if to reactivate it. Or, as James Snead puts it in the article "Repetition as a Figure of Black Culture," "In black culture, repetition means that the thing circulates (exactly in the manner of any flow, including capital flows) there in an equilibrium. In European culture, repetition must be seen to be

not just circulation and flow but accumulation and growth. In black culture, the thing (the ritual, the dance, the beat) is 'there for you to pick it up when you come back to get it'" (Snead 1984: 67).

Later in his book, Middleton introduces his distinction between musematic and discursive repetition. Musematic repetition is the repetition of short units, for example a riff, while discursive repetition is the repetition of longer units "at the level of the phrase, the sentence or even the complete section." Moreover, he says, "Musematic repetition is more likely to be prolonged and unvaried," it tends to have "a one-leveled structural effect," and "the most immediate familiar examples—riffs—are found in Afro-American musics and in rock." Conversely, discursive repetition is usually mixed with contrasting units of different types. Furthermore, it tends to be part of a hierarchically ordered discourse and, last but not least, "discursive processes tend to result in 'developmental structures' most strikingly worked out in the European art tradition" (Middleton 1990: 269).

23. Lidov 1979: 9.
24. Ibid.: 6.
25. Ibid.: 11.
26. Ibid.: 9.
27. Ibid.: 15.
28. Ibid.: 20–21.
29. Middleton 1990: 273–75. For an outline of Middleton's two categories of repetition, musematic and discursive, see note 22.
30. See Gates 1988: xxii–xxiii. See also the discussion in chapter 3.
31. This relation seems analogous to how Heidegger, and later Hubert Dreyfus, describes the "skilled use of equipment," pointing out how both the equipment and the skills become transparent. This way of interacting with the world is referred to by Dreyfus as "absorbed coping"; see Dreyfus 1994: 61–69 and Heidegger 1962: 98–99.
32. Lidov 1979: 21. Lidov's typology is built on the tonal canon of Western art music, as well as on a habitus of listening typical of the confident listener within this field.
33. Ibid.
34. See Adorno 1941, Adorno 1973.
35. This is brilliantly demonstrated in the writings of Søren Kierkegaard. In the essay "Repetition: A Venture in Experimenting Psychology by Constantin Constantius," Kierkegaard (alias Constantius) repeats a journey to Berlin to ascertain whether repetition is possible: "The only repetition was the impossibility of a repetition . . . When this had repeated itself several days, I became so furious, so weary of the repetition, that I decided to return home. My discovery was not significant, and yet it was curious, for I had discovered that there simply is no repetition and had verified it by

having it repeated in every possible way" (Kierkegaard 1983: 170–71). Constantius is experiencing the lack of constancy that follows time, which he has already anticipated earlier in the text through his description of the dialectics of repetition: "The dialectic of repetition is easy, for that which is repeated has been—otherwise it could not be repeated—but the very fact that it has been makes the repetition into something new" (Kierkegaard 1983: 149).

36. Hume quoted in Deleuze 1994: 70.

37. Ibid.: 71. In French the three instances of repetition are described as follows: "La constitution de la répétition implique déjà trois instances: cet en-soi qui la laisse impensable, ou qui la défait à mesure qu'elle se fait; le pour-soi de la synthèse passive; et fondée sur celle-ci, la representation réfléchie d'un "pour-nous" dans les synthèses actives" (Deleuze 1968: 98).

38. Deleuze 1994: 19: "Considérons . . . la répétition d'un motif décoration: une figure se trouve reproduite sous un concept absolument identique . . . Mais, en réalité, l'artiste ne procède pas ainsi. Il ne juxtapose pas de exemplaires de la figure, il combine chaque fois un élément d'un exemplaire avec *un autre* élément d'un exemplaire suivant. Il introduit dans le processus dynamique de la construction un déséquilibre, une instabilité, une dissymétrie, une sorte de béance qui ne seront conjurés que dans l'effet total" (Deleuze 1968: 31).

39. Deleuze 1994: 20: "Car dans l'ordre dynamique, il n'y a plus ni concept représentatif, ni figure représentée dans un espace préexistant. Il y a une Idée, et un pur dynamisme créateur d'espace correspondant" (Deleuze 1968: 32).

40. I refer to these grooves as "closed" even though I know that the opposite is often the case. For instance, van der Merwe describes the repetitive groove as "open ended," due to the fact that it does not end at a certain point predetermined by the musical course (van der Merwe 1989: 107–9). Conversely, closed form is often linked with Kramer's first category, namely "linear teleology." To say that a groove is open ended, however, may actually presuppose a distanced point of view. Only when we can view the musical course as a whole can we say that a repetitive groove is open ended in the sense above. When we are actually *in* a groove, the musical course is anything but open ended; it is experienced instead as a closed circle. The rhythmic dialogue leads back to its own beginning and the basic elements remain unchanged, almost as if they were decided beforehand.

41. Classic funk grooves such as "Ain't That Peculiar" and "Tell Me Something Good" from the live recording *Stompin' at the Savoy* (1983) by Rufus and Chaka Khan are characterized by the same heavy feeling. The time signature appears about to slow down to 2/2 or simply 1/1. In "Ain't That Peculiar" the basic pulse feels like a heavy concentration of energy near

beats one and three, and the snappy pick-up to these heavy beats gives exactly the right contraction to the body. In "Tell Me Something Good" it is perhaps only the One that really matters.

42. Deleuze 1994: 90: "La répétition est une condition de l'action avant d'être un concept de la réflexion" (Deleuze 1968: 121).

Chapter 9. Between Song and Groove (pp. 172–91)

1. One's experience of funk will be different if the context implies a different mode of listening. It can probably also be changed by learning. My own experience has been that the more familiar one gets with the aesthetics of the groove, the more this restlessness seems to fade away. One might presume also that contemporary listeners, who seem not only to have danced to grooves but to have listened to them, may in fact have a different listening habitus than the disco generation to which I belong.

2. In *The Souls of Black Folk* (1903), W. E. B. DuBois writes: "From the double life every American Negro must live, as a Negro and as an American . . . must arise a painful self-consciousness, an almost morbid sense of personality and a moral hesitancy which is fatal to self-confidence. The worlds within and without the Veil of Color are changing, and changing rapidly, but not at the same rate, not in the same way; and this must produce a peculiar wrenching of the soul, a peculiar sense of doubt and bewilderment. Such a double life, with double thoughts, double duties, and double social classes, must give rise to double words and double ideals, and tempt the mind to pretence or revolt, to hypocrisy or radicalism" (DuBois 1989: 142).

3. For a description of the typical dramaturgy of a live funk event, see chapter 10.

4. See chapter 3.

5. The song leaves the impression of James Brown at some point becoming aware of the qualities of this groove and then giving his instructions to the band. The song is also named on the spot, when James Brown, toward the end of the song, states, "The name of this tune is the Funky Drummer." These eight bars are probably among the most frequently sampled breaks in the history of popular music.

6. Rose 1994: 73–74.

7. Grandmaster Flash, quoted in Rose 1994: 73.

8. Rose 1994: 70.

9. Snead 1984: 67.

10. Ibid.: 69.

11. Ibid.: 72.

12. Chernoff 1979: 100.

13. Ibid.

14. Ibid.: 115.
15. This play with relative duration can also be heard in a song such as "Mother Popcorn." This song has a B section, as discussed earlier in this chapter. However, to make the A section have the same effect each time— in order to make it seem like an infinitely running groove—the A section after the B section (A$_2$) has to be longer than the A section before the B section (A$_1$). In his analysis of "Superbad," David Brackett finds that all of the A sections are progressively longer, and he refers to this as "proportional signifyin(g)" (Brackett 1995: 148–53).
16. The sound ends so abruptly that one wonders whether the take actually continued. The material may have been edited afterward, both to give the ending the right feel and to keep the song from getting far too long.
17. See also the discussion in chapter 8.
18. It may not be accidental that the basic unit never exceeds the so-called "psychological or perceptual present," which has been characterized as a temporal span of attention, a sort of window opened on experience that continually shifts its view in time. The perceptual present in listening normally lies in the range of two to five seconds. However, this length may vary with context and can be manipulated by composers and performers within stylistic limits (Dowling and Harwood 1986: 179–81).
19. Chernoff 1979: 112.
20. Ibid.
21. The groove is fundamental in songs with a more traditional melody and form as well, even though the listener may not be primarily focused upon it. However, in some Western contexts that are situated far from African American culture both geographically and culturally, a groove can probably be rather poor without disturbing the experience of the song, simply because most listeners are not particularly aware of it.
22. Michael Jackson's formidable crossover hit "Don't Stop Till You Get Enough" (1979), for example, is organized according to a traditional song format. All of the necessary ingredients are present, like verse, chorus, bridge, and a repeated break played by synthetic horns to assert the formal scheme. Moreover, it has a phrase-based melody that may be sung separate from the accompaniment.
23. The unusual form of the song may be explained by the fact that it was originally recorded as a soundtrack to a film. However, the producer did not think it was funky enough and turned it down. In his autobiography, Brown says, "I knew that the song wouldn't make it without the movie, so I came up with the story line that you could see" (Brown 1997: 241). The story he refers to is probably the one printed on the cover of the double album *The Payback*, released in 1974, which hints at the song by including some of its characteristic verbal expressions.

1. A state is not stable, however. It is better to speak of one continuously changing state in a never-ending stream of previous and possible states of being. One does not skip between states as in a binary structure, and perhaps it is only on occasion that one really forgets one's time and place.

2. Small 1996: 55.

3. James Brown has released three live recordings from the famous Apollo Theatre in Harlem. The first one was recorded in 1962 and went to number two on the *Billboard* pop chart for albums, the second was recorded in 1967, and the third was recorded in 1971. On each of them Brown's opening procedure varies.

4. According to the Western understanding of "presence," this mode of being is actually "absence" (of thinking). I will return to this in the next chapter.

5. Ricoeur 1973: 130–31.

6. Ibid.: 140.

7. Ibid.: 132. Ricœur uses the text as a paradigmatic example of the distanciation that is a part of social life as such: "For me the text is much more than a particular case of interhuman communication, it is the paradigm of the distanciation in all communication" (Ibid.: 130).

8. Ibid.: 132.

9. This figure is analogous to how Derrida interprets the sign as deferred presence in the sense that "the circulation of signs defers the moment in which we can encounter the thing itself," so as to make us believe it is already present (Derrida 1982: 9). "La circulation des signes différe le moment où nous pourrions rencontrer la chose même" (Derrida 1972: 9).

10. Lyotard 1994: 12–13. "Car elle [la pensée: my addition] n'a à juger que selon son état, en jugeant ce qui plaît. Ainsi cet état, qui est 'l'objet' de son jugement, est le même plaisir qui est la 'loi' de jugement. Dans l'esthétique, ces deux aspects du jugement, référentialité et légitimité, pour ainsi dire, ne sont qu'un ... c'est cette disposition remarquable que je nomme la *tautégorie* de la réflexion" (Lyotard 1991a: 26). Lyotard also writes about the tautological structure of feeling in L'*inarticulé ou le différend même;* see Lyotard 1990.

11. Lyotard 1994: 45. "Ne doit-on pas conclure que la réflexion, laissée à elle-même, ne peut rien dire autre que 'je sens, je sens' et 'je sens que je sens,' tautégoriquement?" (Lyotard 1991a: 63).

12. However, feeling in this context does not refer to a personal feeling or an emotion.

13. Deleuze refers to intensity as a difference in quantity, understood as that aspect of a certain quantity that cannot be reduced to the quantitative dimension of the quantity. In the words of Deleuze, it is "that which cannot be canceled in difference in quantity or that which is unequalizable in

quantity itself" (Deleuze 1994: 232). "Ce qu'il y a d'inannulable dans la différence de quantité, d'inégalisable dans la quantité même" (Deleuze 1968: 299). A "difference in quantity" may, in other words, be interpreted in two ways: it can be the difference between two different quantities, and it can be the difference *in* quantity, *in one quantity*, in the sense of a fundamental or original moment present in every quantity. According to Deleuze, the latter is how intensity is to be understood. Intensity is not a relative difference, but difference in itself, or rather the differential of a certain quantity.

14. Deleuze 1994: 222. "Toute intensité est E-E', où E renvoie lui-même à e-e', et e à Ɛ-Ɛ', etc.: chaque intensité est déjà un couplage" (Deleuze 1968: 287).

15. Deleuze 1994: 228. However, even when intensity is summed up as a certain quality, difference is not canceled out as a productive force: "We cannot conclude from this that difference is canceled out, or at least that it is canceled in itself. It is canceled in so far as it is drawn outside itself, in extensity and in the quality which fills that extensity. However, difference creates both this extensity and this quality. Intensity is developed and explicated by means of an extension (*extensio*) which relates it to the extensity (*extensum*) in which it appears outside itself and hidden beneath quality" (Deleuze 1994: 228). "On ne peut pas en conclure que la différence s'annule, du moins qu'elle s'annule en soi. Elle s'annule en tant qu'elle est mise hors de soi, *dans* l'étendue et *dans* la qualité qui remplit cette étendue. Mais cette qualité comme cette étendue, la différence les crée. L'intensité s'explique, se développe dans une extension (*extensio*). C'est cette extension qui la rapporte à l'étendue (*extensum*), où elle apparaît hors de soi, recouverte par la qualité" (Deleuze 1968: 294).

16. Ricoeur 1973: 132.

17. One might also say that the separation (*espacement*) of meaning does now appear as a detour (*temporisation*), while the difference in time (*temporisation*) making the event into something of the past has become a difference in space, another separation (*espacement*); see also Derrida 1982: 18.

18. Kant 1951 (1790).

19. Waterman 1967: 211.

Chapter 11. Presence and Pleasure (pp. 204–18)

1. As Derrida writes, "This privilege is the ether of metaphysics, the element of our thought that is caught in the language of metaphysics. One can delimit such a closure today only by soliciting the value of presence that Heidegger has shown to be the ontotheological determination of Being; and in thus soliciting the value of presence, by means of an interrogation whose status must be completely exceptional, we are also examining the absolute privilege of this form or epoch of presence in general that is consciousness

as meaning in self-presence" (Derrida 1982: 16). "Ce privilège est l'éther de la métaphysique, l'élément de notre pensée en tant qu'elle est prise dans la langue de la métaphysique. On ne peut délimiter une telle clôture qu'en sollicitant aujourd'hui cette valeur de présence dont Heidegger a montré qu'elle est la détermination onto-théologique de l'être; et à solliciter ainsi cette valeur de présence, par une mise en question don't le statut doit être tout a fait singulier, nous interrogeons le privilège absolu de cette forme ou de cette époque de la présence en général qu'est la conscience comme vouloir-dire dans la présence à soi" (Derrida 1972: 17).

2. Derrida 1974: 17. "L'écriture au sens métaphorique, l'écriture naturelle, divine et vivante, est vénérée; elle est égale, en dignité, à l'origine de la valeur, à la voix de la conscience comme loi divine, au cœur, au sentiment, etc." (Derrida 1970: 29).

3. Ibid. "Dans l'intimité de la présence à soi" (Derrida 1970: 30).

4. Ibid. "L'écriture représentative, déchue, seconde, instituée, l'écriture au sens propre et étroit, est condemnée" (Derrida 1970: 29).

5. Ibid. "Comprise comme cela même qui devait être compris" (Derrida 1970: 30).

6. The relation of mediation and musical immediacy is also a central issue in Kai Fikentscher's discussion of underground dance music in New York. Though Fikentscher does not identify exactly how mediation brings about musical immediacy, the relation of mediation, in this case how mediated music is mediated in a dance floor setting, and musical immediacy is pointed out as an important aspect of the disco experience (Fikentscher 2000: 15–16).

7. See Feld 1994.

8. Radano 2003: 236.

9. Frith 1983: 19. See also part I of this study.

10. In his discussion of Ewe drumming, Chernoff also stresses the focus on personal coolness. According to Chernoff, music making in Africa is above all an occasion for the demonstration of character. Entering an ecstatic stage of no control not only spoils the quality of the musical performance but also comes across as both tasteless and ridiculous (Chernoff 1979: 141–51).

11. This probably also led to poor local competence when it came to the task of performing funk and similar black music. When this hot reception is put into action on the production side—when the experienced inner motion, the bodily feeling, is being externalized—it is easy to hear that the music is losing its power. It is almost as if the power is being brought out of the music and transformed into exterior movement, to a collection of oversized "expressive" gestures.

12. In the 1960s and 1970s the Norwegian Broadcasting Company, owned by the state, had a monopoly on radio and TV transmissions. This meant an

almost total absence of commercial popular music on radio and TV, due to the ruling ideology of high culture as a means of enlightening the people. This was changed with the deregulation of broadcasting in 1984, which allowed for private initiatives as well.

13. Chambers 1985: 148.

14. See Small 1987.

15. Lipsitz 1998: 128. George Lipsitz's discussion of how Robert Johnson's life takes on the contours of romanticism in the British blues interpretation in the 1960s is just another instance of how black music changes when it is transferred from one context (in this case production) to another (reception).

16. Chambers 1985: 148.

17. Lipsitz 1998: 118.

18. Lott 1993: 6.

19. Following Lott, it may be that with regard to funk this requirement would eventually wither away, not least because of the marker's—in Lott's case, the minstrel show's—success in introducing the cultures to each other. According to Lott, in the 1920s "an imaginary proximity to 'blackness' was so requisite to white identity and to the culture industry which helped produce that identity . . . that the signifier of blackface had become redundant" (Lott 1993: 240, note 13). In parallel, one might say that today funk and black rhythm in general have been used as a means of negotiating the boundaries between the dominant culture and its internal others for so long a time as to make this music redundant as a signifier of difference.

20. See Pattison 1987.

21. See Adorno 2003.

22. Adorno 1997: 176–77. "Ihre Bewegung muß stillstehen und durch ihren Stillstand sichtbar werden. Objektiv aber ist der immanente Prozeßcharakter der Kunstwerke, schon ehe sie irgend partei ergreifen, der Prozeß, den sie gegen das ihnen Auswendige, das Bloß Bestehende anstrengen" (Adorno 1970: 264).

23. Heidegger 1971: 62. "Die Wahrheit richtet sich ins Werk" (Heidegger 1960: 63).

24. Lyotard 1991b: 107. "La présomption de l'esprit par rapport au temps" (Lyotard 1988: 118).

25. Abrahams 1976: 52.

26. My translation: "Le temps du sentiment est *maintenant*" (Lyotard 1990: 203).

Bibliography

Abrahams, R. D. 1976. *Talking Black*. Rowley, Massachusetts: Newbury House.

Adorno, T. W. 1941. "On Popular Music." *Studies in Philosophy and Social Sciences* 9: 17–48.

———. 1970. *Äestetische Theorie*. Frankfurt am Main: Suhrkamp.

———. 1973. "Leichte Musik." *Einleitung in die Musiksoziologie: Zwölf theoretische Vorlesungen*. Frankfurt am Main: Suhrkamp. 199–218.

———. 1997. *Aesthetic Theory*. London: Athlone.

———. 2003. *Philosophy of Modern Music*. New York: Continuum.

Agawu, K. 1995. "The Invention of 'African Rhythm.'" *Journal of the American Musicological Society* 48(3): 380–95.

Arom, S. 1991. *African Polyphony and Polyrhythm: Musical Structure and Methodology*. Cambridge: Cambridge University Press.

Baker, H. A. J. 1984. *Blues, Ideology and African-American Literature: A Vernacular Theory*. Chicago: University of Chicago Press.

Bakhtin, M. M. 1986 (1952). "The Problem of Speech Genres." *Speech Genres and Other Late Essays*. Austin: University of Texas Press. 60–102.

Barthes, R. 1973. "Théorie du texte [Text theory]." *Encyclopædia Universalis France* 15: 1013–17.

———. 1991. "The Grain of the Voice." *The Responsibility of Forms: Critical Essays on Music, Art, and Representation*. Ed. R. Howard. Berkeley: University of California Press. 267–77.

Bengtsson, I., A. Gabrielsson, et al. 1969. "Empirisk rytmforskning [Empirical research on rhythm]." *Svensk Tidskrift for Musikforskning*. 49–118.

Berman, M. 1982. *All That Is Solid Melts into Air: The Experience of Modernity*. London: Simon and Schuster.

Born, G., and D. Hesmondhalgh, eds. 2000. *Western Music and Its Others. Difference, Representation, and Appropriation in Music*. Berkeley: University of California Press.

Bourdieu, P. 1990. *The Logic of Practice*. Oxford: Polity Press.

Brackett, D. 1995. "James Brown's 'Superbad' and the Double-Voiced Utterance." *Interpreting Popular Music*. Cambridge: Cambridge University Press. 108–156.

———. 2002. "(In Search of) Musical Meaning: Genres, Categories, and Crossover." *Popular Music Studies*. Ed. D. Hesmondalgh and K. Negus. London: Arnold. 65–84.

Brogan, T. V. F. 1993. "Rhythm." *The New Princeton Encyclopedia of Poetry and Poetics.* Ed. A. Preminger and T. V. F. Brogan. Princeton, New Jersey: Princeton University Press. 1066–70.

Brown, J. 1991. "Introduction." Liner notes to *Star Time.* Polygram 849 108–2.

Brown, J., with B. Tucker. 1997. *James Brown. The Godfather of Soul.* New York: Thunder's Mouth Press.

Chambers, I. 1985. *Urban Rhythms: Pop Music and Popular Culture.* Basingstoke: Macmillan.

Chernoff, J. M. 1979. *African Rhythm and African Sensibilities: Aesthetics and Social Action in African Musical Idioms.* Chicago: University of Chicago Press.

Chernoff, J. M., and S. F. J. Johnson. 1991. "Basic Conga Drum Rhythms in African-American Musical Styles." *Black Music Research Journal* 11(1): 55–74.

Corbett, J. 1994. *Sounding Off from John Cage to Dr. Funkenstein.* Durham, North Carolina: Duke University Press.

Dahlhaus, C. 1983. *Foundations of Music History.* Cambridge: Cambridge University Press.

Danielsen, A. 1998. "His Name Was Prince: A Study of Diamonds and Pearls." *Popular Music* 16(3): 275–91.

Deleuze, G. 1968. *Différence et répétition.* Paris: Presses Universitaires de France.

———. 1994. *Difference and Repetition.* London: Athlone Press.

Derrida, J. 1970. *De la grammatologie.* Paris: Les Éditions Minuit.

———. 1972. *Marges de la philosophie.* Paris: Les Éditions de Minuit.

———. 1974. *Of Grammatology.* Baltimore: John Hopkins University Press.

———. 1982. *Margins of Philosophy.* Chicago: University of Chicago Press.

Dowling, W. J., and D. L. Harwood. 1986. *Music Cognition.* San Diego: Academic Press.

Dreyfus, H. 1994. *Being-in-the-World: A Commentary on Heidegger's Being and Time, Division I.* Cambridge, Massachusetts: MIT Press.

DuBois, W. E. B. 1989 (1903). *The Souls of Black Folk.* New York: Bantam Books.

Dyer, R. 1990 (1979). "In Defense of Disco." *On Record: Rock, Pop, and the Written Word.* Ed. S. Frith and A. Goodwin. London: Routledge. 410–18.

Feld, S. 1994. "Communication, Music, and Speech about Music." *Music Grooves.* Ed. C. Keil and S. Feld. Chicago: University of Chicago Press. 77–95.

Fikentscher, K. 2000. *"You Better Work!" Underground Dance Music in New York City.* Hanover, New Hampshire: Wesleyan University Press/University Press of New England.

Floyd, S. A. J. 1995. *The Power of Black Music: Interpreting Its History from Africa to the United States.* New York: Oxford University Press.

Frith, S. 1983. *Sound Effects: Youth, Leisure, and the Politics of Rock 'n' Roll.* London: Constable.

———. 1996. *Performing Rites: On the Value of Popular Music.* Oxford: Oxford University Press.

———. 2004. "'And I Guess It Doesn't Matter Any More': European Thoughts on American Music." *This Is Pop: In Search of the Elusive at Experience Music Project.* Ed. E. Weisbard. Cambridge, Massachusetts: Harvard University Press. 15-25.

Fuller, H. F. 1972. "Towards a Black Aesthetic." *The Black Aesthetic.* Ed. A. J. Gayle. New York: Anchor Books. 3-11.

Garofalo, R. 1993. "Black Popular Music: Crossing Over or Going Under?" *Rock and Popular Music. Politics, Policies, Institutions.* Ed. T. Bennett et al. London: Routledge. 231-48.

Garofalo, R. 1994. "Culture Versus Commerce: The Marketing of Black Popular Music." *Public Culture* 7: 275-87.

Gates, H. L. J. 1987. *Figures in Black: Words, Signs, and the "Racial" Self.* New York: Oxford University Press.

———. 1988. *The Signifying Monkey: A Theory of African-American Literary Criticism.* New York: Oxford University Press.

Gayle, A. J., ed. 1972. *The Black Aesthetic.* New York: Anchor Books.

George, N. 1988. *The Death of Rhythm & Blues.* New York: Plume.

Gran, A-B. 2000. *Hvite løgner / sorte myter: Det etniske på modernitetens scene.* [*White lies / black myths: The ethnic in modern theater.*] Oslo: Unipub.

Hegel, G. W. F. 1980 (1830). *Lectures on the Philosophy of World History.* Cambridge: Cambridge University Press.

Heidegger, M. 1960. *Der Ursprung des Kunstwerkes.* Frankfurt am Main: Reclam.

———. 1962 (1927). *Being and Time.* Oxford: Blackwell.

———. 1969. "Zeit und Sein." *Zur Sache des Denkens.* Tübingen: Niemeyer. 1-26.

———. 1971. "The Origin of the Work of Art." *Poetry, Language, Thought.* New York: Harper and Row. 15-87.

———. 1972. "Time and Being." *On Time and Being.* New York: Harper and Row. 1-24.

Holloway, J. E., ed. 1990. *Africanisms in American Culture.* Bloomington: Indiana University Press.

Hughes, W. 1994. "In the Empire of the Beat: Discipline and Disco." *Microphone Fiends: Youth Music and Youth Culture.* Ed. A. Ross and T. Rose. New York: Routledge. 147-57

Husserl, E. 1991 (1893-1917). *On the Phenomenology of the Consciousness of Internal Time.* Dordrecht: Kluwer.

Jones, A. M. 1959. *Studies in African Music.* London: Oxford.

Jones, L. 1972. "The Changing Same (R&B and New Black Music)." *The Black Aesthetic.* Ed. A. J. Gayle. New York: Anchor Books. 112-25.

Kant, I. 1951 (1790). *Critique of Judgment.* New York: Hafner Press.

Kauffman, R. 1980. "African Rhythm: A Reassessment." *Ethnomusicology* 24(3): 393-415.

Keil, C. 1994a. "Motion and Feeling through Music." *Music Grooves.* Ed. C. Keil and S. Feld. Chicago: University of Chicago Press. 53-76.

——. 1994b. "Participatory Discrepancies and the Power of Music." *Music Grooves*. Ed. C. Keil and S. Feld. Chicago: University of Chicago Press. 96–108.

Kerman, J. 1980. "How We Got into Analysis, and How to Get Out." *Critical Inquiry* 7: 311–31.

——. 1985. *Musicology*. London: Fontana Press/Collins.

Kierkegaard, S. 1962 (1843). "Gjentagelsen." *Samlede værker, Bind 5 & 6*. Copenhagen: Gyldendal. 113–94.

——. 1983. "Repetition: A Venture in Experimenting Psychology by Constantin Constantius." *Fear and Trembling: Repetition*. Princeton, New Jersey: Princeton University Press. 125–231.

Kramer, J. D. 1988. *The Time of Music*. London: Schirmer.

Kvifte, T. 1989. *Instruments and the Electronic Age: Toward a Terminology for a Unified Description of Playing Technique*. Oslo: Solum.

Large, E. W., and J. F. Kolen. 1994. "Resonance and the Perception of Musical Meter." *Connection Science* 6(2/3): 177–209.

Leeds, A. 1991. "From the Inside." Liner notes to *Star Time*. Polygram 849 108-2.

Levine, L. 1978. *Black Culture and Black Consciousness: Afro-American Folk Thought from Slavery to Freedom*. New York: Oxford University Press.

Lidov, D. 1979. "Structure and Function in Musical Repetition." *Journal of the Canadian Association of University Schools of Music* 8(1): 1–32.

Lipsitz, G. 1998. *The Possessive Investment in Whiteness: How White People Profit from Identity Politics*. Philadelphia: Temple University Press.

Lott, E. 1993. *Love and Theft. Blackface Minstrelsy and the American Working Class*. New York: Oxford University Press.

Lyotard, J.-F. 1988. "Le sublime et l'avant-garde." *L'inhumain: Causeries sur le temps*. Paris: Galilée. 101–18.

——. 1990. "L'inarticulé ou le différend même." *Figures et Conflits Rhétoriques*. Ed. M. Meyer and A. Lempereur. Bruxelles: Editions de l'Université de Bruxelles. 201–7.

——. 1991a. *Lecons sur l'analytique du sublime*. Paris: Galilée.

——. 1991b. "The Sublime and the Avant-Garde." *The Inhuman: Reflections on Time*. Cambridge: Polity Press. 89–107.

——. 1994. *Lessons on the Analytic of the Sublime*. Stanford, California: Stanford University Press.

Marcuse, H. 1969. "Repressive Tolerance." *A Critique of Pure Tolerance*. Ed. R. Wolff, B. Moore Jr., and H. Marcuse. Boston: Beacon Press.

Marsh, D. 1992. "Sly and the Family Stone." *The Rolling Stone Illustrated History of Rock & Roll*. Ed. A. DeCurtis and J. Henke. New York: Random House. 435–40.

Maultsby, P. K. 1990. "Africanisms in African-American Music." *Africanisms in American Culture*. Ed. J. E. Holloway. Bloomington: Indiana University Press. 185–210.

Mayfield, J. 1972. "You Touch My Black Aesthetic and I'll Touch Yours." *The Black Aesthetic*. Ed. A. J. Gayle. New York: Anchor Books. 23–30.

McClary, S. 2000. *Conventional Wisdom: The Content of Musical Form*. Berkeley: University of California Press.

McEwen, J. 1992. "Funk." *The Rolling Stone Illustrated History of Rock & Roll*. Ed. A. DeCurtis and J. Henke. New York: Random House. 521–25.

Meyer, L. B. 1956. *Emotion and Meaning in Music*. Chicago: University of Chicago Press.

———. 1967. *Music, the Arts, the Ideas*. Chicago: University of Chicago Press.

———. 1989. *Style and Music: Theory, History and Ideology*. Chicago: University of Chicago Press.

Middleton, R. 1990. *Studying Popular Music*. Milton Keynes: Open University Press.

Mills, D., L. Alexander, et al. 1998. *George Clinton and P-Funk: An Oral History*. New York: Avon Books.

Monson, I. 1996. *Saying Something: Jazz Improvisation and Interaction*. Chicago: University of Chicago Press.

Moore, A. F. 1993. *Rock: The Primary Text*. Buckingham: Open University Press.

Narmour, E. 1989. "The 'Genetic Code' of Melody: Cognitive Structures Generated by the Implication-Realization Model." *Contemporary Music Review* 4: 45–64.

———. 1991. "The Top-Down and Bottom-Up Systems of Musical Implication: Building on Meyer's Theory of Emotional Syntax." *Music Perception* 9(1): 1–26.

Nketia, J. H. K. 1974. *The Music of Africa*. New York: Norton.

Palmer, R. 1992. "James Brown." *The Rolling Stone Illustrated History of Rock & Roll*. Ed. A. DeCurtis and J. Henke. New York: Random House. 163–70.

Pattison, R. 1987. *The Triumph of Vulgarity*. New York: Oxford University Press.

Perry, S. 1988. "Ain't No Mountain High Enough: The Politics of Crossover." *Facing the Music: Essays on Pop, Rock and Culture*. Ed. S. Frith. New York: Mandarin. 51–87.

Radano, R. 2003. *Lying Up a Nation: Race and Black Music*. Chicago: University of Chicago Press.

Radano, R., and P. V. Bohlman, eds. 2000. *Music and the Racial Imagination*. Chicago: University of Chicago Press.

Ramsey, G. P. J. 2003. *Race Music. Black Cultures from Bebop to Hip-Hop*. Berkeley: University of California Press; Chicago: Center for Black Music Research, Columbia College.

Ricoeur, P. 1973. "The Hermeneutical Function of Distanciation." *Philosophy Today* 17: 129–43.

Romanowski, P., and H. George-Warren, eds. 1995. *The New Rolling Stone Encyclopedia of Rock & Roll*. New York: Fireside, Simon and Schuster.

Rose, T. 1994. *Black Noise: Rap Music and Black Culture in Contemporary America*. Hanover, New Hampshire: Wesleyan University Press/University Press of New England.

Said, E. W. 1978. *Orientalism: Western Conceptions of the Orient*. New York: Penguin.

Small, C. 1987. *Music of the Common Tongue: Survival and Celebration in Afro-American Music*. London: Calder/Riverrun Press.

———. 1996. *Music, Society, Education*. Hanover, New Hampshire: Wesleyan University Press/University Press of New England.

Smitherman, G. 1994. *Black Talk: Words and Phrases from the Hood to the Amen Corner*. Boston: Houghton Mifflin.

Snead, J. A. 1984. "Repetition as a Figure of Black Culture." *Black Literature and Literary Theory*. Ed. H. L. J. Gates. New York: Methuen. 59-80.

Solie, R. A. 1980. "The Living Work: Organicism and Musical Analysis." *Nineteenth-Century Music* 4(2): 147-56.

Southern, E. 1997. *The Music of Black Americans: A History*. New York: Norton.

Stewart, J. 1972. "Introduction to Black Aesthetics in Music." *The Black Aesthetic*. Ed. A. J. Gayle. New York: Anchor Books. 77-91.

Straw, W. 1997. "Sizing Up Record Collections: Gender and Connoisseurship in Rock Music Culture." *Sexing the Groove: Popular Music and Gender*. Ed. S. Whiteley. London: Routledge. 3-16.

Tate, G. 1992. *Flyboy in the Buttermilk: Essays on Contemporary America*. New York: Simon and Schuster.

Tomlinson, G. 1991. "Cultural Dialogics and Jazz: A White Historian Signifies." *Black Music Research Journal* 11: 229-64.

Toynbee, J. 2002. "Mainstreaming, from Hegemonic Centre to Global Networks." *Popular Music Studies*. Ed. D. Hesmondalgh and K. Negus. London: Arnold. 149-63.

Van der Merwe, P. 1989. *Origins of the Popular Style: The Antecedents of Twentieth-Century Popular Music*. New York: Oxford University Press.

Vincent, R. 1996. *Funk: The Music, the People, and the Rhythm of the One*. New York: St. Martin's/Griffin.

Walser, R. 1995a. "'Out of Notes': Signification, Interpretation, and the Problem of Miles Davis." *Jazz among the Discourses*. Ed. K. Gabbard. Durham, North Carolina: Duke University Press. 165-88.

Walser, R. 1995b. "Rhythm, Rhyme, and Rhetoric in the Music of Public Enemy." *Ethnomusicology* 39(2): 193-217.

Waterman, R. 1948. "'Hot' Rhythm in Negro Music." *Journal of the American Musicological Society* 1: 24-37.

Waterman, R. A. 1967. "African Influence on the Music of the Americas." *Acculturation in the Americas*. Ed. S. Tax. New York: Cooper Square. 207-18.

Weber, M. 1949. *The Methodology of the Social Sciences*. New York: Free Press.

———. 2001 (1958). *The Protestant Ethic and the Spirit of Capitalism*. London: Routledge.

West, C. 1988. *Prophetic Fragments*. Grand Rapids, Michigan: William B. Eerd-
mans Publishing.

———. 1994. *Race Matters*. New York: Vintage.

White, C., and H. Weinger. 1991. "Are You Ready for Star Time?" Liner notes to
Star Time. Polygram 849 108-2.

White, H. 1972. "The Forms of Wildness: Archaeology of an Idea." *The Wild
Man Within: An Image in Western Thought from the Renaissance to Romanticism.*
Ed. E. Dudley and M. E. Novak. Pittsburgh: University of Pittsburgh Press.
3–38.

Wilson, O. 1974. "The Significance of the Relationship between Afro-American
Music and West African Music." *The Black Perspective in Music* 2(1): 3–22.

———. 1983. "Black Music as an Art Form." *Black Music Research Journal* 3: 1–22.

———. 1992. "The Heterogeneous Sound Ideal in African-American Music."
New Perspectives on Music. Ed. J. Wright. Warren, Michigan: Harmonie Park
Press. 327–38.

Zak, A. J., III. 2005. "Bob Dylan and Jimi Hendrix: Juxtaposition and Transformation in 'All Along the Watchtower.'" *Journal of the American Musicological
Society* 57(3): 599–644.

Index

Page numbers with *f* indicate a figure; those with *p* indicate a picture.

black minstrelsy, 21–24, 212, 213, 221n9, 243n19

Black Talk (Smitherman), 3

blues: adoption by British musicians, 212, 243n15; cyclic progressions, 235–36n22; spiritual-blues impulse in funk, 115; twelve-bar blues pattern, 40–41

"Body Heat" (Brown), 108, 110, 111*f*

Bohlman, P. V., 10, 20, 28

"Bop Gun" (Parliament/P-Funk All-Stars), 137, 233n17

Born, G., 33

Bourdieu, Pierre, 235n12

Brackett, David, 96–97, 231n10, 231–32n21, 234n11, 239n15

the break, 184–88, 199–201

break beat, 182–83

bridge forms, 41, 224n3

British blues, 212, 243n15

"Brother Rapp" (Brown), 89

Brown, James, 4–7, 17–19, 86*p*, 87*p*, 132–33; Afro-modernism, 32–33, 223n46; black identity, 15–16, 32; childhood, 5–6; community work, 7; counter-rhythm, 62–69, 229n9; decline in popularity, 109–11, 138; emergence of funk grooves, 39–42; live performances, 194–95, 240n3; negotiation of song and groove, 149, 174–91; Polydor era, 99–105; proto-funk, 39–40; r&b tunes, 63, 74; shouts as gesture, 47; temporal designs of songs, 18–19, 174–80, 184–88; vocal percussion, 47, 78, 82–84, 230n11, 230n13

Byrd, Bobby, 6, 83

Byrd, Sarah, 6

call-and-response dialogue, 52–55, 134–35, 226n33

Chambers, Iain, 145, 146, 211, 212

Charles, Ray, 30

Chernoff, John M., 17, 220n22, 235n21; on African cross-rhythms, 65–66; on African stylized genres, 57, 59, 226n27, 226n33; on breaks in Takai music, 187; on Brown's groove, 188–90; on discipline, 55; on the internal beat, 55–56; on open spaces, 55; on

repetition in African drumming, 189–90, 242n10; on rhythmic dialogues, 53

Chic, 4, 147

Chocolate City, 114, 117*p*

"Chocolate City" (Parliament/P-Funk), 8, 125, 126*f*, 127

civil rights movement, 7, 8

classical-romantic aesthetics of music, 152–54

Clinton, George, 4–5, 7–8, 18, 116*p*, 117*p*; as Dr. Funkenstein, 8, 114–15; drumming, 194; funk crossover, 234n11; origins of P-Funk, 115; P-Funk's anti-crossover grooves, 137; psychedelic utopias, 113–15, 125, 136–38, 209. *See also* Parliament/P-Funk All-Stars

The Clones of Dr. Funkenstein, 117*p*

"Cold Sweat" (Brown), 6, 18, 39–41, 223n2; ambivalence and ambiguity, 133; basic groove, 76*f*; binary verse and chorus/bridge forms, 41; counter-rhythm, 63, 63*f*; density referent, 75; disparity between upper and lower densities, 88, 90; downbeat of anticipation, 74, 75; modal harmony, 41

Collins, Bootsy, 6, 7–8, 61; displaced rhythms, 167–68, 167*f*, 168*f*, 169*f*; downbeat of anticipation, 73; emergence of funk rhythm, 76–77, 229n7; the JBs, 65; live concerts, 230n15; move to P-Funk, 115, 121; the One, 121; pick-up gestures, 133; strong beat displacement, 80, 85–88

Collins, Phelps "Catfish," 6, 7; emergence of funk rhythm, 76–77; the JBs, 65; live concerts, 230n15

Coltrane, John, 30, 183–84

the consecration phase, 181, 194–95, 240n3

Count Basie, 57

counter-rhythms, 45, 61–72, 228n4; ambivalent rhythmic patterns, 71–72; balanced imbalance, 65–72, 78–79, 229nn9; the basic pulse, 69–70, 229n9; cross-rhythmic tendencies, 62–66; disparity between upper and lower densities, 88–91; 4:3 patterns, 63–66, 78–79, 100–104, 110–11, 126–30, 135,

European experience. *See* white experiences of funk

expectation theory, 150–51

experiential aspects of funk. *See* states of being in funk

the fade, 181

Feld, Steven, 208

"Fight the Power" (Public Enemy), 229n8

figure—gesture, 47–50, 225n12

Fikentscher, Kai, 144, 146, 147, 242n6

"Flash Light" (Parliament/P-Funk All-Stars), 137, 233n17

FM radio, 98

folk music, 156

4:3 patterns, 63–66, 78–79, 100–104, 110–11, 126–30, 135, 138, 165–67. *See also* cross-rhythmic tendencies

Frazier, E. F., 222n40

Frith, Simon, 27, 222n24

Fuller, Hoyt W., 29

Funk: The Music, the People, and the Rhythm of the One (Vincent), 219n4

Funkadelics, 4, 7–8, 109. *See also* Parliament/P-Funk All-Stars

funk bass, 61

the funk groove, xi, 11–12, 17–18. *See also names of specific tunes; rhythm;* states of being in funk

funk riffs, 125–32; cultivation of ambiguity, 127, 130–35; 4:3 patterns, 126–30, 134, 138; the One, 131–33; pick-up gestures, 133; tension between dueling forces, 138–39

"Funky Drummer" (Brown), 182–83, 182*f,* 238n5

"Funky Monks" (Red Hot Chili Peppers), 139

"Funky President" (Brown), 100–103, 101*f,* 102*f,* 229n9

fusion, 138–39

Garafalo, Reebee, 96–97, 232n25

Gates, Henry Louis, Jr., 17, 227nn45–46; on the Black Arts Movement, 28, 31; on signifyin(g) and repetition, 57–60, 227nn45–46, 227–28nn49–50

Gayle, Addison, Jr., 28–29, 222n36

genre and signifyin(g), 56–60, 159, 227nn45–46, 227–28nn49–50

George, Nelson, 96, 97–98, 112

gesture, 47–50, 225n18. *See also* figure—gesture

"Get It Together" (Brown), 165, 166*f*

"Get Up, Get Into It, Get Involved" (Brown), 6

"Get Up Offa That Thing" (Brown), 101, 110

ghost strokes, 74, 229nn4–5

"Give It Up or Turnit A Loose" (Brown), 76, 176

"Give Up the Funk (Tear the Roof Off the Sucker)" (Parliament/P-Funk), 8, 18; cross-rhythmic gestures, 123–25, 123*f*; main groove, 122–25, 123*f,* 124*f,* 233nn10–11; the One, 121–22, 122*f*; riff, 125, 127

"Gotta Do What I Gotta Do" (Public Enemy), 139

Graham Central Station, 61

Gran, A-B., 21

groove mode of listening, 147–49, 172–74, 177–79

grouping of rhythmic dialogues, 52–55, 226n33

habitus, 235n12

hard bop origins, 3

harmony in funk, 41

Hegel, Georg, 21

Heidegger, Martin, 195, 216

Hendrix, Jimi, 7–8

"The Hermeneutical Function of Distanciation" (Ricœur), 17, 195–97

hermeneutics of funk, 12–17, 193, 195–97, 214–18, 220nn20–23, 240n7

Herskovits-Frazier debate, 222n40

Hesmondhalgh, D., 33

heterogeneous sound ideal, 50–52, 111

hip-hop, 4, 98

history of funk, 219n4

the hook, 181

"Hot (I Need to Be Loved, Loved, Loved)" (Brown), 101–4; counter-rhythm and extended One, 103–4, 103*f*; lyrics, 108–9; the One and pick up, 104*f*; song structure, 104, 106*f*

"Hot Pants" (Brown), 64, 65, 65*f,* 68

hot rhythm, 27, 46

Hughes, Walter, 146–47

era, 7, 18, 28; secularization of black
music, 106–9, 231–32n21; tongue in
cheek lyrics, 177–78; Vietnam War, 29.
See also African American contexts of
funk; Black Arts Movement
Polydor record company, 99–105,
230n15; despiritualization of funk,
106–9; polishing of Brown's funk, 99–
105
polyrhythm, 45, 61–62. *See also* counter-
rhythms
popular music, 156. *See also* Anglo-
American pop and rock
primitivist representations of blackness,
9, 16, 17, 20–28, 205–13, 221n7;
African rhythm, 24–26, 208–9; black
minstrelsy, 21–24, 212, 213, 221n9,
243n19; repression of technical qualities, 206–8; response to black otherness, 8–9, 15–16, 21–24, 27–28, 212–18;
sexual aspects of "body music," 24–
25, 27–28, 208–11, 222n24
Prince, 4, 97–98, 139, 161
"The Problem of Speech Genres" (Bakhtin), 17
Public Enemy, 139, 229n8
pure groove, 179–84

r&b: Brown's repertoire, 63, 74; influence
on rock 'n' roll, 97; origins of funk, 3,
39–40; retreat from blackness, 112
race music, 36
racial contexts. *See* African American
contexts of funk; primitivist representations of blackness; white experiences of funk
Radano, R., 10–11, 20, 28, 220n21; on
Gates and signifyin(g), 227n45; on
linking of race and rhythm, 26–27,
208–9; on the scholarly discourse on
black music, 34–36, 223n54
ragtime, 62
Ramsey, Guthrie P., Jr., 32–33
rap, 4, 36, 231n8; break beats, 182–83;
concept of badness, 24, 221n14; the
One, 139; sampling of funk grooves,
183
Ray, Danny, 194
Red Hot Chili Peppers, 139

Reed, Ishmael, 184
Reich, Steve, 161, 235n21
repetition, 58–60, 156–71, 235–36nn21–
22; breaks, 184–88; circular grooves,
170; creation of the groove, 170, 184–
90; Deleuze's three instances of, 162–
64, 170–71, 237nn37–39, 238n42; with
difference, 159–64, 200–201, 235–
36n22, 236–37n35; Lidov's formative
and focal types, 157–58; Lidov's textural repetition, 161, 236n32;
Middleton's categories of, 156–58,
235–36n22; the One, 165–66, 168–71;
production of funk grooves, 164–71,
237nn40–41; productive dissymmetry, 163–65; states of being in funk,
156–71, 192; in Takai music, 187
rhythm, 43–60; call-and-response dialogue, 52–55, 134–35, 226n33;
counter-rhythms, 61–72, 228n4; cross-
rhythmic tendencies, 62–66; density
referents, 46, 74–75; downbeat in anticipation, 73–91; figure—gesture, 47–
50, 225n12, 225n18; as focus of study
of African-American music, 24–26,
34–36; 4:3 patterns 63–66, 78–79, 100–
104, 110–11, 126–30, 135, 138, 165–67;
funk bass, 61; grouping, 52–55;
heterogeneous sound ideal, 50–52,
111; hot jazz rhythm, 27, 205; internal
beat, 55–56, 69–70, 226n39; isoperiodicity, 43–44, 224n2, 224n4; meter, 47,
225n11; multilinear rhythm, 43–46;
musical skill and technique, 206–8;
the One, 61, 73, 103–4, 118–22, 131–32,
229n3; pick-up gestures, 80, 81*f*, 101,
102*f*, 104, 104*f*; racial links, 26–27;
space between notes (silence), 45–46,
54–55; spatial "sound box" dimension, 51–52, 226n24; syncopation, 61–
62, 79; virtual and actual structures,
46–48, 224–25nn9–11; vocal percussion, 47, 78, 82–84, 230n11, 230n13.
See also repetition
rhythm and blues. *See* r&b
"The Rhythmic Basis of Instrumental
Music" (Nketia), 43–46
rhythmic layers. *See* counter-rhythms;
multilinear rhythm

Ricœur, Paul, 16–17, 48; dialectic of event and meaning, 193, 195–97, 214–18, 240n4, 240n7; genre use, 59
riff. *See* funk riff
rock, 97, 231n8; link with rebellion, 27–28; phallic eroticism, 145–46; sexuality and hot rhythm, 27, 222n24. *See also* Anglo-American pop and rock
rock 'n' roll era, 97
The Rolling Stone Illustrated History of Rock & Roll (Palmer), 5, 39
Rose, Tricia, 182–83
Ross, Diana, 4
rumba rhythm, 63, 228n6

Said, Edward, 22–23
Saturday Night Fever, 97, 110, 144
Saussure, Ferdinand de, 48
"Say it Loud, I'm Black and I'm Proud" (Brown), 112
self-knowledge, 220n23
"Serpentine Fire" (Earth, Wind, and Fire), 147
Sex Machine, 87p
"Sex Machine" (Brown), 6, 18–19, 41, 139–40; ambivalence and ambiguity, 133–34; basic groove, 77f; counter-rhythm, 78, 79f; density referent, 84; disparity between upper and lower densities, 88–91; downbeat in anticipation, 75–79; 4:3 pattern, 78–79; the hook, 181; mix of song and groove, 149, 174, 175f, 176, 178–79, 188–90; off-beat phrasing, 80–82, 84; pick-up gestures, 80, 81f, 133, 164; production of groove, 164–65; strong beat displacement, 79–80; vocal percussion, 78, 230n11, 230n13
sexuality in musical styles: disco's gay links, 144, 145–47, 234n10; of funk, 9, 16, 145–46, 205, 213; lyrics, 108–9; primitivist representations of blackness, 24–25, 27–28, 208–13, 222n24; rock's eroticism, 27, 145–46, 222n24
"Shoot'n Up and Gettin' High" (Me'Shell), 139
"Signature Event Context" (Derrida), 17
"The Significance of the Relationship

between Afro-American Music and West African Music" (Wilson), 62
"Signify" (Count Basie), 57
"Signifying" (Oscar Peterson), 57
signifyin(g), 56–60, 159, 216, 227nn45–46, 227–28nn49–50, 235–36n22
The Signifying Monkey (Gates), 17, 57–60, 216, 227n46
simple syncopation, 62
Sly and the Family Stone, 4, 145, 219n3
Small, Christopher, 22, 154–55, 194
Smitherman, Geneva, 3, 219n1
Snead, James, 21, 183–84, 235–36n22
social context of funk. *See* cultural context of funk
the song, 105
song mode of listening, 18, 108–9, 147–49, 172–74, 177–79
soul music, 3–4, 111, 144, 145, 232n26
"Soul Power" (Brown), 6; counter-rhythm, 65–66, 66f, 68, 88–90; disparity between upper and lower densities, 88–90, 230n14; production of groove, 166–68, 167f, 168f, 169f, 170
The Souls of Black Folk (DuBois), 238n2
sound box, 51–52, 226n24
spatial dimension, 51–52
spiritual aspects of funk, 28, 106–9, 204, 208–9
Starks, John "Jabo," 6, 73, 77
states of being in funk, xi, 12–19, 115, 144–49, 192–203, 214–18, 220n19, 220n21, 240n1; being in the groove, 11–12; the consecration phase, 194–95; Deleuze's notion of intensity, 193, 199–201, 240–41nn13–15; Derrida's ether of metaphysics, 205–7, 209–10, 212, 214, 241–42nn1–2; dialectic of event and meaning, 193, 195–97, 214–18, 240n4, 240n7, 240n9; distanciation, 195–96, 201–3, 207–8, 242n6; the feel, 197–99; gender and sexuality, 145–47; listening strategies, 144, 147–54, 172–91, 235n12, 238n1; Lyotard's aesthetics of the sublime, 193, 198–99, 201, 202–3, 240nn10–12; participatory mode of listening, 144, 172–74; performative essence of funk, 17, 18, 125–32, 193–95, 230n15, 233n12,

240n3; P-Funk's psychedelic utopias, 137–38; primitivist renderings by white listeners, 205–13; pure groove, 179–84; repetition and groove, 156–71; response to black otherness, 8–9, 15–16, 21–24, 27–28, 212–18; technical-rhetorical qualities of funk, 206–10; Western dualism of mind and body, 214, 217–18. *See also* dance and movement; temporal experiences of funk; white experiences of funk

Stax record label, 4

Stewart, Jimmy, 30, 31

Stone, Sly, 8

"Stoned to the Bone" (Brown), 63, 64*f*, 65, 66

storytelling, 30

"Structure and Function in Musical Repetition" (Lidov), 157–58, 161, 236n32

Stubblefield, Clyde, 6, 74; in "Funky Drummer," 182–83, 182*f*, 238n5; ghost strokes, 74, 229nn4–5

Studying Popular Music (Middleton), 156–58, 235–36n22

Style and Music (Meyer), 150–54, 234n1

stylistic origins of funk, 3–4

"The Sublime and the Avantgarde" (Lyotard), 17

Summer, Donna, 4

"Super Bad" (Brown), 6, 223n46, 227–28n50, 229–30n9

syncopation, 61–62, 79

"Talkin' Loud and Saying Nothing" (Brown), 6

technofunk, 115, 139. *See also* Parliament/P-Funk All-Stars

"Tell Me Something Good" (Rufus and Chaka Khan), 237n41

temporal experiences of funk, 18–19, 147–71, 192–93, 214–15; dialectic of event and meaning, 193, 195–97, 214–18, 240n7; distanciation, 195–96, 201–3, 207–8, 242n6; eternal present, 155–56, 178–79, 184–88, 203; expectation and closure, 150–52; linear musical time, 150–54, 156, 178–79, 234n9, 237n40; never-endingness, 147–49;

nonlinear musical time, 151–56; repetition and grooves, 156–71, 184–91; teleological motion of music, 150–51, 153, 191, 234n1; vertical time, 154–55, 235n16, 235n21. *See also* states of being in funk

"Thank you (Falettinme Be Mice Elf Again)", 4, 219n3

3+3+2 groupings, 62–64, 228n6

The Time of Music (Kramer), 151–54, 237n40

Tin Pan Alley era, 97, 231n8

Tomlinson, Gary, 220n23

Toynbee, Jason, 96, 231n8

trip-hop, 4

"Try Me" (Brown), 6

twelve-bar blues pattern, 40–41

"Up for the Downstroke" (P-Funk), 18; the One, 118–20, 119*f*, 120*f*, 170–71; tension between dueling forces, 138

urban contemporary music, 232n25

verse and chorus/bridge forms, 41, 224n3. *See also* the song; song mode of listening

vertical time, 154–55, 235n16, 235n21

Vietnam War, 29

Village People, 146–47

Vincent, Ricky, 219n4

vocal percussion, 47, 78, 82–84, 230n11, 230n13

Walser, Robert, 227–28n50, 229n8

Waterman, Richard, 46, 56, 80–82, 220n22

Weber, Max, 42, 224n4

Wesley, Fred, 6

West, Cornel, 24, 106–8, 115, 221n14

West African music, 41, 224n5, 235n21

Western art music, 24–25, 27, 234n10

Western pop/rock. *See* Anglo-American pop and rock

"We Want the Funk" (Parliament/P-Funk), 61, 170, 172–74

Wexler, Jerry, 223n2

White, Hayden, 21

white experiences of funk, 4–5, 8–19, 204–5, 238n1; crossover black dance

white experiences of funk *(cont'd)*
music, 5, 11, 18, 96–112, 205; primitivistic understandings of funk, 205–13;
repression of technical-rhetorical
qualities of funk, 206–8; response to
black otherness, 8–9, 15–16, 21, 27–28,
212–18; rock music values, 9–10;
song-directed listening, 18, 148–49,
162, 171, 178; states of being in funk,
144–49, 205–18; subversion of the
dominant order, 213–14; Western dualism of mind and body, 214, 217–18.
See also crossover era

Wilson, Olly, 31–32, 50–52, 62, 63,
223n46

Wonder, Stevie, 231–32n21

Worrell, Bernie, 126–27, 233n13

"YMCA" (Village People), 147

About the author

Anne Danielsen is in the Musicology Department at the University of Oslo in Norway. She has published articles in *Aesthetic Theory, Art and Popular Culture* and *Popular Music*. She has spent time as a freelance teacher and writer as well as a singer and songwriter in various bands.